Dictionary
of
Counseling

DICTIONARY OF COUNSELING

Donald A. Biggs

With the assistance of Gerald Porter

Greenwood Press
Westport, Connecticut · London

Library of Congress Cataloging-in-Publication Data

Biggs, Donald A.
    Dictionary of counseling / Donald A. Biggs ; with the assistance
of Gerald Porter.
      p. cm.
    Includes index.
    ISBN 0-313-28367-2 (alk. paper)
    1. Counseling—Miscellanea. I. Porter, Gerald.
  II. Title.
    BF637.C6B444   1994
    361.3'23'0973—dc20   93–39352

British Library Cataloguing in Publication Data is available.

Library of Congress Catalog Card Number: 93–39352
ISBN: 0–313–28367–2

First published in 1994

Greenwood Press, 88 Post Road West, Westport, CT 06881
An imprint of Greenwood Publishing Group, Inc.

Printed in the United States of America

The paper used in this book complies with the
Permanent Paper Standard issued by the National
Information Standards Organization (Z39.48-1984).

10 9 8 7 6 5 4 3 2

Contents

Acknowledgments

This dictionary of counseling reflects the collaboration of Professor Gerald Porter and myself. His contributions include a number of the entries found in the dictionary as well as editorial feedback that was important in developing the completed manuscript.

I would like to dedicate this dictionary to two colleagues who have provided me with ideas, support, and constructive criticism over the years. A. Garth Sorenson, Professor Emeritus from the University of California at Los Angeles started out as my advisor in graduate school and became a trusted friend and colleague for over 30 years. The introduction to this dictionary was greatly influenced by many conversations with Professor Sorenson. The second colleague, Mrs. Maribel Gray, came into my life in more recent times. She has worked with me on three books, several chapters, and numerous articles. I would be quite remiss if I failed to note her important contributions to this dictionary. Without her editorial feedback and excellent organizational skills, this manuscript would never have seen "the light of day!" My deepest appreciation to both of these colleagues.

Introduction

Counseling services are available for individuals seeking assistance with a wide range of human problems. However, it is very difficult to evaluate the quality and appropriateness of these services. Students, consumers, and professionals find that much of what is called counseling is not easily distinguished from psychotherapy and friendship. Moreover, there is no clear demarcation as to which clients will benefit from the professional counseling services offered by psychologists, pastoral counselors, mental health counselors, and social workers.

This dictionary of counseling for the United States focuses on the twentieth century, a time when the concept of counseling emerged in a number of different contexts. In psychology, counseling was seen as a "scientifically respectable" way of dispensing personal, social, and educational information and advice. For the most part, the goal of counseling was to provide accurate and scientifically valid information gleaned from empirical observations. The assumption was that the credibility of both the counselor and counseling was a consequence of the scientific and technical characteristics of the data used in the helping process. Counseling, until well after World War II, was part of the psychology of individual differences and utilized data to help individuals and institutions improve decision making.

The concept of counseling was used in another American context involving vocational education and the world of work. In order for the United States to continue its scientific, technical, and economic progress following the Civil War, schools had to do more to prepare students for jobs. Consequently, specially trained personnel called vocational guidance counselors were needed to inform youth about job requirements and opportunities. They were to bridge the gap between school and work opportunities in an industrial society. This emerging profession was to have responsibility for doing surveys of local industries so as to identify job requirements and opportunities and predict changes in the work force. Then these vocational counselors were to use these data to advise the

schools on improving the job relevance of the curricula and to advise youth
regarding vocational training and job opportunities.

Counseling was part of the idealism that characterized the social and educational reform movements of the early 1900s. Many early advocates of counseling
had been exposed to the writing of John Dewey and were interested in how
counseling could be a tool for individualizing educational and occupational experiences. Counseling as described by these early twentieth century writers was
similar to a philosophical position that espoused a humane way of advising and
helping students and workers in a society that was becoming more urban and
industrial. Their goals for counselors included enhancing individual development, increasing the quality of individual thinking, and using social experiences
to develop humane and caring citizens.

The history of mankind reveals a long search to grasp the principles of human
understanding and caring. Some of the most provocative insights on these two
important human phenomena are found in Aristotle's understanding of virtue
and the process of character education.

In the United States, John Whiteley identified five historical foundations for
counseling and counseling psychology: (1) the vocational guidance movement,
(2) the mental health movement, (3) the psychometric movement, (4) the development of nonmedical counseling and psychotherapy, and (5) changes in the
social and economic conditions in the United States (Whiteley, 1984). Counseling psychology emerged on the scene in the United States at about the mid-
point of the twentieth century. Since that time the debate regarding the
credibility of professional counselors versus counseling psychologists has dominated professional and legal discussions of counseling in the United States. This
debate still rages.

The history of counseling in the United States encompasses the fields of
psychology, education, the world of work, and philosophy. Because of this fact,
counseling terms are defined in different ways by different folks at different
times. The language reflects disparate world views and academic perspectives.
As a consequence, counselors in the twentieth century have found different
meanings in what some might consider to be ostensibly the same facts or observations. Throughout this period definitions used in counseling resembled
mini-theories or explanations about human conditions based on a variety of
implicit assumptions. The reader is warned that the realities of counseling during
the last 100 years in the United States mirror different literary traditions that
are based on a variety of personality theories. Very few definitions emphasize
scientific or empirical observations. Still, readers need to be aware that definitions used in counseling are always incomplete if viewed from only one point
of view, and incoherent if viewed from all points of view at the same time.

In the early twentieth century counseling alluded to a generic kind of helping
relationship that included good advice and human concern. Teachers, parents,
friends, and ministers all engaged in counseling or helping. After World War
II, definitions of counseling were derived from professional orientations based

to some degree on personality theories, so that the field became very orthodox in its approach to "professional" definitions. Arguments over definitions of directive and nondirective counseling, as well as cognitive, behavioral, and psychodynamic terms, filled the professional journals.

A perusal of this literature gives the impression that the process of counseling was a very complicated phenomenon about which authorities and experts disagreed and that only a professional counselor could understand all of the subtleties, distinctions, and differences among terms and theories. This array of various counseling approaches left laypersons feeling very inadequate about their knowledge regarding counseling. Furthermore, counseling had increasingly become the province of experts who were certified and licensed to practice. Counseling no longer referred to a generic kind of helping relationship. During the last half of the twentieth century, counseling terms and concepts became associated with psychotherapy and the mental health fields.

As we approach the close of the twentieth century, serious questions have been raised about the differential effectiveness of the various schools or points of view in counseling. Is one approach to counseling superior to others? Is there really such a wide number of different approaches to counseling? Are professional counselors more effective than laypersons? Research in the 1970s, 1980s, and early 1990s suggests that most of the different approaches share a common concern in human understanding and helping clients make decisions about the problem situations in their lives.

Readers are encouraged to use this dictionary to become rational consumers and reasoned observers of counseling in the United States. In trying to evaluate counseling in a specific context, readers will find that there are no unequivocal facts or answers. There are multiple authorities and a wide variety of credible approaches to counseling. However, it is clear that responsible members of this field do not consider themselves to be gurus or priests and priestesses with amazing, almost magical skills in human understanding.

In critically examining different approaches to counseling, the reader should not be intimidated by jargon or obtuse language. Counseling is always about human communication in social situations where there is a person seeking help in improving his/her lot and a person willing to offer help. The major components in counseling have to do with human understanding and caring. Counselors "wear the glasses" of their clients in order to get a tentative glimpse of their worlds. They also care about the welfare of their clients and give them help. It is assumed that counselors feel empathy for people in need and are capable of caring for them for their own sakes. Clearly, clients should expect no less from counselors than such altruistic caring.

WHO ARE CLIENTS?

In trying to define the concept of counseling, it is necessary to describe the position of the client. Since counseling is one kind of helping process, it is logical to ask, "What kinds of persons need this type of help?" The character-istics of potential clients for counseling should be differentiated from the char-acteristics of potential clients for other kinds of helping activities. In trying to decide if persons are candidates for counseling, two sets of diagnostic questions should be asked:

1. What is the nature of the potential client's motivation to change? What are the reasons for his/her distress and discomfort in the present situation? Do counselors have the personal and professional resources and compe-tencies needed to deal with this client's emotional conditions and person-ality deficits?

2. Why has the potential client been unable or unwilling to solve the problem on his/her own? What are the obstacles standing in the way of a client being able to achieve his/her goals? Are the client's views of these obsta-cles reasonable? Does the counselor have the skills and competencies needed to help the client cope effectively with the distress and his/her lack of knowledge and/or inadequate skills?

Counseling is usually limited to those individuals whose problems include reasonable levels of distress or emotional arousal combined with personal def-icits such as inadequate or inappropriate knowledge and skills. The first condi-tion provides motivation for change, while the second provides client desire for help. Counselors primarily offer their services to clients who are motivated to change and want the help of the counselor in gaining knowledge or learning skills needed to make desired changes in their lives. Counselors employ different theoretical and conceptual models of personal problem conditions and causes of problems for deciding who should be defined as clients.

The professional task for counselors is to decide which persons, with what problems, can be helped by counseling. In general, counseling is not considered a preferred mode of treatment for individuals whose problems appear to be physiological in nature or for those individuals whose behaviors have led to difficulties with the law that involve legal representation. In this dictionary, counseling is viewed as basically a process in which clients may learn to (a) develop insights or a new understanding of a problem situation based on con-sideration of alternative perspectives; (b) develop increased awareness of the possible meaning of their behaviors, emotions, and experiences to themselves and others in a problem situation; and (c) learn new behaviors, concepts, and skills that will allow them to achieve their goals in a problem situation.

It is difficult for laypersons to decide if they or others who are confronted with problems may be potential clients for counseling. The answer seems to be that counseling helps persons deal with certain problem situations in which they are unable to achieve their goals, or with situations where they wish to take advantage of opportunities for personal development (Egan, 1990). In both cases the clients are dissatisfied with their present situations and would like to see improvements, but do not know how to achieve the desired changes on their own. Three conditions defining the client position include:

1. A sense of dissatisfaction or distress with present situations.
2. A sense of inadequacy that makes it difficult or improbable to make desired changes without help.
3. An awareness of personal goals that include changes in life situations.

Potential clients for counseling present problem situations as narratives or stories regarding the meaning of certain experiences in their lives. For the most part, their problems are reported in subjective narratives about their experiences, their actions or behaviors in these situations, and their emotions or feelings about the experiences and behaviors.

Problem situations in the lives of clients include problematic behaviors such as behavioral excesses or deficits. If they are to benefit from counseling, they will need to change these problematic behaviors and deal with the obstacles that have prevented them from achieving their goals, caused them personal pain or discomfort such as excessive anxiety, or caused undesirable consequences for themselves and others. In counseling, clients need to identify the nature of their previous ineffective methods of dealing with their problems, and then they need to learn more effective ways of acting on their problems. If the clients' previous modes of dealing with their problems had been effective, there would no longer be a problem situation.

In determining those people for whom counseling is a preferred method of helping, it is also necessary to refer to ethical principles and standards. Counselors accept persons as clients based on a sense of public trust which defines their profession. Certain ethical questions in counseling are rooted in this public trust. Two professional organizations, the American Psychological Association (APA), Division 17 (Counseling Psychology) and the American Counseling Association (ACA), have developed ethical codes and standards for practice for use in deciding whether individuals seeking help for personal problems are suitable clients for counseling.

WHAT IS THE PROCESS OF COUNSELING?

One way to define counseling is to describe generic models used by practitioners. These generalist approaches to defining counseling attempt to isolate stages and steps in helping clients learn more effective ways of managing their problems. They usually describe a systematic approach to problem solving that focuses on helping clients deal with their presenting problems. These are working models of the counseling process and do not necessarily represent any particular theoretical orientation. Most generic approaches to counseling deal with the improvement of clients' problem-solving skills; they identify activities that promote constructive behavior changes, enhance affective conditions, and increase personal control. The outcomes of such counseling, whether done by a teacher, a parent, a counselor, or a therapist, are viewed as the same: more constructive behavior, enhancement of emotional sensitivity, and greater control over one's life.

In a generic model of the helping process (Carkhuff, 1984), clients are seen as moving through stages in learning problem management skills: (a) the pre-helping stage, which increases the level of client involvement in the helping process; (b) the first stage, which involves facilitating client exploration of the meaning of the problem situation; (c) the second stage, which involves facilitating clients' understanding of their problematic behaviors and how these behaviors stand between them and their desired goals; and (d) the third stage, which has to do with clients learning skills for planning and implementing courses of action for achieving desired goals. In this model of counseling, counselors use responding skills to promote client insight into their present problem situations; personalizing skills to promote client understanding of personal deficits or limited capabilities; and initiating skills to promote planning and responsible actions needed for achieving goals.

WHAT IS THE COUNSELING RELATIONSHIP?

Another strategy used to define counseling has been to emphasize the characteristics of the relationship between counselors and clients. Almost all counselors view counseling as involving a unique working relationship between a person seeking help and a person willing to act as a helper. In some cases the relationship is viewed as a means of achieving the goals of counseling, while in other instances the quality of the relationship itself is seen as the basis of counseling. Humanistic counselors argue that the counseling relationship is the major agent of change and as such is the goal of counseling. Although other theoretical approaches don't go quite this far in extolling the centrality of the relationship to successful counseling, most approaches to counseling discuss how various aspects of the relationship can influence the outcomes of counseling.

The counseling relationship includes the feelings and attitudes that counselors and clients have toward each other and the manner in which they are expressed in counseling. All counseling relationships involve three components: (1) a working alliance, or contract; (2) the transference or unreal side of the relationship; and (3) the real side of the relationship as expressed in counselor and client attitudes toward each other (Gelso & Carter, 1985). The importance attached to each of these components varies according to the theoretical perspective of counselors and the specifics of a given case.

Three somewhat different views of the counseling relationship are espoused by counselors with psychoanalytic, humanistic, and learning approaches. Those who identify with these different orientations will emphasize the importance of different parts of the counseling relationship because they assume that there are different mechanisms of change within clients that are facilitated by a specific component of a counseling relationship. For the psychoanalytic counselor, the mechanism of change for clients is their increased insight. With the humanistic counselor, change comes about as a result of client experiences in counseling. Counselors with a learning orientation assume that client changes in counseling are due to learning processes.

Psychoanalytic counselors promote client insight into how they distort and misperceive their present experiences because of their past life. The transference component of a counseling relationship plays a central role in promoting insight. Humanistic counselors emphasize the need to increase awareness of clients to fully experience their present situations. For these counselors, the attitudes of clients and counselors toward each other define the counseling relationship. Counselors with a learning orientation view the relationship in counseling as a means to achieve certain goals. The relationship provides the context for promoting client learning of new attitudes, behaviors, and skills. Counselors who adhere to different theoretical perspectives will develop their own kinds of counseling relationships that support their assumptions about both the mechanisms of change in clients and the processes of change in counseling.

The processes in counseling are intended to change people: to make them think differently, to feel differently, or to act differently. These processes and activities involve both learning and influence dynamics. However, there is no reasoned consensus about which specific processes in counseling constitute the necessary or critical conditions to promote client changes. There are at least 250 different systems or approaches to counseling and psychotherapy. From this rainbow of perspectives, it is not possible to deduce which of them are clearly right and which are wrong, which superior and which inferior.

In evaluating a pluralistic field and profession such as counseling, the intellectual dilemma involves the need to sort out from these various theoretical approaches a perspective on counseling for yourself. Consumers, students, and professionals need to decide which approach is right for them. In coming to such a decision, they will recognize the tentative nature of all evidence involving counseling and the limitations of actuarial data for predicting which approach to counseling is best for an individual client.

WHAT ARE THE GOALS OF COUNSELING?

After surveying the diverse theoretical approaches to counseling, readers need to develop some rules for organizing and making sense of this knowledge and information. One strategy is to differentiate the various approaches to counseling according to their goals:

Psychoanalytic—to help clients be more aware of the unconscious in their lives

Adlerian—to provide encouragement to develop socially useful goals

Existential—to help clients identify obstacles that block their freedom

Person-centered—to provide a climate for clients to engage in self-exploration

Gestalt—to help clients gain awareness of their present experiences

Transactional analysis—to help clients examine early decisions in their lives and to make new decisions about their life scripts

Behavior—to help clients eliminate behaviors and learn more effective behaviors

Rational-emotive—to help clients apply the rational method for solving personal problems

Reality—to help clients evaluate their present behaviors in terms of their effectiveness in meeting goals

In discussing counseling goals, it is useful to differentiate the process goals of counselors and the outcome goals or expectations of clients. Process goals involve the development of the necessary learning conditions for client change. They are mainly the responsibility of counselors and involve the establishment of a particular kind of counseling relationship as well as the choice of particular strategies for helping clients learn to manage problem conditions more effectively. Counselors with different theoretical perspectives will approach counseling relationship and problem management issues with different assumptions about effective counseling processes and appropriate role expectations for themselves and their clients. We expect process goals to be similar for counselors from the same schools of counseling.

Outcome goals of clients are the consequence of joint decisions by counselors and clients, and the counseling contracts or alliances will reflect these agreements. Still, counseling contracts and outcome goals are often modified and refined as the counselor and the client improve their understanding of the presenting problem conditions. Clients come to counselors with problem conditions in mind that they would like to see changed or improved. The outcome goals are first stated in counseling as the concrete and specific expectations of clients. The counselor and client then discuss these expectations and possible counseling interventions that may be most effective in achieving the needed changes. They will develop outcome goal statements by clarifying problem situations, identifying problematic behaviors, and specifying goal situations. In order to achieve these positive outcomes, the client and counselor have to clarify what specific changes are needed in the client's present approach to his/her problems. They should try to select helping strategies that have goals that make sense for the client's goal situation. For example, if goal situations have to do with affective conditions in a client's life, then client-centered or Gestalt strategies and techniques may provide a sensible approach to achieving the client's goals.

WHO ARE COUNSELORS?

Counselors may hold positions in which their job obligations include more than individual counseling. They may be involved in organizational development, consulting, group counseling, assessment, research, and supervision. Although much has been written about the generic responsibilities of individuals who hold positions as counselors, it is probably still a truism that most people who are counselors spend the majority of their time engaged in individual counseling and that most clients expect counselors to provide appropriate help in achieving their personal goals.

Counseling is engaged in by professionals from medicine, psychology, and social work. One might expect there to be some overlap and similarities in their approaches as well as some unique characteristics. You might even expect clients to selectively seek out psychologists, social workers, and psychiatrists depending on their different problems and goals. Contrary to expectations, researchers have found that most psychologists, psychiatrists, and social workers spend most of their time with clients who present the YAVIS syndrome—they are youthful, attractive, verbal, intelligent, and successful.

William Schofield, in his book *Psychotherapy: The Purchase of Friendship,* distinguishes between "visible" and "invisible" counselors and psychotherapists. The invisible helpers are the men and women in any society who, by virtue of their roles and their characters, are regularly turned to for help by persons in need of counsel and support. The clergy and teachers are part of this reserve force of invisible helpers in any society. And so are "good" neighbors, "good" friends, and "good" colleagues. Some persons suffer from philosophical neuroses and need to work with individuals who have insight regarding human wisdom and the meaning of life. In other words, they are in need of "wise counsel," not counseling. Others may be in need of education to be less anxious about human concerns rather than counseling.

THE DICTIONARY

This dictionary focuses on counseling as it developed in the United States during the twentieth century, a period during which the concept of counseling and the terms associated with it have changed in a variety of ways. However, regardless of different theoretical perspectives or historical time periods, counselors have been seen as experts in conversation who are sensitive to affective nuances, able to listen selectively, able to influence the amount and content of conversation, and able to use silence as an effective mode of communication (Schofield, 1986). The dictionary treats counseling and psychotherapy as being qualitatively the same. Any differences that may exist between them can best be described in quantitative terms. We concur with Corsini (1968) that there is nothing that a psychotherapist does that a counselor does not do. In the text, we have chosen to use the term *counseling* rather than *psychother-apy.* We have also used the term *counselor* rather than *psychotherapist.*

The story of counseling in the twentieth century is about the formalization of helping processes that rely on human communication as the mode of treatment. This phenomenon has developed as a part of the culture and has emerged as a cultural program that has influenced how U.S. citizens think about human problems, their causes, and their treatment. This dictionary describes the development of this U.S. cultural perspective on caring and helping processes. Cultural thinking about counseling has been stored in our collective memory at different points in history and describes shifts in how people have defined concepts about counseling, used these concepts to understand people, and then used these counseling concepts to help people. This dictionary describes terms used in contemporary U.S. culture to construe issues of human understanding and caring and how these constructs have changed over time.

The selection of entries in the dictionary is based on their significance in understanding thinking about counseling in the United States during the twentieth century. For the most part, the entries represent concepts or categories of information. When a concept is a significant component of a counseling proposition or a counseling prototype about counseling diagnosis or treatment, the relevant context will be discussed in the entry.

The format for the entries in the dictionary is as follows:

1. General definition of the term;
2. Narrative definition of the term;
3. Cross-references;
4. References.

The emphasis is on how terms have been used as part of our thinking about counseling. Influential figures will be discussed in reference to their contributions to thinking about counseling in the United States during the twentieth century. The dictionary does not contain terms that could be described as popular jargon.

REFERENCES

Carkhuff, R. (1984). *Helping and human relations: Vol. 1.* Amherst, MA: Human Resource Development Press.

Corsini, R. J. (1968). Counseling and psychotherapy. In E. F. Borgotta & W. W. Lambert (Eds.), *Handbook of personality theory and research.* Chicago: Rand McNally.

Egan, G. (1990). *The skilled helper* (4th ed.). Pacific Grove, CA: Brooks/Cole.

Gelso, C. J., & Carter, J. A. (1985). The relationship in counseling and psychotherapy: Components, consequences and theoretical antecedents. *The Counseling Psychologist, 13,* 155–243.

Schofield, W. (1986). 2nd Ed. *Psychotherapy: The purchase of friendship*. New Brunswick, NJ: Transaction Books.

Schofield W. (1964). *Psychotherapy: The purchase of friendship*. Englewood Cliffs, NJ: Prentice Hall.

Whiteley, J. (1984). Counseling psychology: A historical perspective. *The Counseling Psychologist, 12,* 2–110.

Dictionary of Counseling

A

A-B-C THEORY. A counseling procedure used by rational-emotive counselors to help clients understand the philosophic source of their problems and to identify strategies for changing disturbance-creating beliefs.

Albert Ellis (1989) held that when a highly charged emotional consequence (C) followed a significant activating event (A), A may seem to be but is actually not the cause of C. Instead, emotional consequences are largely created by B—the individual's belief system. When an undesirable emotional consequence occurs, such as severe anxiety, this can usually be traced to the person's irrational beliefs; when these beliefs are effectively disputed (at point D) by challenging them rationally and behaviorally, the disturbed consequences become minimal and largely cease to occur.

The real cause of emotional upsets in persons is their beliefs and not what happens to them.

Related entries: AWFULIZING; COGNITIVE RESTRUCTURING; ELLIS, ALBERT; IRRATIONAL BELIEFS; MUSTURBATION; RATIONAL-EMOTIVE COUNSELING.

Reference

Ellis, A. (1989). Rational emotive therapy. In R. J. Corsini & D. Wedding (Eds.), *Current psychotherapies* (4th ed., pp. 197–240). Itasca, IL: F. E. Peacock.

ABREACTION. The reliving of painful emotional experiences in counseling; the process usually involves an increasing conscious awareness of distressing thoughts which have not been consciously expressed.

In Adlerian counseling, abreaction is seen as a way of affording the client relief by freeing him/her from carrying the burden of unfinished business. However, Alexander and French (1946) observed that abreaction may also be a test to determine whether a client should trust a counselor. Lazarus (1989) argued that one of the main mechanisms that promotes change in affect during counseling is abreaction, or reliving and recounting painful emotions in the presence of a supportive, trusted ally. For some clients, the nonjudgmental acceptance of a highly respected person may be sufficient to promote changes in their attitudes.

Abreactive catharsis is a fundamental part of psychodrama. However, these counselors think that every catharsis or abreaction should be followed by catharsis of integration that promotes the development of healthy behaviors to replace unhealthy ones. Psychodrama in a group setting provides opportunities for clients to integrate their needs for both individuation and belonging.

Related entries: ADLERIAN COUNSELING; CATHARSIS; INDIVIDUAL PSYCHOLOGY; MULTIMODAL APPROACH TO COUNSELING; PSYCHODRAMA; PSYCHOTHERAPY.

References

Alexander, F., & French, T. M. (1946). *Psychoanalytical therapy.* New York: Ronald Press.

Lazarus, A. (1989). Multimodal at Therapy. In R. J. Corsini & D. Wedding (Eds.), *Current psychotherapies* (4th ed., pp. 505–546). Itasca, IL: F. E. Peacock.

Moreno, J. L. (1988). *The essential Moreno writings on group method, psychodrama and spontaneity* (J. Fox, Ed.). New York: Springer.

ACCEPTANCE. A nonjudgmental attitude expressed by either the client or the counselor.

In the book *Counseling and Psychotherapy* (1942), Carl Rogers argued that when clients can accept as part of themselves their less praiseworthy feelings and their roles in problem situations, they no longer will find it necessary to keep up compensatory attitudes of a defensive nature. The basis of person-centered counseling involves the counselor communicating acceptance or unconditional positive regard. Rogers (1937) described the counselor-client relationship: "It is in this relationship with a non-critical accepting worker that the client achieves an emotional growth that has not been possible for him as he defends himself in other situations" (p. 240). Acceptance is the recognition of a client's right to have feelings; it is not the approval of all behavior.

In rational-emotive therapy (RET), the basic idea is to help clients avoid self-condemnation. Counselors are to express full acceptance or tolerance; they refuse to evaluate their clients as persons. Unlike person-centered counselors, they do not think that acceptance needs to involve personal warmth or empathic understanding. RET counselors accept clients as imperfect beings without expressing personal warmth.

In analytical counseling (Jungian) it is essential that clients feel accepted by their counselors. Acceptance is communicated through the counselors' genuine openness. Jungian counselors do not see their relationship with clients as being between healthy persons and sick persons. Rather, they view themselves as persons who have an enormous respect for the complexities and hidden resources inherent in their clients. The client-counselor relationship is more like peer confrontation than a healer-patient relationship.

Related entries: ANALYTICAL COUNSELING; AUTHENTICITY; CLIENT-CENTERED COUNSELING; EMPATHY; HUMANISTIC APPROACHES TO COUNSELING; PUNISHMENT; UNCONDITIONAL POSITIVE REGARD.

References

Ellis, A., & Dryden, W. (1987). *The practice of rational-emotive therapy.* New York: Springer.

Kaufman, T. (1989). Analytical psychotherapy. In R. J. Corsini & D. Wedding (Eds.), *Current psychotherapies* (4th ed., pp. 118–152). Itasca, IL: F. E. Peacock.

Rogers, C. R. (1937). The clinical psychologist's approach to personality problems. *Family, 18,* 233–243.

Rogers, C. R. (1942). *Counseling and psychotherapy.* Cambridge, MA: Riverside.

ACHIEVEMENT TEST. A measure of an individual's degree of accomplishment or learning in a subject or task.

Achievement tests give clients an idea of what they have learned in a specific area as compared to what others have learned, and provide them with one type of information they need for making educational and career decisions. These tests may be either teacher-made or standardized. Each mode of measuring achievement has certain advantages. The teacher-made test measures specific units of study emphasized in a particular educational setting, while standardized achievement tests measure more general educational objectives and provide clients with information about how they compare to a wider sample of persons in a particular subject area. Standardized achievement tests are available for elementary and secondary students as well as adults.

Achievement tests typically are subdivided into three types. Single subject matter achievement tests assess the level of knowledge retention for a specific subject area. Survey batteries are collections of single subject matter tests. Achievement test batteries have the same norm group, which facilitates comparisons of achievement across areas. Diagnostic tests are used to determine which reading, writing, or mathematical skills clients can perform adequately.

Although there are conceptual differences between achievement tests and aptitude tests, it is difficult to define clear practical distinctions between these two types of tests. For example, there is considerable debate about whether the Scholastic Aptitude Test is an aptitude test or an achievement test, because scores on this particular test have high positive correlations with students' high school grade point averages, which in turn have high positive correlations with secondary school achievement tests.

Related entries: APTITUDE TEST; INTELLIGENCE TESTS; SCHOOL COUNSELING; TRAIT AND FACTOR COUNSELING.

References

Anastasia, A. (1982). *Psychological testing* (5th ed.). New York: Macmillan.
Karmel, L. J. (1979). *Measurement and evaluation in the schools.* New York: Macmillan.

ACQUIRED IMMUNE DEFICIENCY SYNDROME (AIDS). As of June 30, 1992, 230,179 cases of AIDS had been diagnosed in the United States. The human immunodeficiency virus (HIV) causes a chronic progressive immune deficiency disease, the most severe phase of which is Acquired Immune Deficiency Syndrome (Volberding, 1989).

HIV disease is manifest in a spectrum of conditions, with highly variable expression but with a general consistency of pattern and features. The most advanced phase of HIV disease, called AIDS, has become a critical reason for the premature mortality of male and female adolescents and young adults in the United States (Keeling, 1993).

The AIDS crisis has created a new set of problems that clients bring to counselors. The stigma associated with the HIV illness continuum is related to the fact that many people in society tend to associate the illness with supposedly "immoral" life styles and consequently are apt to blame the victims. Counselors have to be sensitive to the problem of stigmatization and how it may compromise a client's ability to ask for and receive help. In the beginning stages, counseling may focus on crisis intervention, but it is important to move beyond these issues and deal with client concerns about empowerment and quality of life. AIDS clients may find themselves dealing with developmental issues related to integrity and despair even though they may not have fully resolved developmental issues that normally would have occurred earlier in their lives (Gutierrez & Perlstein, 1992).

Related entries: COUNSELING; GAY AND LESBIAN COUNSELING.

References

Dworkin, S. H., & Pincu, L. (1993). Counseling in the era of AIDS. *Journal of Counseling and Development, 71*(3), 275–291.
Gutierrez, F. J., & Perlstein, M. (1992). Helping someone to die. In S. H. Dworkin & F. J. Gutierrez (Eds.), *Counseling gay men and lesbians: Journey to the end of the rainbow* (pp. 259–275). Alexandria, VA: American Association for Counseling and Development.
Keeling, R. P. (1993). HIV disease: Current concepts. *Journal of Counseling and Development, 17*(3), 261–274.
Volberding, P. (1989). Infection as a disease: The medical indications for early diagnosis. *Journal of AIDS, 2,* 421–425.

ACTUALIZING TENDENCY. An innate human predisposition toward growth and fulfilling one's potential.

Individuals will prefer to be healthy rather than sick, to be independent rather than dependent; and, in general, they will try to further the optimal development of the total organism. Carl Rogers, in the book *Client Centered Therapy* (1951), wrote that

> the whole process (of self enhancement and growth) may be symbolized by the child's learning to walk. The first steps involve struggle and usually pain. . . . The child may, because of pain, revert to crawling for a time. Yet, the forward direction of growth is more powerful than the satisfaction of being infantile. . . . In the same way, they will become independent, responsible, self governing, and socialized in spite of the pain which is often involved in these steps. (Pp. 490–491)

In person-centered counseling, the counselor tries to create a climate in which clients can move forward and become what they are capable of becoming. Because these counselors believe that clients have an inherent capacity to move away from maladjustment toward psychological health, they place primary responsibilities for directing the counseling process on the clients. They assume that the urge to move toward psychological maturity is deeply rooted in human nature, so that the principles of person-centered counseling apply to those clients who function at relatively normal levels as well as to clients who experience more psychological difficulties.

Related entries: CLIENT-CENTERED COUNSELING; HUMANISTIC APPROACHES TO COUNSELING; SELF-ACTUALIZATION; SELF-CONCEPT.

References

Rogers, C. (1951). *Client centered therapy.* Boston: Houghton Mifflin.

Rogers, C. (1957). The necessary and sufficient conditions of therapeutic personality change. *Journal of Consulting Psychology, 21,* 95–103.

ADAPTIVE COUNSELING. An integrative model for selecting a progression of counseling styles as clients move through developmental stages during the course of counseling.

The adaptive counseling model is built upon the situational leadership theory in the field of organizational psychology. Counselors are to make intervention decisions based on the characteristics of their clients and on the issues that they bring to counseling. The best counseling relationships are the result of accurately assessing the task readiness of clients and correctly determining the requirements of the presenting problem.

Two dimensions of counselor behavior, direction and support, are combined to identify four different styles of counseling. Progress in counseling involves client movement from being unwilling or insecure about accomplishing goals to being willing, able, and confident to make necessary changes in their lives.

References

Hersey, P. S., & Blanchard, K. H. (1977). *Management of organizational behavior: Utilizing human resources* (3rd ed.). Englewood Cliffs, NJ: Prentice-Hall.

Howard, G., Nance, D. W., & Myers, P. (1986). Adaptive counseling and psychotherapy: An integrative eclectic model. *The Counseling Psychologist, 14,* 363–442.

ADLER, ALFRED (1870–1937). Along with Sigmund Freud and Carl Jung, Adler was a major contributor to the development of the psychodynamic approach in counseling.

He resigned his post as president of the Vienna Psychoanalytic Society in 1911, and in 1912 he founded the Society for Individual Psychology. He incurred the disfavor of Freud when he asserted that humans were motivated by social urges rather than biological urges; their behaviors were goal directed, and they had within them the capacity to both create and influence events in their lives.

Adler was born near Vienna on February 7, 1870, and died while on a lecture tour in Aberdeen, Scotland, on May 27, 1937. He graduated from the University of Vienna in 1895 and entered private practice as an ophthalmologist in 1898. He later changed to general practice and then to neurology. In 1902 he joined Freud's Wednesday evening discussion circle.

In 1922 Adler initiated child guidance centers within the community. These family education centers were located in public schools and were directed by psychologists who served without pay. Twenty-eight such centers existed in Vienna until 1934. The model for such centers was later transported to the United States by Rudolph Dreikurs and his students (Dreikurs, Corsini, Lowe, & Sonstegard, 1959).

In 1926 Adler was invited to the United States to give lectures and provide demonstrations. Until 1934 he divided his time between the United States, where he served on the faculty of the Long Island College of Medicine, and abroad.

In discussing Adler's influence, Henri Ellenberger commented, "It would not be easy to find another author from which so much has been borrowed from all sides without acknowledgement than Adler" (1970, p. 645).

Related entries: ADLERIAN COUNSELING; DREIKURS, RUDOLPH; INDIVIDUAL PSYCHOLOGY.

References

Adler, A. (1930). Individual psychology. In C. Murchison (Ed.), *Psychologies of 1930* (pp. 395–405). Worcester, MA: Clark University Press.
Bottome, P. (1939). *Alfred Adler: A biography.* New York: Putnam.
Dreikurs, R., Corsini, R. J., Lowe, R., & Sonstegard, M. (1959). *Adlerian family counseling.* Eugene: University of Oregon Press.
Ellenberger, H. F. (1970). *The discovery of the unconscious.* New York: Basic Books.

ADLERIAN COUNSELING. The process of Adlerian counseling has four aims: (1) establishing and maintaining a "good" relationship; (2) uncovering the dynamics of a client, including his/her life style and personal goals and how they effect life movement; (3) interpretation culminating in insight; and (4) reorientation.

A good relationship in Adlerian counseling is a friendly one between equals. Counselors inform their clients that human beings play a role in creating their problems, that they are responsible for their actions, and that their problems are based on faulty perceptions and faulty values (Dreikurs, 1957).

Counselors attempt to understand the life style and how it affects the client's current functioning with respect to his/her life tasks. They then try to ascertain the conditions present when the client was forming his/her life style convictions. What position did the client have in the family? How did the client find a place within the family, in school, and among peers? The second aspect of life style assessment has to do with interpreting a client's early recollections. A recollection is treated as a projective technique and represents a single event rather than a group of events.

Adlerian counselors facilitate insight mainly by interpretation of ordinary communications, dreams, fantasies, behaviors, symptoms, the counselor/client transactions, and the client's interpersonal transactions. The emphasis in their interpretations is on purposes rather than causes, on movement rather than description, on uses rather than possession.

Reorientation involves persuading the client that change is in his or her best interest. The client's present manner of living may provide "safety," but it has not provided "happiness." Counselors employ a variety of action techniques such as role playing to assist their clients in reorientation. Given that Adlerians consider clients to be discouraged rather than sick, they make extensive use of encouragement and try to enhance the client's faith in self.

Related entries: ADLER, ALFRED; BASIC MISTAKES; BIRTH ORDER; DREIKURS, RUDOLPH; INDIVIDUAL PSYCHOLOGY.

References

Dreikurs, R. (1957). Psychotherapy as correction of faulty social values. *Journal of Individual Psychology, 13,* 150–158.
Mosak, H. (1989). Adlerian psychotherapy. In R. J. Corsini & D. Wedding (Eds.), *Current psychotherapies* (4th. ed., pp. 65–116). Itasca, IL: F. E. Peacock.

ADOLESCENCE. A period in life between childhood and adulthood that is divided into three parts: puberty (early adolescence), middle adolescence, and late adolescence. Adolescence is a term used to describe the psychological aspects of a developmental stage that falls between childhood and adulthood.

Erikson (1963) outlines the basic challenge of the adolescent period as the individual's development of a self-identity. Adolescent youth need to see themselves as unique persons who are both similar to and different from other persons. Failure to establish their identities during these years may lead to role confusion or even to an identity crisis.

The contemporary view of adolescence places less emphasis on the conditions of storm and stress as a necessary part of adolescent development. Instead, the emphasis is on the stabilizing, goal directed aspects of adolescent development. The development of intimate and mature social relationships comprises the major task of adolescents.

Adolescents may manifest behaviors that are commonly thought to indicate maladjustment or emotional disturbances in adults, such as lying, destructiveness, excessive fears, hyperactivity, and fighting. Adults who find such behaviors disturbing may refer these young persons to counselors. However, many of these behaviors may disappear without any special counseling interventions (see Kazden, 1988). Adolescents will often balk at the idea of seeking counseling because they see no value in or reason for getting help in this way. They tend to respond most positively to counseling when there is support from or minimal opposition from their peers. This is one reason that counselors who work with adolescents should consider including peer approaches, group counseling, and/or cooperative school projects in their program of activities. Positive changes may be found to occur in a group context when adolescent clients are given opportunities to both release their tensions and examine their behaviors with the help of peers (Goodman, 1976, p. 520).

Related entries: DEVELOPMENTAL COUNSELING (BLOCHER); DEVELOPMENTAL COUNSELING (IVEY); IDENTITY.

References

Erikson, E. H. (1963). *Childhood and society* (2nd ed.). New York: Norton.

Goodman, J. (1976). Group counseling with seventh graders. *Personnel and Guidance Journal, 54,* 519–520.

Kazoden, A. (1988). *Child Psychotherapy: Developing and Identifying Effective Treatments.* New York: Pergamon.

ADULT EGO STATE. In transactional analysis (Berne, 1961), the adult ego state is the realistic, logical part of personality that solves problems in a rational manner.

The adult ego state resembles a computer in that it takes in, stores, retrieves, and processes information about self and environment. The adult deals exclusively with facts and logical data in a nonemotional way. The adult has its own observable mannerisms, a special repertoire of words, thoughts, body postures, gestures, voice tones, and expressions.

Related entries: BERNE, ERIC; CHILD EGO STATE; EGO; EGO STATES; EGOGRAM; PARENT EGO STATE; TRANSACTIONAL ANALYSIS.

References

Berne, E. (1961). *Transactional analysis in psychotherapy.* New York: Grove Press.

Berne, E. (1977). *Intuition and ego states.* San Francisco: TA Press.

ADULTHOOD. Three stages that cover the psychosocial aspects of development during the adult period in life are young adulthood—intimacy versus isolation; middle age—generativity versus stagnation; and later life—integrity versus despair (Erikson, 1982).

Erikson believed that we approach adulthood only after we have mastered adolescent conflicts over identity and role confusion. One of the key characteristics of mature young adults is their ability to form intimate relationships. Intimacy involves the ability to share with others the important aspects of our identity. In middle age, adults learn how to live creatively with both themselves and others. Generativity includes creating through a career, family, and leisure time activities, and so on. If middle-aged adults fail to achieve a sense of productivity, they begin to stagnate and die psychologically. The core crisis for older adults is integrity versus despair. Those who achieve a sense of integrity feel few regrets; they have lived a productive and worthwhile life and have coped with their failures as well as their successes.

For Freud, adulthood was considered a continuation of the genital stage (ages 12 to 18). Young adults move into the genital stage of psychosexual development unless they become fixated at some earlier stage. As adolescents advance into mature adulthood, they develop intimate relationships, become free of parental influences, and develop the capacity to be interested in others. Freud considered the goals of *lieben und arbeiten* to be core characteristics of mature adults: that is, the freedom to love and to work and to derive satisfaction from loving and working are very important parts of their lives.

Related entries: DEVELOPMENTAL COUNSELING (BLOCHER); DEVELOPMENTAL COUNSELING (IVEY).

References

Erikson, E. H. (1982). *The life cycle completed.* New York: Norton.
Hall, C., & Lindzey, G. (1979). *Theories of personality* (3rd ed.). New York: Wiley.

ADVICE/ADVICE GIVING. Statements providing information, directions, or recommendations regarding actions that a client should or should not take. In giving advice a person usually recommends or prescribes a particular solution or course of action.

Williamson (1939, 1950) listed advising as one of the five techniques of clinical counseling. Advising was to begin at the point of the client's understanding. The counselor was to marshal the evidence for and against the client's claimed educational or vocational choices and social or emotional habits, practices, and attitudes. Then the counselor was to list those phases of the diagnosis which were favorable to the client's frame of reference and those which were unfavorable. The counselor was to explain why he/she advised a client to shift goals, to change social habits, or to retain the present ones.

In advising their clients, counselors were to state their viewpoints with definitiveness and attempt through exposition to enlighten them. If there were equally desirable alternative actions, counselors were to say so frankly, but they were to avoid taking dogmatic positions. Their advice should consist of activities to be carried out by clients, without stating a single "right" thing to do. Advice involves general suggestions to be tried out by clients that will be evaluated later. Advice should be tentative and subject to revision as contradictory evidence is collected.

Williamson described three methods of advising:

1. *Direct advising.* Counselors stated their opinions regarding the most satisfactory choice, action, or program to be made and followed by clients. This method of advising was recommended for clients who sought the frank opinions of coun-

selors or those who persisted in activities which counselors believed would lead to serious failure and loss of morale.

2. *Persuasive advising.* Counselors were to marshal the evidence in such a reasonable and logical manner that the clients were able to anticipate clearly the outcomes of alternative actions. They were not to dominate their clients' decisions or choices, but they were to persuade them to understand the implications of the diagnostic data.

3. *Explanatory advising.* Counselors were to give more time to explaining the significance of diagnostic data and to pointing out possible situations in which clients' strengths would prove useful and be rewarded. This method of advising was considered the most satisfactory and complete counseling approach.

Carl Rogers (1942) listed two major weaknesses in using advising and persuading techniques in counseling: those clients who had a good deal of independence would reject such advice in order to retain their own integrity, while those clients who had tendencies toward dependency would accept the advice of counselors and become even more dependent and willing to let others make decisions for them. He argued against counselors giving advice to clients because the practice does not promote the growth of clients. He characterized advice giving and persuasion as intervening in and directing the lives of clients.

In emergencies that arise in crisis counseling, counselors will often give advice and information if the welfare and safety of their clients are a matter of concern to them. Knowles (1979) reported that 70 to 90 percent of all responses made by volunteer counselors in crisis counseling involved giving advice.

Related entries: CLINICAL COUNSELING; DIRECTIVE APPROACH TO COUNSELING; EDUCATIONAL COUNSELING; GUIDANCE; TEACHER-COUNSELOR.

References

Knowles, D. (1979). On a tendency of volunteer helpers to give advice. *Journal of Counseling Psychology, 26,* 352–354.
Rogers, C. R. (1942). *Counseling and psychotherapy.* Cambridge, MA: Riverside Press.
Williamson, E. G. (1939). *How to counsel students.* New York: McGraw-Hill.
Williamson, E. G. (1950). *Counseling adolescents.* New York: McGraw-Hill.

AFFECTIVELY ORIENTED APPROACHES TO COUNSELING. These approaches to counseling emphasize the importance of the attitudes that counselors and clients have toward each other. The counselor's basic attitudes and personal characteristics are considered to be critical components in helping clients.

Counseling is considered a human experience characterized by an understanding of human existence. This emphasis on humanistic values is the essence of affectively oriented approaches. Some of these approaches have their roots in philosophy, as is seen in existential counseling.

Affectively oriented approaches assume that clients possess the potential for awareness and freedom to shape their own lives. Counseling evolves from an initial encounter between a counselor and a client and the quality of that relationship. The quality of the relationship between a counselor and a client is considered the major mechanism of change in counseling.

Corey (1977) described the major strengths of affective approaches to counseling as follows: "In my judgment, one of the major contributions . . . is its emphasis on the human-to-human quality of the therapeutic relationship. This aspect of the approach lessens the chances of dehumanizing psychotherapy by making it a mechanical process" (p. 51). However, in a later book Corey (1982) points out one of the major limitations of the person-centered approach to counseling:

> I see the model as an excellent place to begin a counseling relationship, for unless trust is established and attitudes of respect, care, acceptance and warmth are communicated, most counseling interventions will fail. But it is not a good place to remain as the counseling process develops although I see the core conditions that Rogers describes as being necessary for client change to occur. I also see the need for the knowledge and skills of counselors to be applied in a more directive manner, than is called for in the person-centered model. (P. 94)

Related entry: HUMANISTIC APPROACHES TO COUNSELING.

References

Corey, G. (1977). *Theory and practice of counseling and psychotherapy* (1st ed.). Monterey, CA: Brooks/Cole.
Corey, G. (1982). *Theory and practice of counseling and psychotherapy* (2nd ed.). Monterey, CA: Brooks/Cole.

AFRICAN AMERICANS. Counseling interventions should consider both individual behaviors of clients and dysfunctional system relationships.

By one report (Sue, 1977), 52 percent of African Americans, compared with 30 percent of white Americans, drop out of counseling. Counselors and African American clients may differ over their interpretation of time. Among middle-class African Americans, lateness for counseling appointments may reflect resistance, but counselors should consider other possible contextual explanations as well. In some cases, it may be helpful to develop special orientation programs to prepare African American clients and their families for counseling (see Acosta, Evans, Yamamoto, & Wilcox, 1980).

Despite some reports to the contrary, poor African American children and their families have been found to respond positively to "insight" approaches to counseling (see Meers, 1970). In counseling these clients, it is important to be attuned to body language, an aspect of communication generally considered more developed among African Americans than white Americans (Smith, 1981).

The literature has identified four major values of African American families that reflect their experiences in the United States. These values concern the importance of religion and the church, the importance of the extended family and kinship networks, the importance of flexible family roles, and the importance of education (see Gibbs, 1989).

Between 1960 and 1984, the suicide rate for African American male adolescents in the 15–24 age group nearly tripled, from 4.1 to 11.2 per 100,000, while the rate for African American females in this age range nearly doubled, from 1.3 to 2.4 per 100,000 (U.S. Department of Health and Human Services, 1986). The symptoms of suicidal behavior in African American adolescents may be masked by "acting out" and risk-taking behaviors.

African American college level students seek counseling for the same kinds of problems as do their white peers (Gibbs, 1975). However, they are more likely to be concerned about feelings of alienation, academic anxieties, acculturation conflicts, and feelings of victimization.

Surveys of drug and alcohol use show that African American youth have lower rates of alcohol use than whites and equal rates of marijuana use (Dembo, 1988). However, rates of cocaine and heroin use are generally reported to be higher among older African American youth than among whites (Brunswick, 1979).

Short-term ego oriented counseling is an approach recommended for African American adolescents with nonpsychotic disorders (Gibbs, 1989). This approach focuses on problem solving and on strengthening coping skills, and is time limited.

Related entries: BLACK RACIAL IDENTITY DEVELOPMENT; MULTICULTURAL COUNSELING.

References

Acosta, F. X., Evans, L. A., Yamamoto, J., & Wilcox, S. (1980). Helping minority and low income psychotherapy patients "tell it like it is." *Journal of Biocommunication, 7,* 13–19.

Allen, L., & Majidi-Ahu, S. (1989). Black American children. In J. T. Gibbs & L. N. Huang & Assocs. (Eds.), *Children of color: Psychological interventions with minority youth* (pp. 148–178). San Francisco: Jossey-Bass.

Brunswick, A. (1979). Black youths and drug use behavior. In G. Beschner & A. Freidman (Eds.), *Youth and drug abuse: Problems, issues and treatment.* Lexington, MA: Lexington Books.

Dembo, R. (1988). Delinquency among black male youth. In J. T. Gibbs (Ed.), *Young, black, and male in America: An endangered species.* Dover, MA: Auburn House.

Gibbs, J. T. (1975). Use of mental health services by black students at a predominantly white university: A three year study. *American Journal of Orthopsychiatry, 45,* 430–445.

Gibbs, J. T. (1989). Black American adolescents. In J. T. Gibbs & L. N. Huang & Assocs. (Eds.), *Children of color: Psychological interventions with minority youth* (pp. 179–223). San Francisco: Jossey-Bass.

Meers, D. (1970). Contributions of ghetto culture to symptom formation: Psychoanalytic studies of ego anomalies in children. *Psychoanalytic Study of the Child, 25,* 209–230.

Smith, E. (1981). Cultural and historical perspectives in counseling blacks. In D. W. Sue (Ed.), *Counseling the culturally different: Theory and practice.* New York: Wiley.

Sue, S. (1977). Community mental health services to minority groups: Some optimism, some pessimism. *American Psychologist, 32,* 616–624.

U.S. Department of Health and Human Services (1986). *Health, United States 1986.* Washington, DC: National Center for Health Statistics.

ALCOHOLISM. Alcoholics are both physically and psychologically dependent. They spend a great deal of their time drinking to reduce psychological tension and to prevent withdrawal symptoms.

Alcoholism can be described as a disease: "a chronic, primary, hereditary eventually fatal disease that progresses from an early physiological susceptibility into an addiction characterized by tolerance changes, physiological dependence and loss of control over drinking" (Mueller & Ketchum, 1987, p. 9). Freudian counselors argue that alcoholism can be attributed to self-destructive tendencies and to inappropriate dependence (Bennett & Woolf, 1983), while behavioral counselors believe that alcoholism occurs because drinking habits are learned and maintained by certain sociological, psychological, and physiological factors (Miller & Eisler, 1976). For them, tension reduction reinforces alcohol usage.

Cultural groups differ in their patterns of alcohol usage. Jews and Italians have low alcoholism rates, whereas the Irish and French are higher on the scale of alcoholism (Callahan, Cisin, & Crosley, 1969; Valiant & Milofsky, 1982). Native Americans have the highest rates of alcoholism in the United States (Smith-Peterson, 1983).

Many counselors and researchers believe that abstinence is the primary and essential goal of alcoholism counseling. Pietrofesa, Hoffman, and Splete (1984) state this position clearly: "Considering alcoholism is a progressive disease and noting the paucity of research to support the concept of controlled drinking, it is apparent that any implementation of this approach is not in the best interests of the recovering alcoholic" (p. 408). Most counselors treating persons with alcohol problems insist that they join Alcoholics Anonymous. This self-help organization, begun in the early 1930s, developed a spiritually based system to help alcoholics remain sober. The program includes twelve steps in which alcoholics must acknowledge that they need a power greater than themselves to maintain abstinence.

Related entry: CODEPENDENCE.

References

Bennett, G., & Woolf, D. S. (1983). Current approaches to substance abuse therapy. In G. Bennett, C. Vourakis, & D. S. Woolf (Eds.), *Substance abuse: Pharmacologic, developmental and clinical perspectives* (pp. 341–369). New York: John Wiley and Sons.

Callahan, D., Cisin, D. H., & Crosley, H. M. (1969). *American drinking practices: A national study of drinking behaviors and attitudes.* New Brunswick, NJ: Rutgers Center of Alcohol Studies.

Miller, P. M., & Eisler, R. M. (1976). Alcohol and drug abuse. In W. E. Craighead, A. E. Kazdin, & M. J. Mahoney (Eds.), *Behavior modification principles, issues and applications* (pp. 365–393). Boston: Houghton Mifflin.

Mueller, L. A., & Ketchum, K. (1987). *Recovering: How to get and stay sober.* New York: Bantam.

Pietrofesa, J. J., Hoffman, A., & Splete, H. H. (1984). *Counseling: An introduction* (2nd ed.). Boston: Houghton Mifflin.

Smith-Peterson, C. (1983). Substance abuse and cultural diversity. In G. Bennett, C. Vourakis, & D. S. Woolf (Eds.), *Substance abuse: Pharmacologic, developmental and clinical perspectives* (pp. 370–382). New York: John Wiley and Sons.

Valiant, D. E., & Milofsky, C. S. (1982). The etiology of alcoholism: A prospective viewpoint. *American Psychologist, 37,* 494–503.

AMERICAN ASSOCIATION FOR COUNSELING (AAC). The American Association for Counseling is a professional organization for counselors that in 1987 had a membership of over 55,000. From 1983 until 1992 this professional group was known as the American Association for Counseling and Development.

In March 1934 the Council of Guidance and Personnel Associations was established at a meeting in Cleveland, Ohio. This association included the Alliance for Guidance of Rural Youth, the American College Personnel Association, the National Association of Deans of Women, the National Association of Guidance Supervisors, and the National Vocational Guidance Association. In 1951 this association was replaced by the American Personnel and Guidance Association. Its constituencies included the American College Personnel Association, the National Association of Guidance Supervisors and Counselor Trainers, and the National Vocational Guidance Association. The American Personnel and Guidance Association in 1983 became the American Association for Counseling and Development and later the American Association for Counseling.

The AAC publishes the *Journal of Counseling* (JC), formerly the *Personnel and Guidance Journal* (PGJ), and the *AAC Guidepost.* The organization sponsors or coordinates yearly conventions including both workshops and presentations, as well as national task forces to make recommendations about policies and laws dealing with counseling. Members of this association are predominantly master's degree counselors in schools and community agencies.

AAC includes the following divisions:

1. ACPA (American College Personnel Association)

2. ACES (Association for Counselor Education and Supervision)

3. NCDA (National Career Development Association)

4. AHEAD (Association for Humanistic Education and Development)

5. ASCA (American School Counselor Association)

6. ARCA (American Rehabilitation Counseling Association)

7. AMECD (Association for Measurement and Evaluation in Counseling and Development)

8. NECA (National Employment Counselors Association)

9. AMCD (Association for Multicultural Counseling and Development)

10. ARVIC (Association for Religious and Values Issues in Counseling)

11. ASGW (Association for Specialists in Group Work)

12. POCA (Public Offender Counselors Association)

13. AMHCA (American Mental Health Counselors Association)

14. MECA (Military Education and Counselors Association)

15. AADA (Association for Adult Development and Aging)

Related entry: COUNSELING.

References

Aubrey, R. F. (1982). A house divided: Guidance and counseling in twentieth century America. *Personnel and Guidance Journal, 60,* 198–204.
Journal of Counseling and Development (1985, June).

AMERICAN ASSOCIATION FOR MARRIAGE AND FAMILY THERAPY (AAMFT).

This professional association was established in 1945 to develop standards and to upgrade practices in both marriage and family counseling (Horne & Ohlsen, 1982).

In the early 1950s, research by a number of scholars led to the development of counseling for total families, rather than just for disturbed members of families. At about this same time, theories of counseling were being developed that attributed the sources of disturbances in children to family systems.

Pioneers in marriage counseling were instrumental in helping establish the American Association of Marriage Counselors in 1941, which is the predecessor organization to the American Association for Marriage and Family Therapy. These early marriage counselors established a precedent for seeing couples together in conjoint sessions.

Marriage and family counselors have unique confidentiality problems because their clients may be members of a group. As a consequence, the *AAMFT Code of Ethical Principles* (1988) has stated specific limitations regarding confidentiality. Marriage and family therapists cannot disclose client confidences to anyone except (1) as mandated by law; (2) to prevent a clear and immediate danger to a person or persons; (3) where the marriage and family therapist is a defendant in a civil, criminal, or disciplinary action arising from the therapy (in which case client confidences may only be disclosed in the course of that action); or (4) if a waiver has previously been obtained in writing, and then such information may only be revealed in accordance with the terms of the waiver. The ethical guidelines for this professional association also deal with such issues as responsibility to clients; professional competence and integrity; responsibility to students, employees, and supervisees; responsibility to the profession; and fees and advertising.

Related entry: FAMILY COUNSELING.

References

American Association for Marriage and Family Therapy (1988). *AAMFT code of ethical principles for marriage and family therapists.* Washington, DC: American Association for Marriage and Family Therapy.

Horne, A. M., & Ohlsen, M. M. (1982). *Family counseling and therapy.* Itasca, IL: F. E. Peacock.

AMERICAN PSYCHOLOGICAL ASSOCIATION DIVISION 17—COUNSELING PSYCHOLOGY. A professional association of psychologists interested and trained in working with the normal concerns of individuals, groups, and families. Before 1951 this professional group was known as the Division of Counseling and Guidance.

The initial creation of Division 17 in the American Psychological Association stemmed from the 1943 Joint Constitutional Committee of the American Psychological Association and the American Association of Applied Psychology. The original name of this group was the Division of Personnel Psychologists. Between 1944 and 1951 this charter division of the American Psychological Association, under the title of Counseling and Guidance, had five different names.

Division 17 has developed Standards for Providers of Counseling Psychological Services. This association offers workshops, papers, and panels at national conventions and organizes national task forces to work on issues in the field. Members are doctorate level psychologists.

Super (1955) distinguished between counseling psychology and clinical psychology, arguing that counseling psychology is more concerned with normal growth and development, while clinical psychology is concerned with the diagnosis and treatment of psychopathology. He also noted that counseling psychology arose from a merger between a broadening field of vocational developmental counseling and the new humanistic therapeutic approach. Although counseling psychology may have had a difficult time establishing a clear identity within the American Psychological Association (Whitely, 1984), Division 17 has had a major impact on defining the professional role of counseling psychologists in the United States.

Related entry: COUNSELING PSYCHOLOGIST.

References

Super, D. E. (1955). Transition: From vocational guidance to counseling psychology. *Journal of Counseling Psychology, 2,* 3–9.

Whitely, J. M. (1984). Counseling psychology: A historical perspective. *The Counseling Psychologist, 12,* 2–109.

ANAL STAGE. Freud's second phase of psychosexual development, extending from eighteen months to three years of age.

A time in the life of children when most of their erotic pleasure is the outcome of retaining and expelling feces. Their developmental tasks include learning independence, personal power, and autonomy. During this phase in their development, children also learn to recognize and deal with negative feelings.

When toilet training begins during the second year, children have their first major experience with discipline. The method of toilet training and the parents' feelings, attitudes, and reactions toward the child can have an effect on the formation of the child's personality traits. Freud described the characteristics of anal aggressive personalities as including cruelty, the inappropriate display of anger, and extreme disorderliness, while he said that adults with anal retentive personalities were more apt to display such characteristics as extreme orderliness, hoarding, stubbornness, and stinginess. The assumption is that certain adult characteristics can have their roots in children's experiences during their anal phase of psychosexual development.

Related entries: GENITAL STAGE; ORAL STAGE; PHALLIC STAGE; PSYCHOANALYTIC COUNSELING; PSYCHOSEXUAL STAGES OF DEVELOPMENT.

References

Freud, S. (1951). Observations on child development. *Psychoanalytic Study of the Child, 6,* 18–30.

Freud, S. (1961). On transformations of instinct as exemplified in anal erotism. In J. Strachey (Ed. and Trans.), *The standard edition of the complete psychological works of Sigmund Freud* (Vol. 17). London: Hogarth Press. (Original work published 1923)

Hall, C. (1954). *A primer of Freudian psychology.* New York: New American Library.

ANALYSIS. The collection of reliable, valid, and relevant information that can be used by a counselor and client to diagnose characteristics which facilitate or inhibit satisfactory adjustment in school and at work.

E. G. Williamson (1939, 1950) described a first step in counseling as analysis. The counselor and the client collect data into a case history which yields a clear picture of the client as a growing, dynamic, multidimensional individual. Each client's case history portrays a unique combination of general traits which have a characteristic style totally different from that of other clients.

Six analytical tools are cumulative records, the interview, time distribution forms, autobiographies, anecdotes, and psychological tests.

Williamson's model of clinical counseling emphasizes the necessity of collecting complete case data before diagnosis and counseling take place. He cautions counselors that the tendency to rationalize and conceal serious problems is so prevalent that they should analyze and then diagnose in all problem areas, not merely in those areas mentioned by the clients.

Related entries: CLINICAL COUNSELING; DIRECTIVE APPROACH TO COUNSELING.

References

Williamson, E. G. (1939). *How to counsel students.* New York: McGraw-Hill.
Williamson, E. G. (1950). *Counseling adolescents.* New York: McGraw-Hill.

ANALYTICAL COUNSELING. Carl Jung first identified a set of therapeutic interventions that attempt to create, by means of a symbolic approach, a dialectical relationship between consciousness and the unconscious.

Through these specific interventions, communication is facilitated via dreams, fantasies, and other unconscious products between the conscious state of the client and his/her personal as well as collective unconscious. Jung saw counseling as a process of developing self-knowledge, as a reconstruction of the personality or even as education. Jung as a counselor was unorthodox, doing one thing in a given case and doing the opposite in the next one. However, as a rule, analytical counseling begins with a thorough exploration of the client's conscious state. The counselor will discuss the past history of the client, various important influences in his/her life, attitudes, values, and ideas. Clients slowly learn to introspect, and then dreamwork may be introduced. These activities provide clients with a deepened awareness of the workings of their unconscious. They will become acquainted with the compensatory nature of the unconscious and can find how their conscious attitudes may be accompanied by opposite attitudes in their unconscious. This situation creates tension and anxiety as well as the possibilities for transformation and resolution of seemingly contradictory personal beliefs and attitudes.

In analytical counseling the client's unconscious products (dreams, fantasies, artistic productions) are interpreted not only in terms of antecedent causes, but primarily as pointing the way toward further development. The major principle of analytical counseling is for the counselor to follow the guidance of the client's unconscious, and to avoid any preconceptions or fixed ideas. The basis for counseling is experiencing rather than intellectual understanding. In some cases, clients may be asked to stay with their depression and accept it as an unconscious message.

Related entries: ANIMA; ANIMUS; ARCHETYPES.

References

Jung, C. G. (1933). *Modern man in search of a soul.* New York: Harcourt, Brace.
Kauffman, Y. (1989). Analytical psychotherapy. In R. J. Corsini & D. Wedding (Eds.), *Current psychotherapies* (4th ed., pp. 119–154). Itasca, IL: F. E. Peacock.

ANECDOTAL RECORDS. Written observations of some significant aspect of another person's conduct, or records of an episode in the life of a person; narratives of events in which a person takes part that may reveal something significant in understanding his/her personality.

Teachers may be asked to write anecdotal records that are descriptions of student behaviors they have heard or observed—antisocial behaviors, exceptional intellectual behaviors, unusual leadership, or examples of social responsibility. The observations are recorded in a straightforward manner, and followed in some cases by the teacher's inferences as to what the observed behaviors mean. A number of anecdotes coming from different teachers during a school year may be used by counselors in making case studies of specific clients. A synthesis of these anecdotes is necessary to avoid unrepresentative sampling of behaviors.

Related entries: GUIDANCE; SCHOOL PSYCHOLOGIST.

References

Roeber, E. C., Smith, G., & Erickson, C. E. (1955). *Organization and administration of guidance services* (2nd ed.). New York: McGraw-Hill.
Williamson, E. G., & Hahn, M. E. (1940). *Introduction to high school counseling.* New York: McGraw-Hill.

ANIMA. In analytical personality theory, this term represents the feminine component of the male personality (Jung, 1964).

The unconscious feminine side of a male's personality is called the anima. According to Carl Jung, the anima accounts for a man's capacity for relatedness, emotionality, involvement with people and ideas, a spontaneous and unplanned approach to life and its experiences, sensuality, and instinctuality. The anima is symbolized by female figures in a man's unconscious products, appearing as the beloved one, princess, priestess, witch, prostitute, or nymph. If the anima is not integrated into the personality, a man seems abstract, barren, and detached, while those men who are overwhelmed by their anima are easily swayed by moods, depressions, and anxieties.

Men may experience their anima, but they cannot totally control it.

Related entries: ANALYTICAL COUNSELING; ANIMUS; SEX-ROLE STEREOTYPES.

References

Jung, C. J. (1964). *Man and his symbols.* Garden City, NY: Doubleday.
Maduro, R. J., & Wheelwright, J. B. (1983). Analytical psychology. In R. J. Corsini & A. J. Marsella (Eds.), *Personality theories, research and assessment* (pp. 125–188). Itasca, IL: F. E. Peacock.

ANIMUS. In analytical personality theory, the masculine component of the female personality (Jung, 1964).

The unconscious masculine side of a female's personality is called the animus. According to Carl Jung and his followers, the animus accounts for a woman's abilities to discriminate and differentiate, to judge and to act, to be disciplined and to act aggressively. An animus driven woman is characterized by argumentativeness, dogmatism, and behaviors based on prejudices and preconceived notions. A woman's animus is the sum total of her expectations, a system of unconscious standards used in judging and experiencing her world. The animus may be symbolized by male figures appearing in a woman's dreams and fantasies as a husband, son, father, lover, or son.

Women may experience their animus, but they cannot totally control it.

Related entries: ANALYTICAL COUNSELING; ANIMA; SEX-ROLE STEREOTYPES.

References

Jung, C. J. (1964). *Man and his symbols.* Garden City, NY: Doubleday.
Maduro, R. J., & Wheelwright, J. B. (1983). Analytical psychology. In R. J. Corsini & A. J. Marsella (Eds.), *Personality theories, research and assessment* (pp. 125–188). Itasca, IL: F. E. Peacock.

ANOREXIA NERVOSA. A form of eating disorder in which the individual overly restricts his or her caloric intake, leading to severe malnutrition and possible physiological harm.

This disorder is characterized by a constellation of maladaptive beliefs that emphasize one central assumption: "My body weight and shape determine my worth and/or my social acceptability." Anorexic clients often show distortions in information processing. They may misinterpret symptoms of fullness after meals as signs that they are getting fat. They will often misperceive their images in mirrors or photographs as much fatter than they actually are.

Mirkin (1983) presented a successful family treatment approach for anorexia nervosa. In this case the condition was seen as an illness that stemmed from an overprotective family that was suppressing autonomy in an adolescent child. Anorexia nervosa was considered a strategy used by the client to control the family. In counseling, the client's refusal to eat was termed "disobedient behavior" and dealt with as unacceptable by the parents. Weight loss was punished by loss of new privileges, while weight gain allowed her more autonomy.

Related entry: ADOLESCENCE.

References

Beck, A. T., & Weishaar, M. E. (1989). Cognitive therapy. In R. J. Corsini & D. Wedding (Eds.), *Current psychotherapies* (4th ed., pp. 285–322). Itasca, IL: F. E. Peacock.
Mirkin, M. D. (1983). The Peter Pan syndrome: Inpatient treatment of adolescent nervosa. *International Journal of Family Therapy, 5,* 179–189.

ANXIETY. A state of tension that motivates us to do something. Its function is to warn us of impending danger. Typically, anxiety is accompanied by rapid heartbeat, shortness of breath, and similar manifestations of arousal of the autonomic nervous system.

In psychoanalytic approaches to counseling, three kinds of anxiety are differentiated: reality, neurotic, and moral. Reality anxiety is a fear of danger from the external world, and the level of anxiety is appropriate to the degree of threat. Neurotic anxiety is a fear that the instincts will get out of hand and cause one to do something for which one will be punished. Moral anxiety is fear of one's own conscience.

Both psychoanalytic and existential counselors view anxiety as being at the center of the dynamic structure of the personality. Psychopathology is attributed to anxiety and the unconscious defense mechanisms that are generated to deal with anxiety. These psychological mechanisms constitute psychopathology because they provide safety but restrict growth.

To existential counselors, anxiety springs from confrontation with death, freedom, isolation, and meaninglessness. They define anxiety more broadly than do counselors of other theoretical persuasions. Anxiety arises from our personal need to survive, to preserve our being, and to assert our being. May defined anxiety as "the threat to our existence or to values we identify with our existence" (1977, p. 205). Anxiety is considered more basic than fear. One of the goals of existential counselors is to help their clients confront anxiety as fully as possible, thus reducing anxiety to objective fears.

Neurotic anxiety is not appropriate to the situation; it is repressed, it is destructive, and it tends to paralyze an individual. Normal anxiety is an unavoidable part of the human condition. It is appropriate, does not require repression, and can be used for creative purposes.

Behavioral counselors assume that anxiety responses are learned behaviors and may be extinguished. If a response that is contradictory to anxiety results in a more pleasant state or more productive behavior for the client, the new response to anxiety-evoking stimuli will gradually replace the anxiety responses. Cognitive-behavioral counselors utilize coping skills programs that expose their clients to anxiety-provoking situations by means of role play and imagery, then require them to evaluate their anxiety levels, become aware of anxiety-provoking cognitions that they experience in stressful situations, reevaluate their self-statements, and note the level of anxiety following the reevaluations.

Related entry: STRESS.

References

Marks, D. M. (1981). *Cure and care of the neuroses.* New York: Wiley.
May, R. (1977). *The meaning of anxiety* (Rev. ed.). New York: Norton.
Meichenbaum, D. (1977). *Cognitive behavior modification.* New York: Plenum.

APPLIED BEHAVIOR ANALYSIS. A form of behavior therapy that emphasizes changes in observable behaviors rather than changes in cognitive events or experiences.

Single subject experimental designs are used to determine the relationship among specific behaviors, antecedents, and consequences. Applied behavior analysis is a strategy in contemporary behavior therapy that focuses exclusively on observable behaviors and rejects the idea that counselors should deal with the cognitive mediating processes of clients. This approach can be traced to B. F. Skinner (1953), whose fundamental assumption was that behavior is a function of its consequences. As a result, he recommended that counseling procedures alter relationships between behaviors and consequences through the use of techniques based on reinforcement, punishment, extinction, and stimulus control. These behavioral counselors do not deal with covert unobservable elements such as needs, drives, motives, traits, and conflicts.

Skinner's concept of applied behavior analysis is based on the principles of operant conditioning, which assume that changes in behaviors are brought about when those behaviors are followed by certain consequences. Learning, he argued, cannot occur in the absence of reinforcement, either positive or negative. Actions that are reinforced are repeated, while those that are discouraged tend to be extinguished. Applied behavior analysis is based on reinforcement principles, and the goal is to identify and control environmental factors that lead to behavioral changes.

Radical behaviorism as exemplified in applied behavior analysis has been criticized for losing sight of the importance of the person and for lacking a theory of personality. Critics say that clients are seen as controlled only by situational forces rather than being free, self-directed persons who are responsible for their own growth and actions.

Related entries: BEHAVIOR MODIFICATION; BEHAVIORAL ASSESSMENT; BEHAVIORAL COUNSELING; FAMILY COUNSELING.

References

Corey, G. (1991). *Theory and practice of counseling and psychotherapy.* Belmont, CA: Brooks/Cole.

Skinner, B. F. (1953). *Science and human behavior.* New York: Macmillan.

APTITUDE TEST. A measure of a person's potential abilities to function satisfactorily in specific domains of human behavior.

Items in aptitude tests are presumed to be related to learning certain knowledge skills or occupational tasks in the future. Practical distinctions between aptitude and achievement tests are difficult to make because all human performance on tests is contingent upon a client's previous learning and life experiences. Aptitude tests are usually categorized as either single domain or multifactor batteries. The former focus on the assessment of a specific aspect of human performance, while the latter consist of sets of single domain tests having a common format, administration procedure, and norm group. Criterion validity or predictive validity and internal consistency reliability are the most important criteria for judging the usefulness of aptitude tests.

Related entries: ACHIEVEMENT TEST; INTELLIGENCE TESTS.

References

American Psychological Association, American Educational Research Association, and National Council on Measurement in Education (1985). *Standards for educational and psychological testing.* Washington, DC: APA.

Drummond, R. J. (1988). *Appraisal procedures for counselors and helping professionals.* Columbus, OH: Charles Merrill.

ARCHETYPES. An analytical personality theory, this term refers to the primordial images that constitute the nonpersonal unconscious. They are inborn psychic predispositions to perception, emotion, and behavior.

The archetype of the self is an expression of a person's inherent predisposition to experience wholeness, centeredness, and meaning in life. Archetypes, according to Carl Jung, give rise to equivalent forms of imagery in myths, fairy tales, and works of art in many cultures. Archetypes exist in people as potentialities; one's life circumstances (one's particular culture, family, and environment) determine which of the archetypes will be actualized, and in which way. The archetype is a psychic propensity that is evoked by experiences which give it a specific form. Each person experiences ''the heroic struggle'' differently, according to their personality and environment. Under normal circumstances, the archetypical images will express contemporary motifs. Today, people are not likely to dream about slaying dragons, but rather about fighting with their mothers-in-law or walking through dark tunnels. Archetypes can give life a sense of meaning, helping people to deal with suffering that otherwise might seem pointless.

Archetypes are part of the nonpersonal unconscious, a layer of the unconscious not directly amenable to consciousness. The nonpersonal unconscious can be observed indirectly through its manifestations in eternal themes in mythology, folklore, and art. Archetypes include rebirth, the Great Mother, the Wise Old Man, the Trickster, the Divine Child, wholeness, and God. Some archetypes that influence the development of the personality include the persona, the shadow, the animus or anima, and the self.

Related entry: ANALYTICAL COUNSELING.

References

Jung, C. G. (1968). *The archetypes and the collective unconscious: Collected works* (Vol. A, Part I, Bollingen Series 20). Princeton, NJ: Princeton University Press. (Originally published 1934)

Kaufman, G. (1989). Analytical psychotherapy. In R. J. Corsini & D. Wedding (Eds.), *Current psychotherapies* (4th ed., pp. 119–154). Itasca, IL: F. E. Peacock.

ASSERTIVENESS TRAINING. Counseling procedures used to help inhibited persons learn to express their feelings, opinions, and beliefs in a productive and responsible manner.

The concept of assertiveness includes the ability to communicate your wishes, ideas, and intentions in direct and honest ways and to react appropriately to similar communications from others. Assertive behaviors may include expressions of aggression, but they also can include expressions of warm, friendly, affectionate behaviors. Assertiveness behaviors can be contrasted with inhibited behaviors.

Assertive behaviors include ''feeling talk''; ''facial talk''; the ability to make ''contradictory and attack'' statements when one disagrees with someone; the frequent use of I statements; the ability to accept praise and compliments; the ability to praise oneself; and the ability to live for the present and be spontaneous. The expression of these assertive behaviors is thought to inhibit or reduce anxiety because they are incompatible with anxiety responses. If persons do not exercise these assertive behaviors, they may become anxious, develop somatic symptoms, and even develop pathological changes in predisposed organs.

Assertiveness training can include behavioral rehearsal, social modeling, positive reinforcement, and cognitive restructuring. However, assertiveness training does not represent a universally agreed upon set of counseling procedures. Most of these procedures emphasize either anxiety reduction or teaching appropriate social skills to deal with a wide range of interpersonal concerns relating to dating and sexual assertiveness, impotence, and depression. Assertiveness training can be described as a form of social skills training for those persons who want to make friends, for those who want to learn skills for interacting with the opposite sex, or for those who want to improve their relationships with mates, peers, and superiors. Specific counseling strategies used in assertion training include instruction, feedback, modeling, behavioral rehearsal, social reinforcement, and homework assignments.

Related entries: COGNITIVE-BEHAVIORAL COUNSELING; SOCIAL SKILLS TRAINING; SOCIAL LEARNING THEORY.

References

Flowers, J. V., & Booraem, C. D. (1980). Simulation and role playing methods. In F. H. Kanfer & A. P. Goldstein (Eds.), *Helping people change* (2nd ed., pp. 117–209). New York: Pergamon.

Goldfried, M. R., & Davison, G. C. (1976). *Clinical behavior therapy.* New York: Holt, Rinehart and Winston.

Remm, D. C., & Cunningham, H. M. (1985). Behavior therapies. In S. J. Lynn & J. P. Garske (Eds.), *Contemporary psychotherapies: Models and methods* (pp. 221–259). Columbus, OH: Charles Merrill.

Wolpe, J. (1969). *The practice of behavior therapy.* New York: Pergamon.

ASSESSMENT. A set of procedures used for developing impressions and images, making decisions, and checking hypotheses about the pattern of characteristics that determines a person's behavior in interactions with the environment (see Sundberg, 1977).

Three purposes for assessment are to develop descriptions of a person, to help make decisions about the relation of the person to his/her present and/or future environments, and to use in testing hypotheses about personality. These three purposes can be described as image making, decision making, and theory building.

The word *assessment* first appeared as a psychological term in the book *Assessment of Men* (Office of Strategic Services Staff, 1948). The book was a report of the activities of the branch of the U.S. Office of Strategic Services that had been charged with selecting persons to serve on special missions in World War II. Their approach involved using many techniques and many judges to collect information on a group of individuals usually living together in a special testing situation called an assessment center.

The history of assessment includes the history of psychological testing, but tests should be considered as examples of some tools used for assessment purposes. The human problems and decisions that psychological assessment addresses are very old questions about the nature of the human condition. Still, most standardized measures for assessment date from the late nineteenth century and early twentieth century.

Related entries: ANECDOTAL RECORDS; BEHAVIORAL ASSESSMENT; INTAKE INTERVIEW; INTELLIGENCE TESTS; RELIABILITY; VALIDITY.

References

Anastasi, A. (1992). What counselors should know about the use and interpretation of psychological tests. *Journal of Counseling and Development, 70*(5), 610–615.

Goldman, L. (1992). Qualitative assessment: An approach for counselors. *Journal of Counseling and Development, 70*(5), 616–621.

Office of Strategic Services Staff (1948). *Assessment of men.* New York: Holt, Rinehart and Winston.

Sundberg, N. D. (1977). *Assessment of persons.* Englewood Cliffs, NJ: Prentice-Hall.

ATTENDING SKILLS. The counselor's presence or "being with" clients. Eye contact and body language, as well as active and passive listening, are components of attending skills.

Attending is done both psychologically, by listening attentively to and considering what a client says, and physically, by displaying a posture of interest. Egan (1982) described the five major appropriate physical attending skills:

1. Face the client squarely.

2. Provide an open posture.

3. At times, lean toward the client.

4. Maintain eye contact.

5. Relax.

Active listening by counselors allows clients to know that they are being paid attention to; it reassures them and encourages them to explore and define their concerns. Active listening can involve the uses of minimal encouragers such as "uh-huh," "and so," "mmm," and "yes" and restatements or repetitions of all or a selected portion of a client's previous communications. Another important attending skill is passive listening or effectively using silence in a counseling session. This important attending skill often allows the counselor to communicate a sincere and deep acceptance to clients.

Related entries: CLIENT-CENTERED COUNSELING; HELPING MODEL (CARKHUFF); HELPING MODEL (EGAN).

References

Egan, G. (1982). *The skilled helper: Model skills and methods for effective helping* (2nd ed.). Monterey, CA: Brooks/Cole.
Ivey, A. E., & Simek-Downing, L. (1980). *Counseling and psychotherapy: Skills, theories and practice.* Englewood Cliffs, NJ: Prentice-Hall.

ATTNEAVE, CAROLYN (b. 1920). A prominent Native American psychologist who is internationally known for her expertise in cross-cultural issues in counseling and her work in social network counseling for families. Her book *Family Networks: Retribalization and Healing* (with Ross Speck) has been translated into Japanese, Spanish, Dutch, and German.

Carolyn Lewis Attneave was born in El Paso, Texas. She was descended from the Delaware Indian tribe on her mother's side. In 1949 she married Fred Attneave II, and they moved to Oxford, Mississippi, where two children were born to them.

She completed her Ph.D. at Stanford University in 1952 and subsequently took a position as the Director of Student Personnel at Texas Women's University in Denton. Later she accepted a position at the University of Washington as a professor of psychology and the Director of the American Indian Studies Program in 1975. In 1987 she retired from the University of Washington.

Related entries: FAMILY COUNSELING; NATIVE AMERICANS.

References

Attneave, C. (1969). Therapy in tribal settings and urban network intervention. *Family Process, 8,* 192–210.
Lamfrombroise, T. D., & Fleming, C. (1990). Keeper of the fire: A profile of Carolyn Attneave. In P. P. Heppner (Ed.), *Pioneers in counseling and development: Personal and professional perspectives* (pp. 225–231). Alexandria, VA: American Association for Counseling and Development.
Speck, R., & Attneave, C. (1973). *Family networks: Retribalization and healing.* New York: Random House.

AUTHENTICITY. Counselors or clients who are being genuine, real, and congruent in their relationships with others display authenticity. Their inner experiences and their outer expressions of these experiences match.

According to Rogers (1987), one of the essential conditions necessary for constructive personality changes to occur in counseling is a counselor who is genuine, integrated, and authentic. Through authenticity, the counselor serves as a model of a person struggling toward realness and congruence. Authentic counselors are spontaneously experiencing their feelings, both positive and negative. This does not mean that they impulsively share all their feelings, for their self-disclosures must be appropriate. Counselor authenticity or congruence exists on a continuum rather than on an either-or basis.

In Gestalt counseling, according to Perls (1970), it is necessary to go through the various layers of neurosis in order to get to the authentic self. The first layer, or the phony, consists of reacting to others in stereotypical and inauthentic ways. At the second layer, or the phobic, persons avoid the emotional pain that is involved in seeing aspects of themselves that they would prefer to deny. Beneath this layer is the impasse, or the point at which they are stuck and convinced that they do not have the resources to proceed without environmental support. At this impasse, they feel a sense of deadness and feel that they are nothing. If they allow themselves to experience their deadness rather than deny it or run away, then the implosive level comes into being. By getting in contact with their deadness and inauthentic ways, they expose their defenses and make contact with their genuine selves. When they peel back the implosive layer, they contact their explosive layer and let go of phony roles and pretenses. With these actions, they are able to release tremendous amounts of energy that they have been holding on to by pretending to be what they are not. To be authentic, it is necessary to achieve this explosion.

Related entries: ACCEPTANCE; EMPATHY; GESTALT COUNSELING.

References

Perls, F. (1970). Four lectures. In J. Fagan & I. Shepherd (Eds.), *Gestalt therapy now* (pp. 14–38). New York: Harper and Row.

Rogers, C. (1987). The underlying theory drawn from experiences with individuals and groups. *Counseling and Values, 32,* 38–45.

AUTOMATIC THOUGHTS. Personal beliefs or ideas that are spontaneously triggered by particular stimuli and lead to certain dysfunctional responses.

Automatic thoughts come to mind spontaneously; they intercede between an event or stimulus and the individual's emotional and behavioral reactions. They are more stable and less accessible than voluntary thoughts. Cognitive distortions that are evident in thoughts are generated by underlying maladaptive assumptions. The assumption that one is responsible for other people's happiness can produce numerous negative automatic thoughts in people who perceive themselves as causing distress to others.

In the initial stages of cognitive counseling, attention is directed to identifying the influences of automatic thoughts on behavioral and emotional conditions of clients. Clients may be asked to record their automatic thoughts when distressed, and then the counselor will demonstrate connections among thoughts, emotions, and behaviors in the client's life. Clients learn to challenge thoughts that interfere with their living; they then question the underlying assumptions that generate such thoughts. By observing automatic thoughts over time and across situations, the assumptions underlying them can be inferred. Once these are identified, the counseling interventions attempt to modify them by examining their validity, adaptiveness, and utility for the client. Automatic thoughts may be tested by using direct evidence or by logical analyses.

Related entries: COGNITIVE-BEHAVIORAL COUNSELING; COGNITIVE COUNSELING; THOUGHT STOPPING.

References

Beck, A. T. (1976). *Cognitive therapy and the emotional disorders.* New York: International Universities Press.

Beck, A. T., & Weishaar, M. E. (1989). Cognitive therapy. In R. J. Corsini & D. Wedding (Eds.), *Current psychotherapies* (4th ed., pp. 285–320). Itasca, IL: F. E. Peacock.

AVERSIVE TECHNIQUES. Interventions used by behavioral counselors to eliminate problematic behaviors that can interfere with the client's learning new behaviors.

Aversive techniques include:

Time out. An intervention that involves providing a client with a special environment in which he/she has no opportunity to receive positive reinforcement. This procedure is most effective when employed for short periods (five minutes) of time and is carefully monitored.

Overcorrection. An intervention in which a client is asked to restore an environment to its natural state and then make it better than normal. For example, children who throw food in the lunchroom might be required to clean up their mess and then wax the floors.

Covert sensitization. An intervention in which undesirable behaviors are eliminated by associating them with unpleasantness. This technique is used with clients who have problems with smoking, obesity, substance abuse, and sexual deviation. Covert sensitization is a verbal technique in which unpleasant scenes are paired with scenes of deviant behaviors.

Aversive techniques are usually not effective over the long run for three reasons: their emotional effects are soon dissipated; they may interfere with the learning of desired behaviors; and they may encourage the client to try to escape, which, when successful, provides positive reinforcement. Before counselors use any aversive techniques, they should obtain written permission from their clients.

Related entry: BEHAVIORAL COUNSELING.

References

Corey, G. (1991). *Theory and practice of counseling psychotherapy* (pp. 228–323). Pacific Grove, CA: Brooks/Cole.

Wilson, G. T. (1989). Behavior therapy. In R. J. Corsini & D. Wedding (Eds.), *Current psychotherapies* (4th ed., pp. 241–284). Itasca, IL: F. E. Peacock.

AWARENESS. A personality process that represents a person's level of contact with his/her present experiences. Awareness may include a personal report about what is actually being perceived and felt in a current situation.

The goal of Gestalt counseling is to increase awareness, which is considered a form of insight. Insight includes an awareness of the patterns of the perceptual field so that the significant realities are apparent. It also includes the formation of a gestalt so that the relevant factors fall into place with respect to the whole (Heidbreder, 1933, p. 355).

Awareness without exploration is not ordinarily sufficient to develop insight. Gestalt counselors use focused awareness and experimentation to achieve insight. The client learns how to become aware of awareness. The aim of Gestalt counseling is the awareness continuum, where what is of greatest concern and interest to the person comes to the foreground; it can be fully experienced and acknowledged so that it can melt into the background, because it is either forgotten or assimilated. Full awareness is the process of being in contact with the most important events in the individual/environment field. Meaningful awareness is of self in the world, in dialogue with the world, and with awareness of others—it is not an inwardly focused introspection.

Related entry: GESTALT COUNSELING.

References

Corey, G. (1990). *Theory and practice of group counseling* (pp. 318–353). Pacific Grove, CA: Brooks/Cole.

Heidbreder, E. (1933). *Seven psychologies.* New York: Century.

AWFULIZING. An irrational belief that an inconvenient or obnoxious occurrence is also awful, horrible, or terrible.

In rational-emotive counseling, it is assumed that some people become psychologically disordered through a process called awfulizing. When individuals feel upset after experiencing an obnoxious occurrence, they almost always convince themselves using irrational beliefs such as "I can't stand this! It is awful that it exists! I am a worthless person for not being able to ward it off! You are a louse for inflicting it upon me!" This chain of beliefs is irrational because it is hardly awful that this particular event occurred in their lives; *awful* is an essentially undefinable term with surplus meaning and no empirical referent. By calling an event awful, the disturbed individual means, first, that it is highly inconvenient, and, second, that it is more than inconvenient, disadvantageous, and unbeneficial. But what noxious event can be, in point of fact, more than inconvenient, disadvantageous, and unbeneficial?

Awfulizing is an irrational belief beyond the realm of empiricism and established by arbitrary fiat. Awfulizing usually takes the form of a statement: "Because I want something, it is not only desirable or preferable that it exist, but it absolutely should and it is awful when it doesn't."

Related entry: RATIONAL-EMOTIVE COUNSELING.

References

Ellis, A. (1989). Rational emotive therapy. In R. J. Corsini & D. Wedding (Eds.), *Current psychotherapies* (4th ed., pp. 197–240). Itasca, IL: F. E. Peacock.

Prochaska, J. O. (1979). *Systems of psychotherapy: A transtheoretical analysis.* Homewood, IL: Dorsey.

B

BASIC ID. An acronym used in multimodal behavioral counseling to assess client problems and identify appropriate interventions (Lazarus, 1973).

According to Lazarus (1989), there are seven modalities to consider when diagnosing client problems and choosing counseling interventions. Each of these modalities interacts with the others and should not be dealt with in isolation.

1. *Behavior.* Behavior includes simple and more complex motor skills and activities such as smiling, talking, writing, eating, smoking, and having sex.
2. *Affect.* Affect includes felt or reported feelings and emotions.
3. *Sensation.* Types of sensation include visual (sight), kinesthetic (touch), auditory (hearing), olfactory (smell), and gustatory (taste).
4. *Imagery.* Imagery comprises mental pictures that exert influence on a client's life.
5. *Cognition.* Cognitions refer to thoughts and beliefs that may be irrational or illogical.
6. *Interpersonal relationships.* Clients' relationships to other persons, such as the ways that they express and accept feelings or the ways that they behave and react to others.
7. *Drugs.* Neurological and biochemical factors that can affect behavior, affective responses, cognitions, sensations, and so on.

Lazarus (1976) believed that most counselors fail to assess and treat these seven basic modalities. He argued that counseling that includes more modalities will be more effective and will yield more durable results.

BASIC ID profiles identify specific excesses and deficits throughout the various modalities. Anger, disappointment, disgust, greed, fear, grief, awe, contempt, and boredom, as well as love, hope, faith, ecstasy, optimism, and joy can be accounted for by examining components and interactions within a person's

BASIC ID. Individuals will tend to favor some modalities more than others. Some are sensory reactors, others may be imagery reactors or cognitive reactors. This does not mean that persons will always favor or react in a given modality, but over time a tendency to prefer certain modalities can be observed in their actions.

Related entry: MULTIMODAL APPROACH TO COUNSELING.

References

Lazarus, A. A. (1973). Multimodal behavior therapy: Treating the BASIC ID. *Journal of Nervous and Mental Disease, 56,* 404–411.

Lazarus, A. A. (1976). *Multimodel Behavior Therapy.* New York: Springer.

Lazarus, A. A. (1989). Multimodal therapy. In R. J. Corsini & D. Wedding (Eds.), *Current psychotherapies* (4th ed., pp. 503–546). Itasca, IL: F. E. Peacock.

BASIC MISTAKES. In Adlerian counseling, these are the myths, self-defeating perceptions, and irrational beliefs that are part of a person's basic life style. They are faulty, self-defeating, subjective interpretations of childhood experiences that can influence a person's present approach to life tasks.

Basic mistakes may be classified as follows:

1. *Overgeneralizations.* "People are hostile"; "Life is dangerous."

2. *False or impossible goals of security.* "One false step and you're dead"; "I have to please everybody."

3. *Misperceptions of life and life's demands.* Typical convictions might be "Life never gives me any breaks" and "Life is so hard."

4. *Minimization or denial of one's worth.* "I'm stupid" and "I'm undeserving" or "I'm just a housewife."

5. *Faulty values.* "Be first even if you have to climb over others."

An assessment procedure used by Adlerian counselors asks clients to report their early recollections, along with the feelings and thoughts that accompanied these childhood incidents. These early recollections reveal beliefs, basic mistakes, and self-defeating perceptions that may impact clients' present approaches to tasks in their lives. Adlerians assume that clients will selectively recollect from their past those incidents which are consistent with their current views of themselves.

According to Sonstegard and associates (1982), group counseling may be more effective than individual counseling in helping clients gain insight into their basic mistakes and redirecting their lives.

Related entries: ADLERIAN COUNSELING; INDIVIDUAL PSYCHOLOGY.

References

Mosak, H. (1989). Adlerian psychotherapy. In R. J. Corsini & D. Wedding (Eds.), *Current psychotherapies* (4th ed., pp. 65–116). Itasca, IL: F. E. Peacock.

Sonstegard, M., Dreikurs, R., & Bitter, J. (1982). The teleoanalytic group counseling approach. In G. M. Gazda (Ed.), *Basic approaches to group psychotherapy and counseling* (3rd ed.). Springfield, IL: Charles C. Thomas.

BEHAVIOR MODIFICATION. A type of behavioral counseling that attempts systematically to control contingencies in order to shape and maintain adaptive behavior and/or extinguish maladaptive behavior.

This viewpoint in behavioral counseling can be traced to B. F. Skinner (1953) and has emphasized an operant conditioning approach to behavior disorders. Counseling interventions are concerned with changing the contingencies that control behaviors. The name *behavior analysis* is often associated with this viewpoint in counseling, in part because of the negative connotations of the term *behavior modification.*

B. F. Skinner argued that learning does not occur in the absence of reinforcement, either positive or negative. Actions that are reinforced are repeated, while those that are discouraged tend to be extinguished. Human behavior, including maladaptive behavior, is largely controlled by its consequences.

The counseling process is straightforward: change the contingencies and maladaptive behavior will change. Contingency management involves the following six steps (Sherman, 1973):

1. State the general problem in behavioral terms.
2. Identify behavioral objectives, including specific target behaviors.
3. Develop behavioral measures and take baseline measures to determine if counseling is effective.
4. Observe clients in their natural environments to determine existing contingencies and effective reinforcements.
5. Specify the conditions under which reinforcements are to be given.
6. Chart the rate of responses and compare the results to baseline measures to determine the effectiveness of specific counseling interventions.

Contingency management procedures can be categorized according to (a) institutional control; (b) self-control; (c) mutual control or contracting; (d) counselor control; and (e) aversive control.

Related entry: BEHAVIORAL COUNSELING.

References

Sherman, A. (1973). *Behavior modification: Theory and practice.* Monterey, CA: Brooks/ Cole.
Skinner, B. F. (1953). *Science and human behavior.* New York: Macmillan.

BEHAVIORAL ASSESSMENT. The identification of particular antecedent and consequent events that influence or are functionally related to the client's defined problem behaviors.

The ABC model is used to describe the relationship between problem behaviors and environmental events (Thoresen & Mahoney, 1974). This model suggests that problem behaviors (B) are influenced by both the events that precede them, called antecedents (A), and by different types of events that follow them, called consequences (C). What function as antecedents or consequences for one person may be very different for someone else. Two clients might complain of anxiety, and the assessments could reveal very different components of the problem behavior and different antecedents and consequences.

A behavioral counselor utilizes a functional analysis to diagnose which client behaviors need to be modified. Three steps in problem identification are similar to those described by Kanfer and Saslow (1967, p. 367):

1. Which specific behavior patterns require change in their frequency of occurrence, their intensity, their duration, or in the conditions under which they occur?

2. What are the best practical means which can produce the desired changes in this individual (manipulation of the environment, of the behavior, or [of] the self-attitudes of the patient)?

3. What factors are currently maintaining the problem behaviors and what are the conditions under which these behaviors were acquired?

This kind of behavior analysis permits a counselor to utilize environmental events to explain a client's problem condition in terms that can be evaluated objectively. The counselor can also then use these environmental events to help promote the types of behavior which the client needs to learn in order to solve his/her problems. A functional assessment of behavior includes analysis and clarification of the problem situation, the individual's motivation for change, his/her biological condition, self-control, social relationships, and social/cultural environment. The counselor uses terms such as frequency, intensity, and duration to describe excesses and deficits in client behaviors (Kanfer & Saslow, 1967).

The interview is one of the most common behavioral assessment procedures (Nelson, 1983). Successful assessment interviews require specific guidelines and training in order to obtain accurate and valid information from clients that will make a difference in planning their counseling treatments.

Behavioral assessment can also involve a client keeping a record of when and under what circumstances a particular behavior occurs. For example, a counselor might ask a client to keep a record of when and in what room of the house the urge to overeat occurs.

Behavioral counselors rely heavily on the self-reports of clients, particularly in assessing thoughts, fantasies, and feelings. Such self-reports often prove to be superior predictors of behavior compared to judgments of counselors or even scores on personality tests (Mischel, 1981). In general, behavioral counselors do not use standardized psychodiagnostic tests, because such measures do not usually provide the kind of information necessary for a functional analysis of a problem or for the planning of specific behavioral counseling interventions. They do use checklists about fears, self-report scales of depression, assertion inventories, and measures of marital satisfaction. These measuring devices are found useful in establishing the initial severity of a client's problem and for charting the effects of various counseling treatments.

Related entries: BASIC ID; FUNCTIONAL ANALYSIS.

References

Kanfer, F. H., & Saslow, G. (1967). Behavioral analysis: An alternative to diagnostic classification. In T. Million (Ed.), *Theories of psychopathology.* Philadelphia: W. B. Saunders.

Mischel, W. (1981). A cognitive social learning approach to assessment. In T. V. Merluzzi, C. R. Glass, & M. Genest (Eds.), *Cognitive assessment* (pp. 479–500). New York: Guilford Press.

Nelson, R. O. (1983). Behavioral assessment: Past, present and future. *Behavioral Assessment, 5,* 195–206.

Thoresen, C. C., & Mahoney, M. J. (1974). *Behavioral self control.* New York: Holt, Rinehart and Winston.

BEHAVIORAL COUNSELING. An approach to counseling that emphasizes the provision of corrective learning experiences in which clients can acquire new coping skills, improve communication competencies, and learn how to break maladaptive habits and overcome self-defeating emotional conflicts.

In behavioral counseling, clients may be asked to do things such as practice relaxation training, self-monitor daily caloric intake, engage in assertive acts, confront anxiety-eliciting situations, and refrain from compulsive acts. The main defining features and basic procedures of contemporary behavioral counseling are discussed by Berkowitz (1982). This approach:

- focuses on selecting target behaviors to be changed and specifying the nature of the changes desired;

- studies the observable events in the environment that are maintaining the behavior;

- clearly specifies both the environmental changes and the intervention strategies that can modify behavior;

- insists on data-based assessment and evaluation of treatment;

- asks the question, "Once a new behavior is established, how can it be maintained and generalized to new situations over a period of time?"

Behavioral counseling refers to the application of a diversity of techniques and procedures that are rooted in a variety of learning theories. A basic assumption of the behavioral perspective is that all problematic behaviors, cognitions, and emotions have been learned and can be modified by new learning. Behavioral counselors assume that clients do not necessarily have to achieve insight in order to make needed changes in their behaviors. Behavioral changes can well lead to an increased level of self-understanding.

The term *behavioral counseling* was used by John Krumboltz at a 1964 annual American Psychological Association convention to remind counselors that their activities should be focused on changes in client behaviors (Krumboltz, 1965). Thoresen (1966) provided impetus for the direct application of behavioral views to school counseling when he outlined the basic propositions of behavioral counseling and their application to the case of a high school student.

The various approaches in contemporary behavior counseling include (a) applied behavior analysis, (b) a neo-behavioristic mediational stimulus-response model, (c) social learning theory, and (d) cognitive behavior modification. These four approaches differ in the extent to which they use cognitive concepts and procedures. At one end is applied behavior analysis, which focuses solely on observable behavior and rejects all cognitive mediating processes. At the other end are social learning theory and cognitive behavior modification, which rely heavily on cognitive theories (Wilson, 1989).

Related entries: APPLIED BEHAVIOR ANALYSIS; ASSERTIVENESS TRAINING; AVERSIVE TECHNIQUES; BEHAVIOR MODIFICATION; BEHAVIORAL ASSESSMENT; BIOFEEDBACK; FUNCTIONAL ANALYSIS.

References

Berkowitz, S. (1982). Behavior therapy. In L. E. Abt & I. R. Stuart (Eds.), *The newer therapies: A sourcebook.* New York: Van Nostrand Reinhold.

Krumboltz, J. D. (1965). Behavioral counseling: Rationale and research. *Personnel and Guidance Journal, 44,* 383–387.

Thoresen, C. E. (1966). Behavioral counseling: An introduction. *The School Counselor, 14,* 13–21.

Wilson, G. T. (1989). Behavior therapy. In R. J. Corsini & D. Wedding (Eds.), *Current psychotherapies* (4th ed., pp. 241–284). Itasca, IL: F. E. Peacock.

BERNE, ERIC (1910–1970). Eric Berne, the originator of transactional analysis, received his M.D. from McGill University in 1935. He did his psychiatric residency at Yale from 1936 to 1941.

As transactional analysis, which was originally developed by Berne (1961), has evolved, its concepts and techniques have become particularly suited for group counseling. In 1964 Berne's book *Games People Play* became an international best seller. This new therapeutic approach, which represented a radical departure from psychoanalysis, achieved wide popularity by the late 1960s. Steiner referred to Berne as a "far reaching pioneer, a radical scientist in the field of psychiatry" (p. 1). Berne has been both a pioneer and a radical thinking scientist in the field of counseling and psychotherapy.

Related entries: GAMES; TRANSACTIONAL ANALYSIS (TA).

References

Berne, E. (1961). *Transactional analysis in psychotherapy.* New York: Grove Press.

Berne, E. (1964). *Games people play.* New York: Grove Press.

Steiner, C. (1974). *Scripts people live: Transactional analysis of life scripts.* New York: Grove Press.

BIBLIOTHERAPY. The guided reading of selected literature in order to help individuals gain a better understanding of self, others, and problems in daily living.

Multimodal counselors may ask clients to read a book, underline points that seem important, and perhaps even summarize their reading in a notebook that can be kept as a ready reference. These readings are often discussed during counseling sessions so that counselors may ascertain their impact on their clients (Lazarus, 1989).

According to Schrank and Engels (1981), bibliotherapy includes three fundamental processes: identification, catharsis, and insight. In their review of the literature on counselor use of bibliotherapy, they concluded that research supports its use as being effective in modifying attitudes, promoting behavioral changes, fostering self-development, and facilitating gains from counseling. Schrank (1982) provides a review of the literature on the uses of bibliotherapy in elementary schools.

Related entries: MULTIMODAL APPROACH TO COUNSELING; RATIONAL-EMOTIVE COUNSELING.

References

Lazarus, A. (1989). Multimodal therapy. In R. J. Corsini & D. Wedding (Eds.), *Current psychotherapies* (4th ed., pp. 503–546). Itasca, IL: F. E. Peacock.

Schrank, F. A. (1982). Bibliotherapy as an elementary school counseling tool. *Elementary School Guidance and Counseling, 16,* 218–227.

Schrank, F. A., & Engels, O. W. (1981). Bibliotherapy as a counseling adjunct: Research findings. *Personnel and Guidance Journal, 54,* 225–226.

BIOFEEDBACK. A counseling technique that uses instrumentation to provide a person with immediate and continuing signals concerning body functions of which that person is not normally conscious.

Biofeedback provides external feedback from visceral organs such as the heart or blood vessels as well as feedback from any physiological functions, including central nervous system activity (brain waves) and peripheral striate muscular activity, which may not be providing normal feedback (after a stroke, for instance).

Biofeedback has been used as a specific form of treatment for somatic disorders such as headaches, high blood pressure, and migraine as well as more common disorders such as anxiety and tension. Biofeedback includes the measurement, quantification, and feedback of responses that represent the final common paths of at least three different segments of the nervous system. Brain wave feedback involves direct assessment of central nervous system cortical activity; heart rate, blood pressure, and peripheral vascular and skin temperature feedback involves the assessment and quantification of responses mediated by the autonomic nervous system; and Electromyogram (EMG) biofeedback represents assessment and quantification of responses mediated by the peripheral somatic nervous system. The primary purpose of biofeedback is to use instrumentation to strengthen a client's ability to discriminate and therefore control otherwise nondiscriminable responses.

Shapiro and Surwit (1976), in their review of the biofeedback literature, concluded that "there is not one well controlled scientific study of the effectiveness of biofeedback and operant conditioning in treating a particular physiological disorder" (p. 113). A little later, Katkin and Goldband (1980) reached a similar conclusion: "Biofeedback may provide future generations with important new weapons against disease. The current state of evidence neither supports nor denies that hope" (p. 572).

Related entry: BEHAVIORAL COUNSELING.

References

Katkin, E. S., & Goldband, S. (1980). Biofeedback. In F. H. Kanfer & A. P. Goldstein (Eds.), *Helping people change* (2nd ed., pp. 537–578). New York: Pergamon.

Shapiro, D., & Surwit, R. S. (1976). Learned control of physiological function and disease. In H. Leitenberg (Ed.), *Handbook of behavior modification and behavior therapy.* Englewood Cliffs, NJ: Prentice-Hall.

BIRTH ORDER. The person's birth ordinal position in a family and its psychological significance to him/her.

Family constellation refers to the influence of the birth order on a child. Position in the family constellation provides the child with a unique perspective on social relationships and on personal abilities (Adler, 1927). Adlerian counselors consider the meaning a person gives to his/her position in the family to be of central importance. Family constellation is influenced by factors such as emotional ties between family members, age differences, sex of siblings, size of family, and characteristics of each sibling (Shulman & Nikelly, 1971).

Family positions are not static or unchanging; instead, they reflect each sibling's interpretation of his/her position. Family constellation is considered to be an especially important influence on a person's life style.

An only child may often act responsibly and even like an adult at an early age. Firstborns all have the experience of being dethroned from a favored position, while second children may often feel that they are in a constant race and believe that they should try to be first in certain areas so as to surpass the first child. The differences in the way parents and siblings treat an oldest and youngest child can have obvious repercussions on the development of the children's personalities. Although it is possible to make generalizations or inferences about birth order and life style, it is important to remember that the child's interpretation of his/her position in a family is more important than his/her chronological position alone.

Many studies have been published concerning birth order and personality, but most are relatively meaningless since they do not consider the child's attitude and movement, the formation of alliances and opposing groups within the family, and the unique ways children approach the social situation in their search for a place for themselves. For the most part, these studies fail to take into account the impact of perceptions of birth order and the fact that personality development is an active process that each person molds in a unique way.

Related entries: ADLERIAN COUNSELING; INDIVIDUAL PSYCHOLOGY.

References

Adler, A. (1927). *Understanding human nature.* New York: Greenberg.
Shulman, B. H., & Nikelly, A. G. (1971). Family constellation. In A. G. Nikelly (Ed.), *Techniques for behavior change.* Springfield, IL: Charles C Thomas.

BLACK RACIAL IDENTITY DEVELOPMENT. Black racial identity development is characterized by movement across a series of sequential life stages. Changes are influenced by the interaction among social/environmental circumstances and individual variables such as thoughts, feelings, and behaviors.

Cross (1971, 1978) contended that the development of a black person's racial identity includes movement through four distinct psychological stages. They lie along a continuum from negative to positive self-perceptions and are identified as pre-encounter, encounter, immersion-emersion, and internalization.

> *Pre-encounter.* At this stage, individuals view the world from a white frame of reference. They may devalue or deny their blackness.
>
> *Encounter.* Individuals experience shocking events that are inconsistent with their frame of reference. Their self-image is shaken as they find that a "Be like white" frame of reference is inappropriate and not realistic. As a result, they definitely decide to develop a black identity.
>
> *Immersion-emersion.* Individuals begin to immerse themselves in total blackness and the various elements of black culture. They withdraw from interactions with other ethnic groups and seem to have a minimal degree of internalized security about their blackness. They tend to denigrate white people and glorify black people and are intensely concerned with the personal implications of their black identity. Anything of value is black or relevant to blackness.
>
> *Internalization.* This stage is characterized by the individuals' achievement of a sense of inner security and self-confidence with their blackness. They reflect psychological openness, ideological flexibility, and a more pluralistic nonracist perspective. These persons are less hostile, more open, and less defensive.

The development of black racial identity attitudes is a lifelong process that usually begins in late adolescence and early adulthood. The initial racial identity attitudes of an individual may reflect any one of the four identity statuses. His or her subsequent development will be influenced by experiences with blacks as well as whites.

Parham (1989) argues that the development of the racial identity of a black person is not simply a reaction to oppressive racist elements in society. Rather, black/African identity is actualized through personal thoughts, feelings, and behaviors rooted in the values of black/African culture itself. Both Baldwin (1984) and Nobles (1986) have suggested that the core of black people's personality is essentially African in nature; the love of the African self motivates one to seek actualization toward natural development of the self. When one's racial identity is more Eurocentric than Afrocentric it violates the core of the person's African makeup and creates dissonance.

Parham (1989) described how the stages of racial identity are manifested at three phases of life (late adolescence/early adulthood, middle adulthood, and late adulthood) and how each of these phases of life reflects different themes. In the late adolescence phase individuals are confronted with the task of trying to define themselves in relation to their social environment. An individual's blackness is displayed in activism and overt behaviors. Middle adulthood is a period in life when individuals confront and successfully integrate the outcomes of earlier physical, social, and psychological developmental tasks. Middle adulthood is a time when a black person manifests his or her racial identity within the various institutions of family, work, church, and civic groups. Issues faced by black persons in middle adulthood are often phenomenological in nature and may reflect perceptions different from those of white persons. Late adulthood is a period when black individuals begin to gain an appreciation for the fullness of their lives. They engage in self-assessment and reflection on past activities and accomplishments in life. At this time the meaning of frustration, discrimination, and degradation may even become the pain associated with their lives.

Racial identity attitudes of black clients can affect their mental health and can influence the dynamics of counseling. Black clients are often confronted with questions regarding how much to compromise their blackness in order to successfully assimilate into the white culture. Blacks struggle with issues regarding (a) self-differentiation versus preoccupation with assimilation; (b) body transcendence versus preoccupations with body image; and (c) ego-transcendence versus self-absorption. In working with black clients on these issues, counselors should be prepared to deal with topics regarding conditions of worth (Parham, 1989).

Smith (1985) offers ten propositions as a basis for a theory of racial identity development, which she considers to be one small part of ethnic identity development. For her, the ethnic identity of each person consists of the signs, symbols, and underlying values that point to a distinctive group—shared identity. The outward signs of ethnic identity are similar race, religion, and national origin. Culture is seen as one aspect of ethnic identity that will influence the particular world views or outlooks that different persons develop. The extent to which people use their ethnic identity as a reference standard for determining the stressfulness of life events and their responses to them is based on their level of ethnic identity. A person can be committed as much or as little as he or she chooses to a particular ethnic group. Most individuals show a situational use of ethnic identity. They use ethnic identity when and if they perceive it as advantageous for their welfare. Black Americans, after experiencing severe racial discrimination, may evidence a heightened sense of identification with their ethnic group and may even seek support from it.

Smith (1989) argues that racial identity development is a process of coming to terms with one's racial membership as a salient reference group. Through shared historical circumstances race can serve as a common referent for a sense of peoplehood. A racial reference group denotes a person's psychological relatedness to a particular group to which the individual commits his or her identity. Reference group perspectives can help to establish a person's goals and to regulate his or her behaviors. Individuals will differ in their racial reference group identifications, ranging from little or no identification to high identification.

Members of racial minorities who are going through the process of anticipatory socialization into American society may vacillate between giving their allegiance to their racial membership group or to the nonracial membership group in which they desire to gain admittance. Acceptance of one's racial membership as a positive reference group can lead to positive self-esteem and adaptive psychological behaviors. The tendency for individuals to develop a positive or negative racial identity will be affected by the status of their racial reference group in society. Negative racial identity development is often characteristic of individuals who use majority group standards to judge themselves as acceptable or not. The process of racial identity development consists of the individual's changing or maintaining certain racial reference group perspectives as he or she passes through the various life stages. The stressor stimuli in a minority person's life are based on one's out-group status in relation to the dominant ethnic-cultural group. In the United States those racial minority groups that are seen to personify the id in humans are treated with greater social distance than are those groups that personify the superego.

Related entries: AFRICAN AMERICANS; MULTICULTURAL COUNSELING; PREJUDICE.

References

Baldwin, J. A. (1984). African self-consciousness and the mental health of African Americans. *Journal of Black Studies, 15,* 177–194.

Cross, W. E. (1971). The Negro to black conversion experience: Toward a psychology of black liberation. *Black World, 20*(9), 13–27.

Cross, W. E. (1978). The Cross and Thomas models of psychological Negrescence. *Journal of Black Psychology, 5*(1), 13–19.

Nobles, W. (1986). *African psychology: Toward its reclamation, reascension and revitalization.* Oakland, CA: Black Family Institute.

Parham, T. (1989). Cycles of psychological Negrescence. *The Counseling Psychologist, 17,* 187–226.

Smith, E. M. J. (1985). Ethnic minorities: Life stress, social support and mental health issues. *The Counseling Psychologist, 13,* 537–579.

Smith, E. M. J. (1989). Black racial identity development: Issues and concerns. *The Counseling Psychologist, 17,* 277–288.

C

CAREER COUNSELING. Individual or group counseling concerned with the relationships between the cognitive, emotional, and behavioral needs of clients and their development, fulfillment, or frustration over the life span in a variety of roles.

Careers are viewed as the sequence of positions that a person occupies during a lifetime, and roles are the expectations that others have for persons who occupy these positions. An occupational career is the sequence or combination of occupational positions held during the course of a person's lifetime.

Traditionally, career counseling involved the matching of individuals with jobs using a model suggested by Frank Parsons (1909):

In a wise choice there are three broad factors:

(1) a clear understanding of yourself, your attitudes, abilities, interests, ambitions, resources, limitations and their causes;

(2) a knowledge of the requirements and conditions of success, the advantages and the disadvantages, compensation opportunities and the prospects in different lines of work;

(3) true reasoning of the relations of these two groups of facts.

Parsons envisioned three components to vocational guidance: testing, information giving, and decision making through "true reasoning." Psychometric methods were to be used to measure abilities, interests, and other characteristics. The contemporary trait and factor models for vocational counseling resemble Parsons' early model of vocational guidance. For example, Weinrach (1979) describes a three-step model for vocational counseling:

Step 1. Discovering individual traits or characteristics.

Step 2. Analyzing occupational requirements.

Step 3. Matching individuals to the job.

Holland's theory of vocational choices (1973) and his various measures provide an example of a well-developed systematic approach to matching individuals and educational/vocational environments.

Super (1951) defined career counseling as "the process of helping a person to develop and accept an integrated and adequate picture of himself and of his role in the world of work, to test this concept against reality and to convert [it] into a reality, with satisfaction to himself and benefit to society" (p. 92). Crites (1981) identified five models of career counseling as trait and factor, client-centered, psychodynamic, developmental, and behavioral. He then presented a comprehensive model of career counseling that integrates aspects of these five approaches. Crites' model identifies three stages in career counseling as diagnosis, intervention, and evaluation.

Related entries: CAREER DEVELOPMENT; CHOOSING A VOCATION; *DICTIONARY OF OCCUPATIONAL TITLES* (DOT); HOLLAND'S THEORY OF VOCATIONAL CHOICE; INTERESTS; KUDER GENERAL INTEREST SURVEY (FORM E); KUDER OCCUPATIONAL INTEREST SURVEY (FORM D-1956 AND FORM DD-1966); OCCUPATIONAL INFORMATION; PARSONS, FRANK; SELF-DIRECTED SEARCH; STRONG-CAMPBELL INTEREST INVENTORY; VALUES.

References

Crites, J. O. (1981). *Career counseling: Models, methods and materials.* New York: McGraw-Hill.

Holland, J. L. (1973). *Making vocational choices: A theory of careers.* Englewood Cliffs, NJ: Prentice-Hall.

Parsons, F. (1909). *Choosing a vocation.* Boston: Houghton Mifflin.

Super, D. E. (1951). Vocational adjustment: Implementation of self-concept occupations. *Occupations, 30,* 88–92.

Super, D. E. (1980). A life span life space approach to career development. *Journal of Vocational Behavior, 16,* 282–298.

Weinrach, S. G. (1979). Trait and factor counseling: Yesterday and today. In S. G. Weinrach (Ed.), *Career counseling* (pp. 59–69). New York: McGraw-Hill.

CAREER DEVELOPMENT. A sequence of career decision-making tasks that occur from childhood to late adulthood.

Ginzberg, Ginsburg, Axelrad, and Herma (1951) provided a theory of occupational choice after criticizing vocational counselors for trying to counsel clients without any theory as to how vocational choices are made. The original theory had four elements:

1. Occupational choice is a developmental process which typically takes place over a period of ten years.

2. The process is largely irreversible.

3. The process ends in a compromise among interests, capacities, values, and opportunities.

4. There are three periods of occupational choice: fantasy choice, tentative choice, and realistic choice.

Their reformulated theory (1972) proposed that occupational choice is a lifelong process of decision making in which the individual seeks to find the optimal fit between his/her career preparation and goals and the reality of the world of work.

Super's (1957, 1981) model of career development assumes that career development is the process of implementing a self-concept; it unfolds in five stages that are defined by specific developmental tasks:

1. *Growth.* This period lasts from birth to age 14. The major tasks are to form a mental picture of the self in relationship to others and to develop an orientation to the world of work.

2. *Exploration.* This period lasts from ages 15 to 24. The major task is to explore the world of work and to specify a career preference.

3. *Establishment.* This period lasts from ages 25 to 44. The major task is to become established in a preferred and appropriate field of work.

4. *Maintenance.* This period lasts from ages 44 to 64. The task is to preserve achieved status and gains.

5. *Decline.* This period lasts from age 64 on. The task is to disengage from work and to seek other sources of personal satisfaction.

Related entries: CAREER COUNSELING; HOLLAND'S THEORY OF VOCATIONAL CHOICE; LIFE CAREER DEVELOPMENT; SUPER, DONALD E.; WORK ADJUSTMENT THEORY.

References

Ginzberg, E. (1972). Occupational choice: A restatement. *Vocational Guidance Quarterly, 20,* 169–176.

Ginzberg, E., Ginsburg, S. W., Axelrad, S., & Herma, J. L. (1951). *Occupational choice: An approach to a general theory.* New York: Columbia University Press.

Super, D. E. (1957). *The psychology of careers.* New York: Harper's.

Super, D. E. (1981). The relative importance of work. *Bulletin—International Association of Educational and Vocational Guidance, 37,* 26–36.

CATHARSIS. The expression and discharge of repressed emotions; sometimes used synonymously with abreaction. Catharsis was used by Freud as the technical term for the "talking cure."

Freud (1923/1961), in his early studies of hysteria, advanced the principle of emotional catharsis. He argued that the discharge of pent-up emotions could have a beneficial therapeutic effect. However, Freud later concluded that this method of treatment had limited value and was, in the long run, ineffectual. In the expressive forms of counseling, the group experience often plays an important role in mitigating anxiety, because it is assumed that expressing in the presence of others what is ordinarily not expressed can lessen guilt feelings.

However, if catharsis involves no essential insight or psychological restructuring, there is a tendency for relapse once the group experience is discontinued (see Arlow, 1989).

Catharsis has one of the longest traditions as a change process that contributes to therapeutic outcomes in persons. The ancient Greeks believed that evoking emotions was one of the best means for promoting personal relief and improvement. Prochaska (1979) describes catharsis as being based on a hydraulic model of emotions in which unacceptable feelings are blocked from direct expression; this condition results in pressure from affects being released in some manner, no matter how indirectly. If the emotions could be released more directly in counseling, then the reservoir of energy would be discharged and the person would be freed from a source of symptoms. Many approaches to counseling try to help clients break through their emotional blocks and express the dark side of themselves in the presence of another person.

The term *corrective emotional experiences* is used to describe those cathartic reactions that are elicited from stimuli within the person. Rogers (Rogers, Gendlin, Keisler, & Truax, 1967) proposed that the curative processes in counseling can be attributed to the direct and intense expression of feelings that result in corrective emotional experiences.

Related entries: ABREACTION; PSYCHOANALYTIC COUNSELING.

References

Arlow, J. (1989). Psychoanalysis. In R. J. Corsini and D. Wedding (Eds.), *Current psychotherapies* (4th ed., pp. 19–64). Itasca, IL: F. E. Peacock.

Freud, S. (1961). Studies on hysteria. In J. Strachey (Ed. and Trans.), *The standard edition of the complete psychological works of Sigmund Freud* (Vol. 2). London: Hogarth Press. (Original work published 1923)

Prochaska, J. O. (1979). *Systems of psychotherapy: A transtheoretical analysis.* Homewood, IL: Dorsey.

Rogers, C., Gendlin, E., Keisler, D., & Truax, C. (1967). *The therapeutic relationship and its impact: A study of psychotherapy with schizophrenics.* Madison: University of Wisconsin Press.

CHILD EGO STATE. A basic ego state in the personality that consists of feelings, impulses, and spontaneous acts; this ego state is a coherent system of thoughts and feelings manifested in corresponding patterns of behaviors.

In transactional analysis, the child (C) ego state is conceptualized as the little boy or girl within each person who may feel, think, act, talk, and respond just the way he or she did when a child of a certain age (Berne, 1972), which may be between two and five years. Berne considered the child ego state to be the most valuable part of the personality.

When people are in the child ego state they sit, stand, speak, think, perceive, and feel as they did in childhood. Their behaviors may be impulsive and not mediated or delayed by reasoning. Throwing temper tantrums, being irresponsible or irrational, and engaging in wishful thinking or daydreams are some expressions of the child. However, the child is also the source of spontaneity, creativity, humor, and fun, and thought to be the part of personality that truly enjoys life.

The child ego state can be differentiated into the natural child, which is the most emotional, spontaneous, and powerful expression of the child; the adapted child, which is the obedient child who conforms to parental demands; and the little professor, which is the inquisitive and intuitive child who acts like a precocious adult. The child ego state can be adaptive in those situations that involve creativity or having fun.

Related entries: ADULT EGO STATE; BERNE, ERIC; EGO; EGO STATES; EGOGRAM; PARENT EGO STATE; TRANSACTIONAL ANALYSIS (TA).

References

Berne, E. (1961). *Transactional analysis in psychotherapy.* New York: Grove.
Berne, E. (1972). *What do you say after you say hello?* New York: Grove.

CHINESE AMERICANS. In counseling Chinese American children or adolescents, it is important to include the family. Level of acculturation and immigration history are relevant social-cultural factors that need to be considered by counselors.

The literature on psychological and behavioral disorders of Chinese American children and adolescents is quite limited, because Asian Americans have not been the focus of many studies on mental health issues. Touliatos and Lindholm (1980) reported that children of Chinese, Japanese, or Southeast Asian descent exhibited fewer disorders having to do with conduct problems or inadequacy and immaturity than a comparison group of native born Caucasian children.

For many Chinese Americans, contacting mental health services is seen as a last-ditch effort to solve their problems. The Chinese American family may be reluctant for members to seek help because of feelings of shame and embarrassment, lack of familiarity with mental health services, or a defensive pattern of denial (see Huang & Ying, 1989). A major problem in counseling Chinese Americans is their tendency to drop out after an initial session because they do not see the value of talking, and they do not see counseling as an effective means of relieving their stress. The appropriate pacing of self-disclosure and the management of specific communication requests are issues of importance in counseling Chinese Americans.

In counseling Chinese American youth, it is very important that the counselor establish a working relationship with the parents. They may even be engaged as partners in the helping process.

Related entries: CULTURE; MULTICULTURAL COUNSELING.

References

Huang, L. N., & Ying, Y. W. (1989). Chinese American children and adolescents. In J. T. Gibbs, L. N. Huang, & Associates (Eds.), *Children of color: Psychological interventions with minority youth* (pp. 30–66). San Francisco: Jossey-Bass.

Lee, E. (1982). A social systems approach to assessment and treatment for Chinese American families. In M. McGoldrick, J. R. Pearce, & J. Giordana (Eds.), *Ethnicity and family therapy.* New York: Guilford.

Sue, D., Sue, D. W., & Sue, D. M. (1983). Psychological development of Chinese American children. In G. J. Powell, J. Yamamoto, A. Romero, & A. Morales (Eds.), *The psychological development of minority group children.* New York: Brunner/ Mazel.

Touliatos, J., & Lindholm, B. (1980). Behavior disturbance of children of native born and immigrant parents. *Journal of Community Psychology, 8*(1), 28–33.

CHOOSING A VOCATION. A book published by Frank Parsons in 1909 elaborated a concept of vocational guidance which in later years became known as the trait and factor approach to counseling.

He described vocational counseling as a process of helping individuals to study both themselves and possible occupational alternatives, and to work out a compromise among their abilities, interests, and opportunities. Parsons' book focused on the need for vocational guidance for those youth who left school to go to work between the ages of 12 and 14. He envisioned three basic components in vocational guidance: testing, information giving, and career decision making through "true reasoning." The goal was to help young persons relate their occupational aptitudes and interests to their vocational choices.

The long-range importance of Parsons' book was not felt until many years later, when it was recognized in the pioneering work of the Minnesota Employment Stabilization Research Institute during the 1930s (Crites, 1981). He was given credit for having identified the three basic variables in the career decision-making process as the individual, the occupation, and the relationship between them. Contemporary approaches to career counseling still must deal with these three components in career decision making, for, as Holland (1973) points out, "the goal of vocational guidance—matching men and jobs—remains the same despite much talk, research and speculation. Our devices, techniques, classifications and theories are more comprehensive than in the days of Parsons, the founder of vocational guidance, but the goal is still one of helping people find jobs that they can do well and that are fulfilling" (p. 85).

Parsons argued that vocational guidance was one way in which society could become more humane in dealing with youth. He believed that it was better for youth to select a vocation scientifically than to drift through a variety of jobs. Indeed, Parsons considered vocational guidance to be a strategy or means of social reform. His prescriptions about how counselees should examine themselves and their lives certainly reflected his humanitarian social philosophy.

Related entries: CAREER COUNSELING; CAREER DEVELOPMENT; PARSONS, FRANK.

References

Crites, J. O. (1981). *Career counseling: Models, methods and materials.* New York: McGraw-Hill.

Holland, J. (1973). *Making vocational choices: A theory of careers.* Englewood Cliffs, NJ: Prentice-Hall.

Parsons, F. (1909). *Choosing a vocation.* Boston: Houghton Mifflin.

CLIENT-CENTERED COUNSELING. The necessary and sufficient conditions for client-centered counseling are contained in the therapeutic relationship. Six conditions are held to account for therapeutic changes in counseling:

1. Two persons are in a relationship in which each makes a perceived difference to the other.

2. The client in the relationship is vulnerable to anxiety or is, in fact, anxious.

3. The therapist is congruent, integrated, and genuine, which means that he/she is freely and deeply him/herself, with his/her experiences being accurately represented in his/her awareness.

4. The therapist experiences unconditional positive regard for the client.

5. The therapist experiences an accurate empathic understanding of the client's inner world and strives to communicate this understanding to the client.

6. The client perceives, at least to a minimal degree, the acceptance and understanding of the therapist. (Rogers, 1959)

According to Grummon (1979), the central hypothesis of client-centered counseling is that the growth potential inherent in all individuals tends to be released in a relationship in which the helping person experiences and communicates genuineness, caring, and a sensitive nonjudgmental understanding of the client's inner flow of experiencing.

Rogers (1959) proposed that when the six therapeutic conditions are present in a counseling relationship the following changes will occur in clients:

1. They will become freer in expressing feelings that refer increasingly to themselves.

2. They will symbolize their experiences more accurately, and they will gradually become more aware of experiences that had been denied or distorted.

3. Their expressions of feelings will increasingly refer to the incongruity between their experiences and their self-concepts and, because of this condition, they will experience threat and anxiety.

4. Their self-concepts will begin to include experiences that have previously been denied or distorted in awareness. As a result, they will feel less need to be defensive.

5. They will feel positive self-regard and react to experiences less in terms of conditions of worth based on the values of others and more in terms of their own organismic valuing process.

In his book *Client Centered Therapy,* published in 1951, Carl Rogers changed the name of his approach to counseling from nondirective to client-centered theory. With this change, he was trying to emphasize that the person seeking help in counseling was not to be treated as a dependent patient but, instead, as a responsible client. In 1990 Rogers' model was identified as the person-centered approach. This change in name was to indicate that the theory had wider applicability than helping relationships. He and his followers argued that the principles underlying person-centered theory were of relevance in every aspect of the behavior of human beings. For instance, the effectiveness of the person-centered approach was demonstrated in the research completed by Aspy and Roebuck (1974) in the field of education.

Related entries: AUTHENTICITY; HUMANISTIC APPROACHES TO COUNSELING; ROGERS, CARL RANSOM.

References

Aspy, D. N., & Roebuck, F. N. (1974). From humane ideas to humane technology and back again many times. *Education, 95,* 163–171.

Grummon, D. L. (1979). Client centered theory. In H. M. Berks, Jr. & B. Stefflre (Eds.), *Theories of counseling* (3rd ed., pp. 28–90). New York: McGraw-Hill.

Rogers, C. R. (1951). *Client centered therapy.* Boston: Houghton Mifflin.

Rogers, C. R. (1959). A theory of personality and interpersonal relationships as developed in the client-centered framework. In S. Koch (Ed.), *Psychology: A study of science: Vol. 3: Formulations of the person and the social context.* New York: McGraw-Hill.

Raskin, N. J., & Rogers, C. R. (1989). Person centered therapy. In R. J. Corsini & D. Wedding (Eds.), *Current psychotherapies* (4th ed., pp. 155–196). Itasca, IL: F. E. Peacock.

CLINICAL COUNSELING (Williamson, 1939, 1950). This model of counseling is divided into six steps: analysis, synthesis, diagnosis, prognosis, counseling (treatment), and follow-up.

Analysis refers to the collection of data from a variety of sources.

Synthesis refers to summarizing and organizing the data to reveal assets, liabilities, adjustments, and readjustments. A case history or cumulative form may be used for this purpose.

Diagnosis includes tentative conclusions regarding the characteristics and causes of the student's problem.

Prognosis refers to the counselor's prediction regarding the future development of the student's problem.

Counseling refers to the steps taken by the student and the counselor to bring about needed adjustments.

Follow-up has to do with the counselor's assistance with new problems or recurrences of the original problem and with efforts to determine the effectiveness of counseling.

This "scientific" approach to counseling assigns to both counselor and client the role of a learner, which includes collecting, sifting, and evaluating and classifying relevant facts to arrive at a description that provides insight regarding the nature and circumstances surrounding the client's problem condition. The client takes full responsibility for participating in the process of learning about self, while the counselor is the teaching assistant who aids the client pupil. Insight was defined as a deep understanding of the results of applying the cause-effect concept of relationships to all aspects of the client's life.

The counselor and counselee play the following roles in counseling: (a) definition of the problem and possible causes; (b) identification of client level of ego involvement and attitudes about the problem; (c) acceptance of the roles of counselor and client as a working team; (d) collection and verification of relevant facts; (e) interpretation of facts and drawing implications; (f) learning new ways of adjustment by the client with the encouragement of the counselor.

Counseling is that general method of helping clients that allows them to increase their probabilities of achieving satisfying adjustments in their lives. It is not merely a way of preventing maladjustments by avoidance of affectively sensitive experiences. Counselors are to help clients deal with a variety of transitional, situational, and developmental problems by providing encouragement and information, as well as by teaching skills of problem solving and personal remediation of learning needs.

It is interesting to note that Williamson's model of clinical counseling included the use of techniques to help students learn to play and work with students of other races, religions, political beliefs, and economic and cultural backgrounds. For him, individual counseling should help students gain insights into their social attitudes and evaluations of those who are different from them.

Related entries: ANALYSIS; DIRECTIVE APPROACH TO COUNSELING; TRAIT AND FACTOR COUNSELING; WILLIAMSON, EDMUND G.

References

Williamson, E. G. (1939). *How to counsel students.* New York: McGraw-Hill.
Williamson, E. G. (1950). *Counseling adolescents.* New York: McGraw-Hill.

CODEPENDENCE. The "co-alcoholic" behavior of spouses and children in chemically dependent family systems. Family members take on the psychological defenses and survival behaviors of the alcoholic, thereby expanding the disease from the individual to the entire family system.

The construct of codependency has been expanded in recent years to include addictive behaviors in sexual disorders, intimate relationships, and organizational systems. Many problems of identity development or impulse control have been associated with codependency.

The first National Conference on Codependency defined codependence as "a pattern of painful dependence on compulsive behaviors and on approval from others in an attempt to find safety, self-worth, and identity" (Laign, 1989, p. 2). Behaviors that typify codependence include (a) martyrdom—sacrifice of one's own needs to meet needs of others; (b) fusion—loss of one's own identity in intimate relationships; (c) intrusion—control of others' behaviors through caretaking, guilt, and manipulation; (d) perfection—unrealistically high expectations of oneself and others that often result in overachievement or inadequacy; and (e) addiction—use of compulsive behaviors for self-management (Cermak, 1986).

Contradependence is a behavioral tendency to separate oneself from others to prevent being emotionally hurt. Contradependent persons put up a wall around themselves, use emotional distancing, and give the message, "I don't need anyone else." The codependent person suffers a loss of personhood, while the contradependent person suffers the pain of aloneness.

Like codependence, contradependence is assumed to develop through the shaming behaviors of families and peer groups. Contradependence shares an emotional commonality with codependence and is the other side of the same psychological coin. Many codependent clients swing to the contradependent end of the continuum in the early stages of counseling.

Related entry: ALCOHOLISM.

References

Cermak, T. (1986). *Diagnosing and treating codependence.* Minneapolis: Johnson Institute.
Hogg, J. A., & Frank, M. L. (1992). Toward an interpersonal model of codependence and contradependence. *Journal of Counseling and Development, 70,* 371–375.
Laign, J. (1989). A consensus on codependency. *Contact, 2,* 2.

COGNITIVE-BEHAVIORAL COUNSELING. Cognitive-behavioral counseling helps clients to define their problems in terms that render them more amenable to solutions; learn how to execute or produce incompatible and adaptive thoughts and behaviors; and develop a sense of responsibility for positive changes in their lives that allows them to cope with future problems.

In cognitive-behavioral counseling, the client is treated like a student who is learning to deal with problems as a personal scientist. Beck, Rush, Shaw, and Emery (1979) have described this kind of relationship as collaborative empiricism. The counselor works with clients to help them identify the interdependence of their thoughts, feelings, behaviors, and environmental consequences; to view their thoughts as hypotheses that should be tested; to perform such personal experiments and collect data; and to explore the beliefs or schema that have given rise to their emotional disturbances and/or maladaptive behaviors.

Cognitive-behavioral counselors assume that the change processes in counseling are facilitated by having clients engage in extra-counseling experiences that lead to consequences that are incompatible with the client's prior expectancies. Components of cognitive events, processes and structures, behavioral acts, feelings, and interpersonal and intrapersonal consequences all come into play in contributing to changes in a client's behaviors (Meichenbaum, 1985).

Cognitive-behavioral counseling interventions are usually active, time-limited, and fairly structured. A goal of counseling is to help a client identify, reality test, and correct maladaptive, distorted conceptualizations and dysfunctional beliefs. This approach is essentially educational, and the counselor functions like a coach who supplies guidance, offers specific training exercises, corrects mis-conceptions, tries to modify faulty styles, provides up-to-date information, and displays caring support and encouragement. However, most of the responsibility for change still rests with the clients, who are to practice between counseling sessions (Lazarus & Fay, 1982; Meichenbaum, 1985).

Related entries: ASSERTIVENESS TRAINING; BEHAVIORAL COUN-SELING; COGNITIVE COUNSELING; SELF-INSTRUCTIONAL TRAIN-ING.

References

Beck, A., Rush A. J., Shaw B. F., & Emery S. (1979). *Cognitive therapy of depression.* New York: Guilford.

Lazarus, A., & Fay, A. (1982). Resistance or rationalization? A cognitive behavioral perspective. In P. Wachtel (Ed.), *Resistance: Psychodynamic and behavioral ap-proaches.* New York: Plenum.

Meichenbaum, D. (1985). Cognitive behavioral therapies. In S. J. Lynn & J. P. Garske (Eds.), *Contemporary psychotherapies: Models and methods* (pp. 261–286). Co-lumbus, OH: Charles Merrill.

COGNITIVE COUNSELING. This approach to counseling is a collaborative process of empirical investigation, reality testing, and problem solving between a counselor and a client. The goal is to modify the dysfunctional interpretations of the client.

Cognitive counseling began in the early 1960s as a result of Aaron Beck's research on depression (Beck, 1963, 1964, 1967). Beck observed a negative bias in the cognitive processing of depressed clients. He proposed a cognitive model of depression that included three specific concepts: the cognitive triad, schemas, and cognitive errors. He and his colleagues have conducted research that pro-vides support for this model as well as support for the use of cognitive coun-seling with depressed clients.

Each individual is assumed to have a set of idiosyncratic vulnerabilities and sensitivities that predisposes him or her to psychological distress. Personality is composed of schemas or cognitive structures consisting of fundamental beliefs and assumptions that develop early in life from personal experiences and iden-tification with significant others. Schemas become active when triggered by spe-cific stimuli, stressors, or circumstances. They may be adaptive or dysfunctional.

Cognitive distortions are evident during periods of psychological distress, and they reflect systematic errors in reasoning. Beck assumes that a bias in infor-mation processing is a characteristic of most psychological disorders.

Examples of cognitive distortions include:

• arbitrary inference

• selective abstraction

• overgeneralization

• magnification and minimization

• personalization

• dichotomous thinking

The cognitive approach to counseling initially addresses symptom relief, including problems and distortions in logic. However, the ultimate goal is to remove systematic biases in thinking. A client's beliefs are seen as testable hypotheses to be examined through behavioral experiments. Cognitive changes occur at several levels: in voluntary thoughts, in automatic thoughts, and in assumptions.

Automatic thoughts come to the client's mind spontaneously and intercede between stimulus events and client responses. They are generated from underlying assumptions that shape perceptions into cognitions, determine goals, and provide interpretations and meanings to events. By observing automatic thoughts over time and across situations, the client and the counselor can identify or infer the nature of underlying assumptions. These automatic thoughts can be tested by direct evidence or by logical analysis.

Related entries: COGNITIVE-BEHAVIORAL COUNSELING; COGNITIVE RESTRUCTURING.

References

Beck, A. T. (1963). Thinking and depression: 1. Idiosyncratic content and cognitive distortions. *Archives of General Psychiatry, 9,* 324–333.

Beck, A. T. (1964). Thinking and depression: 2. Theory and therapy. *Archives of General Psychiatry, 10,* 561–571.

Beck, A. T. (1967). *Depression: Clinical, experimental and theoretical aspects.* New York: Holber. (Republished as *Depression: Causes and treatment,* 1972, Philadelphia, University of Pennsylvania Press)

Beck, A. T., & Weishaar, M. E. (1989). Cognitive therapy. In R. J. Corsini & D. Wedding (Eds.), *Current psychotherapies* (4th ed., pp. 285–322). Itasca, IL: F. E. Peacock.

COGNITIVE RESTRUCTURING. This type of counseling intervention is designed to help clients identify, reality test, and correct maladaptive, distorted conceptualizations and dysfunctional beliefs. The assumption is that an individual's affect and behavior are largely determined by the ways in which he or she construes his or her world.

Cognitive restructuring was described by Lazarus (1971) and has its roots in rational-emotive therapy (Ellis, 1962). It has been developed by Meichenbaum (1972) under the name cognitive behavior modification and by Goldfreid, Decentecco, and Weinberg (1974) under the name systematic rational restructuring.

Cormier and Cormier (1991) present cognitive restructuring in six major parts:

1. Rationale, purpose, and overview of the procedure.

2. Identification of client thoughts during problem situations.

3. Introduction and practice of coping thoughts.

4. Shifting from self-defeating to coping thoughts.

5. Introduction and practice of positive or reinforcing self-statements.

6. Homework and follow-up.

During the process of cognitive restructuring, the counselor trains the client to identify self-defeating thoughts and beliefs and to replace them with more objective, self-enhancing problem-solving thoughts and behaviors. In this process, clients become more aware of the impact of their negative thoughts and beliefs and learn to produce incompatible, adaptive thoughts, feelings, and behaviors.

Ellis (1962) has clients focus on their beliefs and how they contribute to maladaptive appraisals. He uses an A-B-C framework to illustrate how irrational beliefs play a role in and perpetuate emotional upsets.

Beck's (1976) approach to cognitive restructuring emphasizes the influence of automatic thoughts on problematic behaviors of clients. These thoughts accompany unpleasant feelings or sensations, are often vague and unformulated, and are not generated voluntarily. Automatic thoughts, no matter how illogical, are completely believed and difficult to stop. Negative, self-denigrating thoughts can exert a strong impact on how a person feels and believes; reciprocally, how one feels and believes may influence what a person thinks. If we are depressed, we are likely to selectively recall and attend to negative events.

Related entries: A-B-C THEORY; COGNITIVE-BEHAVIORAL COUNSELING; COGNITIVE COUNSELING.

References

Beck, A. (1976). *Cognitive therapy and the emotional disorders.* New York: International Universities Press.

Cormier, W. H., & Cormier, L. S. (1991). *Interviewing strategies for helpers* (3rd ed.). Pacific Grove, CA: Brooks/Cole.

Ellis, A. (1962). *Reason and emotion in psychotherapy.* Secaucus, NJ: Lyle Stuart.

Goldfried, M. R., Decentecco, E. T., & Weinberg, L. (1974). Systematic rational restructuring as a self-control technique. *Behavior Therapy, 5,* 247–254.

Lazarus, A. A. (1971). *Behavior therapy and beyond.* New York: Macmillan.

Meichenbaum, D. H. (1972). Cognitive modification of test anxious college students. *Journal of Consulting and Clinical Psychology, 39,* 370–380.

COMMUNITY. A community is a territorially organized system coextensive with a settlement pattern in which (a) an effective communication network operates; (b) people share common facilities and services distributed within this settlement pattern; and (c) people develop a psychological identification with the locality symbol (the name; see Sanders, 1966, p. 26). A community serves to provide the means of satisfying both individual and societal needs.

Warren (1972) described a community in terms of the following social functions: (a) local participation in the processes of producing, distributing, and consuming goods and services that are a part of daily living; (b) socialization; (c) social control; (d) social participation opportunities; and (e) mutual support.

Bernard (1973) stated that the major component in defining the concept of "the community" is locale, whereas the major components of the concept of "community" are the common ties and social interactions. To understand the concept of community as client for the mental health counselor, it is necessary to assume that a certain degree of interaction of relationships exists within a community and that there are factors of social cohesion and emotional ties among the members. The community contains both resources for the generation and development of "wellness" and conditions that can become obstacles to full human development.

For the mental health counselor, community can be viewed as an environment that is the object of intervention efforts or as an environment in which people who have serious mental health problems can get better. When the United States Congress passed the Community Mental Health Centers Act in 1963, it instituted the first national policy of community care for the mentally disabled. After this act was passed a community based system developed under the umbrella term *deinstitutionalization.* This approach is based on the argument that psychiatric patients are entitled to live in the least restrictive environment possible and to lead their lives as normally and independently as they can.

Related entry: COMMUNITY COUNSELING.

References

Bernard, J. (1973). *The sociology of community.* Glenville, IL: Scott, Foresman.

Hershenson, D. B., & Power, P. W. (1987). *Mental health counseling: Theory and practice.* New York: Pergamon.

Sanders, D. T. (1966). *The community: An introduction to a social system* (2nd ed.) New York: Ronald Press.

Warren, R. L. (1972). *The community in America* (2nd ed.). Chicago: Rand McNally.

COMMUNITY COUNSELING. The community counseling model developed by Lewis and Lewis (1977, 1983) provides a fourfold framework for counselor involvement at the community level: (1) direct community services, (2) indirect community services, (3) direct client services, and (4) indirect client services. The focus of community counseling is on preventing the occurrence or experience of conditions and behaviors that clients could find to be dysfunctional.

According to Lewis and Lewis (1983), primary prevention provides the most important rationale for community counseling. Community counselors try to help community members to live more effectively and thereby prevent problems that might otherwise occur in their lives. Blocher and Biggs (1983) outlined how counseling psychology could be involved in community life by providing direct and indirect services to the community at large as well as to individuals and groups.

Related entries: COMMUNITY; PRIMARY PREVENTIVE COUNSELING.

References

Blocher, D., & Biggs, D. (1983). *Counseling psychology in community settings.* New York: Springer.

Coyne, R. K. (1987). *Primary preventive counseling: Empowering people and systems.* Muncie, IN: Accelerated Development.

Lewis, J., & Lewis, M. (1977). *Community counseling: A human services approach* (1st ed.). New York: Wiley.

Lewis, J., & Lewis, M. (1983). *Community counseling* (2nd ed.). New York: Wiley.

CONFIDENTIALITY. A professional obligation of counselors that protects clients from disclosure of information given in confidence without the express consent of the clients.

Before clients actually begin counseling, counselors should inform them that confidentiality does not exist under certain specified conditions. Clients should be able to make informed decisions about what they will or will not reveal to counselors.

Privileged communication is a legal term that indicates that client communications cannot be disclosed in a court of law without the client's consent. Most states grant privileged communication to clients of legally certified mental health professionals.

Schurtzgebel and Schurtzgebel (1980) proposed four criteria to use for establishing if communications are privileged:

1. The communications were given in confidence with an assurance that they would not be disclosed.

2. Confidentiality was essential to the maintenance of the relationship.

3. The relationship must be one that, in the opinion of the community, should be sedulously fostered.

4. The injury to the relationship by disclosure of the communication must be greater than the benefit gained by correct disposal of the litigation.

Corey (1991) identified the following circumstances when client information must legally be reported by counselors:

- when clients pose a danger to others or themselves;
- when counselors believe that a child under the age of 16 has been the victim of rape, child abuse, or some other crime;
- when counselors determine that a client needs hospitalization;
- when information is made an issue in a court action.

Related entries: ETHICAL GUIDELINES FOR GROUP COUNSELORS; ETHICS; TARASOFF VS. BOARD OF REGENTS AT THE UNIVERSITY OF CALIFORNIA.

References

Corey, G. (1991). *Theory and practice of counseling and psychotherapy* (4th ed.). Pacific Grove, CA: Brooks/Cole.

Schurtzgebel, R. L., & Schurtzgebel, R. K. (1980). *Law and psychological practice.* New York: John Wiley.

CONFRONTATION. A counselor communicates verbally to a client that he/she experiences some inconsistencies in the client's communications and/or behaviors.

Confrontations fall into three categories, all of which are based on the counselor's awareness of inconsistencies in the client:

1. confrontation of a discrepancy between the client's expression of what he/she wishes to be and his/her perceptions of self (ideal versus real self);

2. confrontation of a discrepancy between the client's verbal expressions of self-awareness (insight) and observable or reported behaviors;

3. confrontation of a discrepancy between how the counselor experiences the client and how the client experiences self.

An example of a fairly high-level confrontation involves the counselor making a direct and explicit statement: "You say you want to succeed at higher levels yet you've been unable to get up enough energy to succeed at your present level" (Carkhuff, 1984, p. 191).

Confrontation is a technique often used in group counseling to challenge members to take an honest look at themselves. Skillful confrontation specifies the behaviors or the inconsistencies between messages that are being challenged and is done with a caring attitude. A major task for the transactional analysis counselor is to confront clients on the different ways that they abdicate personal responsibility in their lives. Adlerian counselors use confrontation to challenge clients to translate what they have learned in the group process into new beliefs and behaviors, while Gestalt counselors use challenges and positive confrontations. In some cases Gestalt counselors help members recognize the ways in which they are blocking their strengths and not living as fully as they might.

Related entry: HELPING MODEL (CARKHUFF, 1987).

References

Carkhuff, R. R. (1984). *Helping and human relations* (Vol. 1). Amherst, MA: Human Resource Development Press.
Corey, G. (1990). *Theory and practice of group counseling* (3rd ed.). Pacific Grove, CA: Brooks/Cole.

CONJOINT FAMILY COUNSELING. An approach to family counseling that deals with both individual issues and family relationships. Counseling interventions focus on improving communication and helping client families to see and hear all that is communicated by family members.

Virginia Satir (1967), the founder of conjoint family counseling, thought that poor self-esteem manifested itself in poor communication among family members. In a dysfunctional family all members fear that they will be hurt or hurt others. All comments are taken as attacks on self-esteem. Family members are unable to handle differentness. Satir has moved away from this early emphasis on correcting deficient self-esteem to an approach that emphasizes growth enhancement and producing changes in family interaction.

The counselor attempts to reduce the need for defenses by interpreting anger as hurt, and by allowing pain to be expressed openly in counseling. The counselor also completes gaps in communication and interprets messages. Attempts are made to separate the content of a message from its relationship message. For example, when a father says to his child, "You are a good student," two messages are communicated. The first is a message about the son's performance, and the second is a message about their relationship: the father is in a position to judge the son.

Related entries: ELLIS, ALBERT; FAMILY CRISIS COUNSELING.

References

Satir, V. (1967). *Conjoint family therapy.* Palo Alto, CA: Science and Behavior Books.
Woods, M. D., & Martin, O. (1984). The work of Virginia Satir: Understanding her theory and technique. *American Journal of Family Therapy, 12,* 3–11.

CONSULTATION. Consultation involves the provision of knowledge and/or training in professional skills to a consultee who is responsible for delivery of counseling services to a client group.

Consultation can include identifying and diagnosing a problem, selecting and implementing intervention strategies, and specifying responsibilities. Consultants sometimes provide direct services to a client group, but usually they try to facilitate the consultees' uses of their own professional skills and knowledge to resolve problems or make decisions about issues that they have identified as important to them (Brokes, 1975).

The empowerment model of consultation argues that consultants should provide support for consultees while avoiding doing tasks for them (Witt & Martens, 1988). For example, a consultant to teachers might direct their efforts at influencing the antecedent conditions of effective teaching and then try to assist the teachers in skill development and learning classroom management procedures. The improvements resulting from consultation in such instances are attributed to consultees' skills and efforts. Consultation thus becomes a process that enhances consultee empowerment, with the goal of building a social structure within a system to support and promote consultee learning and performance.

Four models of school consultation are mental health consultation; behavioral consultation or ecological consultation; organizational development consultation; and instructional consultation. The pediatric psychology literature describes three models of consultation: resource consultation or independent functions consultation; indirect psychological consultation; and collaborative team consultation (Woody, LaVoie, & Epps, 1992).

Gerald Caplan (1970, 1974) was an influential figure in the development of psychological consultation. His approach incorporated both environmental and psychodynamic perspectives. He paid particular attention to identifying and treating those personality factors in consultees that could interfere with their professional functioning and reduce their effectiveness with clients. He discussed four types of mental health consultation: client-centered case consultation; consultee-centered case consultation; program-centered administrative consultation; and consultee-centered administrative consultation. He advocated a nonhierarchical relationship between the consultant and the consultee.

The ethical code of the American Association for Counseling and Development views consultation as "a voluntary relationship between a professional helper and an individual, group, or social units. Consultants provide help to the consultees in defining and solving work-related problems or potential problems with a client or client system" (AACD, 1988).

Drapela (1983) provided a model of consultation in which he emphasized that it is an "indirect service to individual clients or groups for whose benefits the helping intervention is undertaken" (p. 159). There are many models of consultation, among which are the four prototypes described by Kurpius (1978):

1. *Expert or provision model.* The consultant provides a direct service to consultees and directly deals with the identified problems.

2. *Doctor-patient or prescription model.* The consultant advises the consultee about the causes of a client's problem and then recommends remedial actions to be taken.

3. *Mediation model.* Consultants act as coordinators and try to integrate the services of a variety of helpers who are working on a specific problem. Consultants may choose either to coordinate client services or to create an alternative approach to coordinating the services that more effectively integrates them.

4. *Process consultation or collaboration model.* Consultants facilitate problem-solving activities of the consultees. They help them define their problems, analyze their options thoroughly, design a plan to solve their problems, and then implement and evaluate their plan of action.

Consultation services may be implemented through individual, group, or organizational/community interventions. One form of individual consultation involves teaching self-management skills. The idea is for individuals to learn self-management skills so that they can later take preventive and remedial actions on their own. An example of a group-level consultation could involve presenting new knowledge about children or adolescents to parents in a group setting. These groups encourage parents to work together (collaboration), to give and receive input from each other (consultation), to understand the relationships among beliefs, feelings, and attitudes (clarification), to share openly with each other (confrontation), to empathize with one another (concern), to keep information within the group (confidentiality), and to make plans for specific changes (commitment). Groups composed entirely of adults who share information and provide mutual support will, it is hoped, have a very important effect on parent-child relationships (Dinkmeyer, Dinkmeyer, & Sperry, 1987).

Organizational community interventions attempt to change the structure of social systems rather than the persons in the systems. Sometimes mental health consultants will try to build helping relationships with existing community agencies in order to foster trust to a point of mutual enhancement. In other cases intensive environmental programs may be used to intervene in the environments of specific individuals or groups so that their special needs can be met.

Related entries: COMMUNITY COUNSELING; MEDIATION; PRIMARY PREVENTIVE COUNSELING.

References

American Association for Counseling and Development (1988). *Ethical standards* (Rev. ed.). Alexandria, VA: American Association for Counseling and Development.

Brokes, A. A. (1975). Process model of consultation. In C. A. Parker (Ed.), *Psychological consultation: Helping teachers meet special needs.* Minneapolis: Leadership Training Institute.

Caplan, G. (1970). *The theory and practice of mental health consultation.* New York: Basic Books.

Caplan, G. (1974). *Support systems and community mental health.* New York: Behavioral Publications.

Dinkmeyer, D. C., Dinkmeyer, D. C., Jr., & Sperry, L. (1987). *Adlerian counseling and psychotherapy.* Columbus, OH: Charles Merrill.

Drapela, V. J. (1983). Counseling, consultation, and supervision: A visual clarification of their relationship. *Personnel and Guidance Journal, 62,* 158–162.

Kurpius, D. J. (1978). Consultation theory and process: An integrated model. *Personnel and Guidance Journal, 56,* 335–338.

Witt, J. C., & Martens, B. K. (1988). Problems with problem solving consultation: A reanalysis of assumptions, methods, and goals. *School Psychology Review, 17,* 211–226.

Woody, R. H., LaVoie, J. C., & Epps, S. (1992). *School psychology: A developmental and social systems approach.* Needham Heights, MA: Allyn and Bacon.

CONTRACTS. Counselors may use explicit written treatment contracts that define goals, procedures, and expected outcomes. Counseling contracts may have two forms: contingency contracts or informational contracts. Contingency contracts identify bonuses and sanctions if the client succeeds or fails to succeed in performing certain agreed upon actions. Informational contracts specify the parameters of the counseling relationship and provide a standard for evaluating outcomes.

Informational treatment contracts are often used as a tool for building a counseling relationship. They are vehicles for informing clients about the purpose of counseling and the nature of the client-counselor relationship. Such contracts usually include five elements: (1) information about treatment strategies; (2) statements about goals (outcomes, expectations); (3) client intention statements stipulating agreement to participate fully in treatment; (4) duration (weeks or sessions of the contract); and (5) an informed consent statement (Cormier & Cormier, 1991).

Counselors with a behavioral, transactional analysis, or reality therapy orientation will usually begin group counseling by having each member state his or her goals as clearly and concretely as possible. They will then help group members to formulate contracts for their own work that in turn provide a direction for their group (Corey, 1990).

Transactional analysis (TA) is largely based on the capacity and willingness of group participants to understand and design treatment contracts that require them to state their intentions and set personal goals. The personal contracts place the responsibility on members for clearly defining what, how, and when they want to change. Contracts describe what clients will do in a group to change their actions and experiences, when they will do it, and how many times (Corey, 1990).

Clients may employ self-contracts in counseling as a means of helping them to make commitments to new courses of action. These contracts represent promises clients make to themselves to behave in certain ways and to attain certain goals. They can provide both the structure and the incentives clients need in order to act (Egan, 1990).

References

Corey, G. (1990). *Theory and practice of group counseling* (3rd ed.). Pacific Grove, CA: Brooks/Cole.
Cormier, W. H., & Cormier, L. S. (1991). *Interviewing strategies for helpers.* Pacific Grove, CA: Brooks/Cole.
Egan, G. (1990). *The skilled helper.* Pacific Grove, CA: Brooks/Cole.

CORRECTIONAL COUNSELING. Clinical interventions using specialized psychological skills aimed at assisting incarcerated individuals in solving or otherwise coping with personal and social problems that interfere with their abilities to function effectively in school, work, and interpersonal relationships. Correctional counseling is also concerned with enabling incarcerated individuals to make a successful transition from prison to community life.

The actual services provided by correctional counselors may range from counseling involving professional support of essentially normal persons in coping with situational pressures to treatment of individuals suffering from serious mental disorders (Brammer & Shostrom, 1977). The services that correctional counselors provide are determined by the requirements of the employing agency and their professional training and expertise.

Some responsibilities of correctional counselors may include mental health services required by the correctional setting or criminal justice system. They might conduct pretrial evaluations to determine competency to stand trial or to determine an appropriate placement within the criminal justice system. Counselors might be responsible for crisis intervention and treating suicidal inmates, as well as consultation to security staff on mental health issues (Wettstein, 1988). Juvenile offenders may require additional counseling and mental health services, including psychoeducational assessment for determination of appropriate educational services, guidance counseling, and occupational counseling.

Related entry: INVOLUNTARY CLIENTS.

References

Brammer, L., & Shostrom, E. (1977). *Therapeutic psychology: Fundamentals of counseling and psychotherapy* (3rd ed.). Englewood Cliffs, NJ: Prentice-Hall.

Wettstein, R. (1988). Psychiatry and the law. In J. Talbott, R. Hales, & S. Yudofsky (Eds.), *Textbook of psychiatry* (pp. 1057–1084). Washington, DC: American Psychiatric Association.

COUNCIL FOR ACCREDITATION OF COUNSELING AND RELATED EDUCATIONAL PROGRAMS (CACREP).

The accrediting body for counselor education programs. On the master's level CACREP accredits programs in community/agency counseling, school counseling, and student personnel services in higher education. It also accredits counselor education programs that offer the Ph.D. or Ed.D. The council became the official accrediting body of the American Counseling Association in 1981. In 1988 the council included in its standards specific guidelines for the preparation of group work specialists.

Related entries: AMERICAN ASSOCIATION FOR COUNSELING (AAC); COUNSELING.

References

Altekruse, M. (1989). History of standards development. Unpublished data presented at a meeting of the North Central Association for Counseling and Development, Milwaukee, WI.

Herr, E. L. (1989). *Counseling in a dynamic society: Opportunities and challenges.* Washington, DC: American Association for Counseling and Development.

Hollis, J. W., & Wantz, R. (1986). *Counselor preparation 1986–1989.* Muncie, IN: Accelerated Development.

COUNSELING.

A helping process in which one person, a helper, facilitates exploration, understanding, and actions about developmental opportunities and problem conditions presented by a helpee or client.

In 1938 Paterson, Schneidler, and Williamson defined the guidance counselor as that person "who attempts to obtain a picture of all the complex lines of influence which bear down upon the individual student in order that the student may be helped to adjust to his present problems and to plan wisely for the future" (p. 1). From this definition of the role of the guidance counselor, counseling would appear to include diagnostic, adjustment, and planning processes. The authors listed the following duties for guidance counselors: (a) diagnostic services; (b) treatment; (c) analysis of students' needs; and (d) coordination of personnel services in the interests of students.

About a year later, in 1939, Williamson published a book entitled *How to Counsel Students.* Clinical counseling was defined as a form of individualized teaching that included advice which was based upon an adequate diagnosis of student problems. The content of counseling might deal with emotional and social maladjustments, parent and child conflicts, and educational/vocational choices and adjustments.

In his definition of clinical counseling, Williamson identified six steps: analysis, synthesis, diagnosis, prognosis, counseling (treatment), and follow-up. The specific definition of counseling as treatment included forcing conformity, changing the environment, selecting the appropriate environment, learning needed skills, and changing attitudes.

In 1942 Carl Rogers published *Counseling and Psychotherapy,* in which he used the term *counseling* to define interviews that bring about constructive changes of attitudes on the part of clients. He employed the terms *counseling* and *psychotherapy* interchangeably because he thought that they both referred to the same basic method—''a series of direct contacts with the individual which aim to offer him assistance in changing his attitudes and behavior'' (p. 3).

In 1945 Good defined counseling as ''individualized and personalized assistance with personal, educational problems in which all the pertinent facts are studied and analyzed, and a solution is sought often with the assistance of specialists, school and community resources and personal interviews in which the counselee is taught to make his own decisions'' (p. 104). In a later edition of the *Dictionary of Education,* Good's definition of counseling is less structured. Counseling is considered ''a relationship in which one or more persons with a problem or concern desire to discuss and work toward solving it with another person or persons attempting to help them reach their goals'' (1973, p. 144).

The 1950s saw attempts being made to define more clearly the processes in professional counseling. Gustad (1953) emphasized the role of learning in his definition of counseling:

> Counseling is a learning-oriented process carried on in a simple one-to-one social environment in which a counselor professionally competent in relevant psychological skills and knowledge, seeks to assist the client by methods appropriate to the latter's needs, and within the context of the total personnel program to learn more about himself, to learn how to put such understanding into effect in relation to more clearly perceived, realistically defined goals to the end that the client may become a happier and more productive member of society. (P. 17)

Williamson (1950) argued that growing from childhood through adolescence to adulthood was a complex learning process in which education may act as either a facilitator or an inhibitor of the development of individuals. Based on this premise, he defined counseling as a part of modern education that involves ''the personalized and individualized processes designed to aid the individual to learn school subject matter, citizenship traits, social and personal values and habits, and all the other habits, skills, attitudes and beliefs which go to make up a normally adjusted human being'' (p. 2). Counseling involved:

1. assisting high school and college students to identify and achieve desired and desirable goals;

2. eliminating or modifying disabilities which act as obstacles to learning through developing basic skills;

3. aiding individuals to select personal goals which can facilitate their further learning.

Williamson (1950) proposed that counseling was a fundamental technique for assisting individuals to achieve a style of living that was satisfying to themselves and congruent with their status as citizens in a democracy. At that time, he thought that the objectives of modern education were being broadened to include knowledge that was useful to students in their personal lives. Thus, he concluded that it was now possible for counseling and instruction "to join hands in a new type of teamwork" (p. 3). He envisioned instruction and counseling being combined in a comprehensive education program that was dedicated to the full development of each individual citizen in a democratic society.

In the 1960s the American Psychological Association's Division of Counseling Psychology (1961) defined the content of counseling as primarily involving role problems and helping clients to understand their role commitments and how to carry them out successfully. The authors of this report said that counseling psychology "focuses on plans individuals must make to play productive roles in their social environments. Whether the person being helped with such planning is sick or well, normal or abnormal is really irrelevant. The focus is on assets, skills, strengths, possibilities for further development. Personality difficulties are dealt with only when they constitute obstacles to the individual's forward progress" (p. 6).

Numerous attempts have been made in the literature to make a clear distinction between counseling and psychotherapy. For example, Tyler (1969, p. 20) argued that the counseling profession was mainly concerned with helping normal persons to make choices that would further their development, while psychotherapists were mostly concerned with productive personality changes and overcoming adjustment difficulties. However, Tyler rejected the idea that counseling and psychotherapy could be clearly differentiated based on either client populations or settings.

Cottone (1992) proposed that the one area in which the distinction between counseling and psychotherapy has some meaning is that of insurance reimbursement. Medical insurance companies are hesitant to provide coverage for any mental health services other than psychotherapy. Cottone went on to predict that in the future all distinctions between counseling and psychotherapy will become moot.

Ivey and Simek-Downing (1980) attempted to clarify distinctions among the terms *helping, interviewing, counseling,* and *psychotherapy. Helping* was defined as a general framework in which one person offers another person or group assistance, usually in the form of interviewing, counseling, or psychotherapy.

Interviewing was a method of information gathering that was typically employed in welfare offices, employment agencies, and placement services. *Counseling* was a more intensive process than interviewing, concerned with assisting normal people to achieve their goals or to function more effectively. *Psychotherapy* was a longer-term process that was concerned with reconstruction of the person and larger changes in personality structure. These suggested distinctions between terms have often become confused in the literature because they do not reflect any professional consensus among counselors.

Related entries: CORRECTIONAL COUNSELING; COUNSELING ECOLOGIST MODEL; COUNSELING PSYCHOLOGIST; CUBE MODEL OF COUNSELING; GERONTOLOGICAL COUNSELING; HANDICAPPED CHILDREN AND ADOLESCENTS (COUNSELING); RECREATIONAL COUNSELING; REHABILITATION COUNSELING.

References

American Psychological Association, Division of Counseling Psychology Special Committee (1961). *The current status of counseling psychology.* Washington, DC: APA.

Cottone, R. R. (1992). *Theories and paradigms of counseling and psychotherapy.* Boston: Allyn and Bacon.

Good, C. V. (Ed.) (1945). *Dictionary of education.* New York: McGraw-Hill.

Good, C. V. (Ed.) (1973). *Dictionary of education* (3rd ed.). New York: McGraw-Hill.

Gustad, J. W. (1953). The definition of counseling. In R. F. Berdie (Ed.), *Roles and relationships in counseling.* Minneapolis: University of Minnesota Press.

Ivey, A. E., & Simek-Downing, L. (1980). *Counseling and psychotherapy.* Englewood Cliffs, NJ: Prentice-Hall.

Paterson, O. G., Schneidler, G. G., & Williamson, E. G. (1938). *Student guidance techniques.* New York: McGraw-Hill.

Rogers, C. R. (1942). *Counseling and psychotherapy.* Boston, MA: Houghton Mifflin.

Tyler, L. E. (1969). *The work of the counselor* (3rd ed.). New York: Appleton-Century-Crofts.

Williamson, E. G. (1939). *How to counsel students.* New York: McGraw-Hill.

Williamson, E. G. (1950). *Counseling adolescents.* New York: McGraw-Hill.

COUNSELING ECOLOGIST MODEL. This model combines both the systems and persons change emphases (Coyne, 1985). The goal is to promote individual competence through an integrated person-by-environment perspective. Interventions may provide the necessary conditions for either individual growth in competence or the fostering of responsive human environments.

In the counseling ecology model, the interventions target the relevant level of the person and the environment simultaneously or sequentially. They combine a specific direct or indirect method with an identified purpose—remedial, developmental, or preventive. Generally, this model will place primary emphasis on prevention and development and secondary emphasis on remediation.

Direct methods of intervention involve face-to-face contacts between a counselor and an individual or system. Indirect methods of intervention try to effect change through other individuals or through instrumentation and/or research and evaluation.

Related entries: COMMUNITY COUNSELING; PRIMARY PREVENTIVE COUNSELING.

References

Coyne, R. K. (1985). The counseling ecologist: Helping people and environments. *Counseling and Human Development, 18*(2), 1–12.

Coyne, R. K. (1987). *Primary preventive counseling: Empowering people and systems.* Muncie, IN: Accelerated Development.

COUNSELING PSYCHOLOGIST. A professional doctoral level psychologist who provides individual and group guidance and counseling services in schools, colleges and universities, hospitals, clinics, rehabilitation centers, and industry, to assist individuals in achieving more effective personal, social, educational, and vocational development.

Counseling psychologists have three complementary roles: the remedial or rehabilitative, the preventive, and the educative and developmental. Counseling psychologists, in addition to professional practice, engage in research, teaching, and administrative activities.

The stated mission of counseling psychologists is to work with persons in the normal range of emotional adjustment, offering counseling in the personal, interpersonal, and career areas. The American Board of Professional Psychology (ABPP) certifies specialists in counseling psychology. A candidate must have coursework in (a) research design and methodology; (b) ethics and standards; (c) statistics; (d) psychometrics; (e) biological bases of behavior; (f) cognitive-affective bases of behavior; (g) social bases of behavior; and (h) individual differences. In addition, there must be evidence of relevant coursework in counseling psychology and supervised clinical experiences.

Related entry: AMERICAN PSYCHOLOGICAL ASSOCIATION DIVISION 17—COUNSELING PSYCHOLOGY.

References

American Psychological Association (1981). *Specialty guidelines for the delivery of services by counseling psychologists.* Washington, DC: American Psychological Association.

Whitely, J. M. (Ed.) (1980). Counseling in the year 2000 A.D. *The Counseling Psychologist, 8*(4), 2–62.

Whitely, J. M., & Fretz B. R. (Eds.) (1980). *The present and future of counseling psychology.* Monterey, CA: Brooks/Cole.

COUNTER-TRANSFERENCE. Counselors' experience, unconscious wishes, and fantasies toward clients: this tendency for a counselor to respond to a client as though the client was a significant other in the counselor's life.

Counter-transference often refers to the irrational reactions that counselors may have toward their clients. These reactions to clients can stand in the way of helping clients deal effectively with their own problems. Counselors are expected to develop some level of objectivity and not to react irrationally in the face of anger, love, adulation, criticism, and other intense feelings of clients. However, since counselors are humans, they should realize that their own areas of vulnerability and unresolved problems may sometimes intrude into counseling sessions. Still, one should not label all positive and negative feelings that counselors experience toward clients as counter-transference. Counter-transference occurs in counseling only when counselors experience inappropriate affect or respond in irrational ways because they relate to a client as if the person were a mother, father, or lover.

Searles (1979) suggests that there can be some positive outcomes from counter-transference. These reactions of counselors can provide an important means for understanding the world of clients. For example, a counselor who experiences irritability toward a client can possibly learn something about a client's tendencies toward being demanding.

Related entries: PSYCHOANALYTIC COUNSELING; TRANSFERENCE.

References

Corey, G. (1991). *Theory and practice of counseling and psychotherapy* (4th ed., Chapter 4). Pacific Grove, CA: Brooks/Cole.

Searles, H. F. (1979). *Counter transference and related subjects: Selected papers.* New York: International Universities Press.

CUBE MODEL OF COUNSELING. This model describes three dimensions of counselor intervention: the target, the purpose, and the method (Morrill, Oetting, & Hurst, 1974).

The cube model describes counseling interventions that vary from individual, direct therapeutic interventions to attempts at creating more humane environments through effective use of media strategies. The model describes thirty-six potential areas of counseling that cover development, prevention, and remediation.

Related entry: PRIMARY PREVENTIVE COUNSELING.

Reference

Morrill, W. H., Oetting, E. R., & Hurst, J. C. (1974). Dimensions of counselor functioning. *Personnel and Guidance Journal, 52,* 354–359.

CULTURE. The shared values, world views, and symbols of a group that provide the members with plans, scripts, and meaning-making rules for social living. Kroeber and Kluckholn (1952, p. 191) suggested that the various definitions of culture contained these common elements: "patterns, explicit and implicit, of or for behavior transmitted by symbols, constituting the distinctive achievements of human groups . . . [and] ideas and their attached values."

Triandis (1972) makes a distinction between physical and subjective culture. The former includes the objects made by humans, while the latter includes cognitions, attitudes, and behaviors associated with those objects that take the form of different values, roles, and beliefs.

In trying to understand cultural differences, it is important to consider how persons differ in the ways they construct their sensible worlds and live in them. For example, Foster (1969) said that culture is "a logically integrated functional sense making whole. It is not an accidental collection of customs and habits thrown together by chance. It can be compared to a biological organism in that each of its parts is related in some way to all other parts. Each fulfills a definite function in relation to the others" (p. 88).

Bruner (1990) reminds us that "the major activity of all human beings everywhere is to exact meaning from their encounters with the world. What is crucial about this process of creating meanings is that it affects what we do, what we believe, even how we feel" (p. 345). Cultural comparisons are about how different cultures, subcultures, and historical circumstances shape the human mind. Still, Bruner cautions that culture is used differently by each person who enters into its life, depending upon genetic predispositions.

Kroeber and Kluckhohn (1952), in their review of literature, identified 164 definitions of the word *culture*. However, certain limits should be observed when using this term. Culture does not refer to almost any kind of shared belief held by any kind of group. The term *shared sentiments* can be used to distinguish between truly cultural groups and those groups that simply have a lot in common. These latter groups may have similar ideas about sexuality or a common bond reflected by their similar handicaps, yet they may not necessarily be cultural groups. To be sure, distinctions should also be made between the culture of poverty/deprived minority status and one's ethnic and cultural group. Confusing the culture of poverty with the culture of ethnic minority groups leads to "overculturalizing" or mistaking people's reactions to poverty and discrimination for their cultural patterns.

When working with ethnic minority clients, a counselor should think in terms of multiple interactive factors—minority status, rapid cultural change, low socioeconomic status, and sociocultural disintegration—and not just a cultural difference framework (Smith & Vasquez, 1985).

Related entries: AFRICAN AMERICANS; CHINESE AMERICANS; MULTICULTURAL COUNSELING; NATIVE AMERICANS.

References

Bruner, J. (1990). Culture and human development: A new look. *Human Development, 33,* 344–355.

Foster, F. M. (1969). *Applied anthropology.* Boston: Little, Brown.

Kroeber, A. L., & Kluckhohn, C. (1952). A review of culture: A critical review of concepts and definitions. *Papers of the Peabody Museum of American Archeology and Ethnology, 4*(1).

Smith, E. M. J., & Vasquez, M. J. T. (1985). Introduction to special issue. *The Counseling Psychologist, 13,* 531–536.

Triandis, H. C. (1972). *The analysis of subjective culture.* New York: Wiley.

D

DASEIN ANALYSIS. In German, Dasein analysis means analysis of existence, an approach to existential counseling that views individuals as constantly growing, responsible, and interactive as they create and attribute meaning to selves, others, and environments.

Martin Heidegger (1889–1976) differentiated Das Man, or conventional herd mentality, from Dasein, or the ability to reach high levels of consciousness through reflecting upon self, others, and the natural environment. Dasein is that form of human experiencing that includes discomforting conditions such as anxiety and awareness of death, as well as more pleasant states such as those involved in active caring and concern.

Related entries: EXISTENTIAL COUNSELING; EXISTENTIALISM; MAY, ROLLO.

References

Heidegger, M. (1962). *Being and time* (J. MacQuarrie & E. S. Robinson, Trans.). New York: Harper and Row.

Kobasa, S. C., & Maddie, S. R. (1983). Existential personality theory. In R. J. Corsini & A. J. Marsella (Eds.), *Personality theories, research and assessment* (pp. 399–446). Itasca, IL: F. E. Peacock.

DECISION-MAKING MODEL OF COUNSELING. A decision-making model of the counseling process that is similar in many approaches to counseling has three stages: The Problem Definition Phase, The Work Phase, and The Action Phase (see Ivey & Simek-Downing, 1980).

Decision-making tasks in the first stage involve defining the problem, consideration of alternative definitions, and making a commitment to the most suitable definition. Tasks in the work phase include examining the problem from different perspectives in order to identify facts, including personal thoughts and feelings about what is occurring in the client's life. Counselors with different theoretical orientations may use different approaches to the tasks in the work phase. However, most counselors will consider alternative theoretical frameworks, select a primary mode of operation, and then help the client to examine the definition of the problem and generate new ways of looking at issues, answers, and solutions. The tasks in the action stage are concerned with generating further alternative solutions, reflecting on their advantages and disadvantages, and choosing a solution to test in the home environment.

This type of decision-making model of the counseling process has the advantage of allowing for creative choices, providing an emphasis on client-counselor consensus, and suggesting a structure for the interview that provides a system for regenerating the interview when the session falters or fails (Ivey & Simek-Downing, 1980).

Brammer (1973) defined ten steps for systematic decision making that gave attention to the quality of the counselor-client relationship as well as issues regarding value clarification and decision making. Carkhuff (1973) presented a problem-solving model that included suggestions for weighing alternatives.

Janis and Mann (1977) identified five types of decision patterns: (1) unconflicted adherence (a person who adheres resolutely to one way to solve a problem); (2) unconflicted change (a person who changes ideas rapidly without thought); (3) defensive avoidance (a person who denies problems or simply doesn't want to look at them); (4) hypervigilance (a person who is aware of many possibilities but is so emotionally involved that key issues can be missed); and (5) vigilance (a person who is sufficiently aroused and motivated to engage in all of the essential cognitive tasks of decisionmaking).

They also provided seven criteria for decision making. However, they caution that decision making is often so stressful that emotional factors can preclude the implementation of crucial choices.

Related entry: INTENTIONAL COUNSELING.

References

Brammer, L. (1973). *The helping relationship.* Englewood Cliffs, NJ: Prentice-Hall.

Carkhuff, R. (1973). *The art of problem solving.* Amherst, MA: Human Resources Development.

Ivey, A. E., & Simek-Downing, L. (1980). *Counseling and psychotherapy: Skills, theories and practice.* Englewood Cliffs, NJ: Prentice-Hall.

Janis, I., & Mann, L. (1977). *Decision-making: A psychological analysis of conflict, choice and commitment.* New York: Free Press.

DECISION-REDECISION METHODS. Clients in transactional analysis reexperience decision moments in their childhood and then choose to redecide as a consequence of these self-confrontations.

This treatment is used with nonpsychotic individuals. The client confronts those early childhood decisions in which the child, based upon parental injunctions, decides to be an "OK" or a "Not OK" person. These childhood decisions result from injunctions such as "don't be you," "don't think," "don't feel," "don't be a child," "don't grow up," and "don't be." These early decisions and the associated racket feelings or habitual patterns of emotion (e.g., sadness, fear, anger) that are carried throughout life, and a client in counseling will protect them. Redecision techniques can include the use of double chairs, which allow the client to separate the negative and positive parts of self that oppose one another.

Related entry: TRANSACTIONAL ANALYSIS (TA).

References

Goulding, R., & Goulding, M. (1976). Injunctions, decisions, and redecisions. *Transactional Analysis Journal, 6,* 41–48.

Goulding, M., & Goulding, R. (1979). *Changing lives through redecision therapy.* New York: Brunner/Mazel.

DEFENSE MECHANISMS. The strategies or mental maneuvers used by individuals to protect their personalities from the unpleasant affect of anxiety. Typically these mechanisms are repetitive, stereotyped, automatic means used by the ego to ward off anxiety arising from either the id or the superego.

Psychodynamic theory views the defense mechanisms as perceptual, attitudinal, or attentional shifts that aid the ego in dealing with anxiety. These psychic processes provide safety but restrict personal growth. The ultimate aim of all defenses is to achieve repression and keep certain impulses and feelings from becoming conscious. The concept of repression is central to the theory of defenses. It is both a defense and the aim of defenses. Defenses are neutral maneuvers set in motion by anxiety, which in turn is a response to internal danger. Defenses are hypothetical mechanisms or abstract concepts, the manifestations of which can be observed and are known as character traits or symptoms. Defenses can be arranged in a hierarchical continuum so that those which characterize a well-structured ego are at the top. Further down are the more primitive defenses that are characteristic of early developmental phases. The most important criterion for determining whether a defense is relatively sophisticated or primitive is the amount of reality testing. Rationalization, at the top end of the continuum, distorts reality only minimally, whereas denial, which is at the bottom, totally disavows reality. Rationalization is used to explain a person's behavior in a socially accepted manner so as to maintain self-esteem. By way of contrast, the person who uses denial does not acknowledge certain aspects of reality.

Different psychopathological conditions are characterized by a dominant use of particular defenses. Repression, displacement, and conversion are typical of hysteria; isolation, reaction formation, and undoing characterize the obsessive-compulsive neurosis; and introjection, depression, projection, and denial characterize paranoid and other psychotic states. If a particular defense has become the chief modality by which a person maintains a balance between his/her inner psychic world and the external world, then it may be possible to diagnose a specific type of emotional disorder. However, a person is not necessarily paranoid just because he/she uses projection on occasion.

Defense mechanisms include:

—*Repression.* Keeping certain impulses and feelings from becoming conscious.

—*Displacement.* Replacing the object of an impulse (usually a person capable of gratifying the impulse) by a substitute object.

—*Identification.* Taking on the character traits of another person and making them your own.

—*Conversion.* Transforming a psychological disturbance or symptoms that may include paralysis, areas of anesthesia, blindness, and deafness.

—*Isolation or intellectualization.* Dealing with disturbing thoughts in a calm, detached manner.

—*Reaction formation or overcompensation.* Destructive and hostile feelings are expressed as kindness and sweetness.

—*Undoing.* Unacceptable impulses are expressed and then actions are taken to undo the original destructive or hostile actions. Hostile acts are followed by atonement.

—*Introjection.* Some aspects of the outer world, usually persons whom you perceive in an ambivalent manner, are internalized. The loss of a loved person is defended against by preserving a memory of the person in your psyche.

—*Projection.* Something unacceptable in self is attributed to someone else.

For the existential counselor, anxiety springs from confrontation with death, groundlessness (freedom), isolation, and meaninglessness. Individuals use two types of defense mechanisms to cope with such anxiety. The first type includes the conventional defense mechanisms described in the above paragraphs. The second type includes those defense mechanisms that serve to help persons cope with primary existential fears. For example, Yalom (1981) describes two kinds of irrational beliefs that act as defense mechanisms. First is the belief in personal "specialness," and second is the belief in an "ultimate rescuer." The defense of specialness, immortality, and invulnerability is used to ward off anxiety about death. These persons do not believe that the ordinary laws of biology apply to them. The other defense mechanism that blocks the anxiety that arises from awareness of death is a belief that someone is guarding and protecting your welfare.

Related entries: ANXIETY; EXISTENTIAL COUNSELING; MASOCHISM; PSYCHOANALYTIC COUNSELING.

References

Giovacchini, P. L. (1983). Psychoanalysis. In R. J. Corsini & A. J. Marsella (Eds.), *Personality theories: Research and assessment* (pp. 25–68). Itasca, IL: F. E. Peacock.

Yalom, I. (1981). *Existential psychotherapy.* New York: Basic Books.

DELIBERATE PSYCHOLOGICAL EDUCATION. A curriculum or set of educational experiences that is designed to affect personal, ethical, aesthetic, and philosophical development in adolescents and young adults. Counselors act as developmental instructors or as psychological educators.

An example of deliberate psychological education is a course designed to promote psychological growth in young women entitled "A Study of Women Through Literature."

Related entry: PSYCHOEDUCATION.

References

Erickson, V. L. (1975). Deliberate psychological education for women from Iphigenia to Antigone. *Counselor Education and Supervision, 14,* 297–309.
Mosher, R. L., & Sprinthall, N. A. (1971). Deliberate psychological education. *The Counseling Psychologist, 2,* 3–82.

DEPRESSION. Persons experiencing depression report that they feel helpless and discouraged, have little self-esteem, and may have suicidal ideation. Physical symptoms of sleeping and eating problems, as well as fatigue, are also common. The *Diagnostic and Statistical Manual of Mental Disorders* (DSM-III-R) lists depression as a type of mood disorder. These disorders may be characterized by both manic and depressive syndromes (bipolar disorder and cyclothymia) or by depression alone (major depression dysthymia) (Meyer, 1983).

Treatment of mood disorders depends on whether mania or depression is predominantly observed. When it is mania, treatments might include lithium therapy, antipsychotic drugs, or electroconvulsive therapy. A wide range of approaches may be effective for treatment of depression, including a combination of medication and counseling.

Person-centered counselors will work to develop a climate of trust and acceptance in which the depressed client can express his/her feelings. The counselor provides an example of accepting attentiveness. Psychoanalytic counselors might focus their efforts on examining the dependencies that a depressed client exhibits during counseling. In exploring their reactions to the counselor, clients may recognize the same dynamics in other relationships outside of counseling and understand how the past is influencing the present problem conditions. The reality approach to counseling encourages depressed clients to examine what it is that they are doing in the present situation that contributes to their feelings of depression. This approach does not look for causes of depressive symptoms in the past, nor do these counselors seek to identify unconscious reasons for depressive symptoms.

Cognitive therapy (Beck, 1987) began as a treatment for depression that focused on the client's negative thinking and interpretations. Beck (1967, 1975) described the cognitive triad as a pattern of thinking that contributed to depression. The first component is the negative view depressed clients have of themselves. They are convinced that they lack the personal qualities that are essential to bring them happiness. The second component is a tendency to interpret experiences in a negative manner. Depressed clients select certain facts that conform to their negative conclusions. The third component is a gloomy vision or negative view of the future. They expect their present problems to continue and anticipate only failures in the future. They set rigid perfectionistic goals for themselves and screen out successful experiences that are not consistent with their negative self-image.

Related entries: COGNITIVE COUNSELING; *DIAGNOSTIC AND STATISTICAL MANUAL OF MENTAL DISORDERS*—THIRD EDITION, REVISED.

References

Beck, A. T. (1967). *Depression: Clinical, experimental and theoretical aspects.* New York: Harper and Row.

Beck, A. T. (1975). *Depression: Causes and treatment.* Philadelphia: University of Pennsylvania Press.

Meyer, R. G. (1983). *The clinician's handbook: The psychopathology of adulthood and late adolescence.* Boston: Allyn and Bacon.

DESENSITIZATION. A counseling intervention designed to help clients overcome phobias. The client and the counselor identify a list of scenes, ranging from least scary to most scary, that is referred to as the "fear hierarchy." The client is then taught to relax, and the elements of the fear hierarchy are presented one at a time. A scene is said to be desensitized when the client is able to imagine it for twenty to twenty-five seconds without anxiety.

The theory of desensitization described by Wolpe (1958) is based on classical conditioning and is called counter conditioning. Goldfreid (1971) views desensitization as essentially a coping or self-control technique. He tells clients to "relax away" any increases in anxiety that are associated with specific scenes in a fear hierarchy.

Kazden and Wilcoxen (1976) argue that desensitization works because it sounds like a plausible technique and clients expect it to work.

Related entries: BEHAVIORAL COUNSELING; STRESS; STRESS MANAGEMENT.

References

Goldfreid, M. R. (1971). Systematic desensitization and training in self-control. *Journal of Consulting and Clinical Psychology, 37,* 228–234.

Kazden, A. E., & Wilcoxen, L. A. (1976). Systematic desensitization and nonspecific treatment effects: A methodological evaluation. *Psychological Bulletin, 83,* 729–758.

Wolpe, J. (1958). *Psychotherapy by reciprocal inhibition.* Stanford, CA: Stanford University Press.

DEVELOPMENTAL COUNSELING (Blocher, 1966, 1974). The basic assumption of developmental counseling is that human personality unfolds in terms of a largely healthy interaction between the person and the culture or environment.

The task of the developmental counselor is to help a client become more self-aware of how he or she reacts to the influences in the environment, and to establish a set of goals and values for future behavior. Developmental counseling tries to maximize human freedom and human effectiveness.

Developmental counseling is based on the following assumptions about clients and counselors:

—Clients are not mentally ill. They are capable of choosing goals, making decisions, and assuming responsibilities.

—Counselors should be concerned with where clients are going, not where they have been. Development is about the future, not the past.

—A client is not a patient, and the counselor is essentially a teacher who helps clients move toward mutually defined goals.

—Counselors are not amoral; they have values, feelings, and standards that they do not hide from their clients.

—The counselor is concerned with changing behaviors, not just creating insights. The counselor assigns tasks, arranges try-out experiences, serves as a consultant to the client, and provides a helping relationship.

Developmental counseling is an approach to changing human behavior that is aimed at facilitating human development. It is based on the assumption that clients are capable of choosing the desired directions of their own development. Developmental counseling is educational in its orientation, but it concentrates on the personal meaning of events and experiences rather than on any so-called objective meaning of them.

Blocher (1974) describes the following characteristics of developmental groups:

—*Mutuality of purpose.* Members are willing to abide by majority decisions.

—*Effectiveness of leadership.* Leaders are facilitators who assure maximum participation of all members in the decision-making process.

—*Flexibility of group organization.* Members have opportunities to play a variety of roles and assume leadership roles from time to time because of their unique contributions.

—*Mutuality of climate.* The group does not exploit, neglect, or reject a group member. There is mutuality of support and caring.

—*Positiveness of social control.* Forms of social control are exercised in open and positive ways that intend to both change deviant behavior and contribute to the development of individual group members.

Related entry: DEVELOPMENTAL THERAPY (IVEY, 1986).

References

Blocher, D. H. (1966). *Developmental counseling.* New York: Ronald Press.
Blocher, D. H. (1974). *Developmental counseling* (2nd ed.). New York: Ronald Press.

DEVELOPMENTAL THERAPY (Ivey, 1986). A structured approach to the systematic development of consciousness. It involves person-environment transactions in which two realities are met and accommodated and assimilated by the two parties, counselor and counselee (Ivey, 1986).

The counselor may accommodate to the client through empathic responding (perspective taking) or may assimilate client data through a preexisting theoretical lens (behavioral, Rogerian, psychodynamic). The client working with an accommodating counselor will have the opportunity to have his or her past assimilations fed back (mirrored) and may develop a new construction of reality with these clarified data. The client with an assimilating counselor may learn to accommodate to and to adopt the counselor's construction of reality, one that is presumably more workable.

Assimilation is that cognitive process used by individuals to integrate new information into their lives. For example, persons are able to identify certain objects as trees because they have certain preexisting mental structures that can be used for this task. Assimilation implies an incorporation of the environment with one's own frame of reference. Overassimilators distort their experiences so as to fit their frames of reference.

In accommodation, a person modifies or transforms certain preexisting cognitive structures of meaning so as to accommodate to an environment. It is possible to overaccommodate to one's environment; as a result, a person may lose a sense of self as a unique person. Clients must have a balance of assimilation and accommodation if they are successfully to adapt and cope with their worlds.

Dialectics is central to change in developmental counseling, and pointing out contradictions is critical to the dialectical process. Unless clients can experience these contradictions in their own lives, it will be difficult for them to move to or find a new creative synthesis, explanation, or meaning.

A major task of the developmental counselor is to assess client developmental level and then to provide appropriate therapeutic environments. A client may be magical and preoperational on one level, concrete operational on another, formal operational on another, and dialectical on still another.

Therapeutic environments include environmental structuring, coaching, consulting, and dialectics designed to match differences in client developmental levels. In a single interview, the counselor may have to provide several therapeutic environments at multiple levels.

Related entry: DEVELOPMENTAL COUNSELING (BLOCHER).

Reference

Ivey, A. E. (1986). *Developmental therapy.* San Francisco: Jossey-Bass.

DIAGNOSTIC AND STATISTICAL MANUAL OF MENTAL DISOR-DERS—THIRD EDITION, REVISED (DSM-III-R, 1987). DSM-III-R consists of descriptions of various mental and psychological disorders; they are categorized into sixteen major diagnostic classes which include additional subcategories.

Diagnostic criteria provide guidelines for evaluating and classifying client problems. Five codes or axes are used:

Axis I. Clinical syndromes and conditions not attributable to a mental disorder that are a focus of attention or treatment.

Axis II. Personality disorders (adult) and specific developmental disorders (child).

Axis III. Physical disorders or conditions.

Axis IV. Severity of psychological stressors.

Axis V. Highest level of adaptive functioning during past year.

Axis IV provides for a seven-point rating or assessment of the overall severity of stress that may have been a contributor to the development or exacerbation of the current disorder. Axis V uses a seven-point scale to assess adaptive functioning in three areas: social relations, occupational functioning, and uses of leisure time.

The DSM-III-R (APA, 1987) has decision trees for differential diagnoses that provide a recommended sequence for determining a specific disorder. Consideration is given to family background factors, levels of education, intelligence, and environmental factors.

The DSM-III-R describes mental disorders as clinically significant behavioral or psychological syndromes that are associated with present distress or disability or with an increased risk of suffering death, pain, disability, or an important loss of freedom. This syndrome is not merely an expectable response to a particular event, it is a manifestation of a behavioral, psychological, or biological dysfunction in the person. Neither deviant behavior nor conflicts between an individual and society are mental disorders unless the deviance or conflict are symptoms of a dysfunction in the person.

The DSM-III-R does allow for behavioral or psychological factors in the definition of a disorder. However, for the most part disorders are viewed as dysfunctions in a person.

Related entries: DEPRESSION; MANIA.

Reference

American Psychiatric Association (1987). *Diagnostic and statistical manual of mental disorders* (3rd ed. rev.). Washington, DC: American Psychiatric Association.

DIAGNOSTIC CATEGORIES IN COUNSELING. Bordin (1946) and Pepinsky (1948) identified the following diagnostic constructs in counseling:

A. Lack of assurance (client has made a decision but wants to play safe by checking up with others)

B. Lack of information
C. Lack of skill
D. Dependence
E. Self-conflict (conflict between self-concepts or between a self-concept and some other stimulus function)
   —cultural self-conflict
   —interpersonal self-conflict
   —intrapersonal self-conflict
F. Choice anxiety (necessity of deciding among several alternative plans, all of which upset his/her present life)

Pepinsky's research (1948) showed that lack of assurance was the most clear-cut category. However, in the thirty-nine cases diagnosed as lack of assurance, the three judges agreed unanimously on the diagnosis less than a third of the time.

Robinson (1950) described the sociological and causal approaches to diagnosis in counseling. In the first model for diagnosis, the problems of clients are viewed in terms of the places where frustrations occurred. In the second, the content of counseling is selected so as to eliminate or overcome the causes of problems. Robinson (1950) goes on to present an alternative approach to diagnosis of client problems that is based on dynamics of learning. He proposed that the interactions between counselors and clients will differ in terms of three major types of problems: adjustment problems, skill problems, and maturity problems.

Although adjustment problems include such diverse concerns as vocational choice, curricular planning, social acceptance, financial problems, religious confusion, and personal adjustment, the client's difficulty in all these cases is that he or she is unable to decide upon a course of action which is adequate for dealing with a frustrating situation. Consequently, the counselor's task is the same in treating clients with any of these adjustment problems. He or she must help clarify the client's thinking so that the client can see the issues more clearly and accept their implications for decision making. Robinson envisioned the process of clarification as including seeing and accepting one's self in relation to the world, with emphasis on both feelings and intellectual insight. Clients have to discover and integrate the elements in their problem through their own conscious efforts. Clients need to recognize that their particular adjustment problem is primarily due to difficulties in their own manner of thinking and adjusting. The reasons that a client is not aware of relevant information, attitudes, and experiences should be a most important determinant of the methods used in counseling. Robinson goes on to explain how the counseling strategies used when clients have skills problems or problems of maturity will differ in several ways from those used with clients who present adjustment problems.

Related entry: TRAIT AND FACTOR COUNSELING.

References

Bordin, E. S. (1946). Diagnosis in counseling and psychotherapy. *Educational and Psychological Measurement, 6,* 169–184.

Pepinsky, H. B. (1948). *The selection and use of diagnostic categories in clinical counseling* (Applied Psychology Monographs, No. 15). Washington, DC: American Psychological Assoc.

Robinson, F. P. (1950). *Principles and procedures in student counseling.* New York: Harper and Bros.

DICTIONARY OF OCCUPATIONAL TITLES (DOT). This book, which is a resource for counselors who are helping clients learn about different jobs, began publication in 1939. The original publication by the United States Employment Service coded and defined more than 18,000 occupations in the United States.

The DOT facilitates the bridging of client characteristics and occupational characteristics. Each entry includes a six-digit *Dictionary of Occupational Titles* (DOT) number.

Related entry: CAREER COUNSELING.

References

Fine, S. A., & Heinz, C. A. (1957). The functional occupational classification structure. *Personnel and Guidance Journal, 37,* 180–192.

United States Employment Service (1991). *Dictionary of occupational titles* (2 vols.). Washington, DC: U.S. Department of Labor, Employment and Training Administration, U.S. Employment Service.

DIRECTIVE APPROACH TO COUNSELING. The focus of the counseling process is on problem causes and treatment. The counselor defines the problem, takes responsibility for discovering the causes of the condition, and makes suggestions for correcting the difficulties.

According to Rogers (1942), directive counselors assumed that they should select the desirable and socially approved goals that clients should attain. This viewpoint was seen as placing a high value on social conformity and the right of the more able to direct the less able. Directive counselors attempted to solve problems of their clients. Counseling techniques were characterized by the use of highly specific questions and the provision of information and explanations.

By way of contrast, Rogers (1942) described counseling of a nondirective sort as being characterized by a preponderance of client activity. The client did most of the talking about his or her problems. The counselor's primary techniques involved helping the client to recognize his or her feelings, attitudes, and reaction patterns more clearly and encouraging the client to talk about them. The counselor sometimes restated or clarified the subjective content of a client's statements.

Robinson (1950) proposed that the distinction between directive and nondirective counselors was fundamentally a matter of the emphasis placed on the principles of acceptance and interpretation. He described the directive approach to counseling in less authoritarian terms than did Rogers. For example, he pointed out that directive counselors did not expect to take entire responsibility for helping clients. They were careful to take responsibility only at crucial points in the counseling process. This counselor was generally to act as a helpful listener by using acceptance, clarification, and open lead remarks. Only when clients encountered blocks was it necessary for counselors to introduce tentative queries and suggestions. In brief, directive or traditional counselors were seen as varying the degree of responsibility depending on the progress that clients were making in solving their problems.

Related entries: CLINICAL COUNSELING; WILLIAMSON, EDMUND G.

References

Robinson, F. P. (1950). *Principles and procedures in student counseling.* New York: Harper and Bros.

Rogers, C. R. (1942). *Counseling and psychotherapy.* Boston, MA: Houghton Mifflin.

DIRECTIVES. The counselor's messages to a client to do something or to not do something. Directives can be given explicitly, or they can be given implicitly by vocal intonation, body movement, or well-timed silences.

According to Haley (1987), whatever a counselor does is a message for the client to do something, and in that sense is a directive. If the client says, "I feel unhappy," and the counselor says, "I understand that you feel unhappy," this reply is seen as a directive because the counselor indicates interest in such client statements and indicates that such statements are all right to talk about.

Directives have three purposes in counseling: to get people to behave differently and so to have different subjective experiences; to intensify the client-counselor relationship by increasing counselor involvement in the proposed client actions; and to gather information about a client's approach to tasks.

Two ways of giving directives are for counselors to tell clients what to do when they want them to take certain actions, and to tell clients what to do when they do not want them to take certain actions. If counselors want clients to do something different, they may give good advice or they may try to change the sequence in a family. For example, if a mother and daughter were fighting about when the daughter was to come in at night, the counselor might direct the father to take charge of the problem. This kind of directive changes the sequence of relationships in the family.

Directives should be clearly given rather than suggested (unless there is a particular reason to be confusing). In family counseling it is important to give everyone something to do in a task. Someone is needed to do the task, someone to help, someone to supervise, someone to plan, someone to check to see that it is done, and so on. After giving a task, the counselor will ask for a report at the next session.

Sometimes clients are more willing to follow a directive if they do not have to concede that they have received one. Talking in metaphor is one way to give such a directive. A counselor might want family members to behave in a certain way. He or she then gets them to behave in some other way that resembles the actions the counselor desires. Then the family members may "spontaneously" behave the way the counselor wants them to.

Related entries: FAMILY COUNSELING; STRATEGIC PROBLEM-SOLVING COUNSELING.

References

Haley, J. (1976). *Problem solving therapy: New strategies for effective family therapy.* San Francisco: Jossey-Bass.

Haley, J. (1987). *Problem solving therapy* (2nd ed.). San Francisco: Jossey-Bass.

DOUBLE BIND. A situation in which a person is put into a position where whatever choice he/she makes is unacceptable. No good choice is possible. In schizophrenic families, double binds occur regularly. Repeated episodes of double binding produce bewilderment and ultimately withdrawal.

In family counseling, a counselor may create a benign double bind by telling a client to continue doing voluntarily what he or she claims is involuntary. The person is faced with either (a) stopping the behavior, or (b) continuing the behavior but now doing it under the control of the counselor. In either case it is voluntary. Frankl (1960) called this technique paradoxical intention.

Related entry: FAMILY COUNSELING.

References

Bateson, G., Jackson, D., Haley, J., & Weakland, J. (1956). Towards a theory of schizophrenia. *Behavioral Science, 1,* 251–264.

Frankl, V. (1960). Paradoxical intention: A logo-therapeutic technique. *American Journal of Psychotherapy, 14,* 320–535.

DREIKURS, RUDOLPH (1897–1972). Dreikurs founded the Alfred Adler Institute in Chicago and provided an explanation of misbehaviors in children which he related to their goals of attention, power, revenge seeking, and display of inadequacy.

Rudolph Dreikurs immigrated to the United States in 1927 to escape the Nazis. He was largely responsible for developing and refining Adler's concepts into a practical counseling approach that he transplanted to the United States. He was a key figure in developing Adlerian child-guidance clinics in the United States and in pioneering group therapy as a way of facilitating insights into participants' life styles. Dreikurs' rationale for group counseling is as follows: "Since man's problems and conflicts are recognized in their social nature, the group is ideally suited not only to highlight and reveal the nature of a person's conflicts and maladjustments but to offer corrective influences" (1969, p. 43).

Related entry: ADLERIAN COUNSELING.

Reference

Dreikurs, R. (1969). Group psychotherapy from the point of view of Adlerian psychology. In H. M. Ruitenbeek (Ed.), *Group therapy today: Styles, methods and techniques.* Chicago: Aldine-Atherton.

DRIVES. This term in psychoanalytic theory applies to libidinal and aggressive impulses (Arlow, 1989). These are states of central excitation in response to stimuli. They are physiological demands that impel the mind to activity with the ultimate aim of bringing about the cessation of tension and a sense of gratification.

According to Arlow, it is important to distinguish drives in humans from instinctive behaviors in animals. Instincts are stereotyped responses evoked by specific stimuli in particular settings. Drives are capable of a wide variety of complex transformations. In psychoanalytic theory, libidinal and aggressive drives are differentiated. However, the terminology used to describe the development of drives originally applied only to the libidinal drives. The early phases of libidinal drives are distinct and related to specific zones of the body. For any individual, given an average expectable environment, one may anticipate a more or less predictable sequence of events constituting the steps in the maturation of the drives.

Adler held that the important problems in human beings do not deal with drive satisfaction (Ansbacher, 1983). Drives become merged with cultural conceptions and an individual's own ideas as to how a specific need should be met to satisfy his/her own striving for success. For example, there is an infinite variety of ways in which individuals and various cultures satisfy the hunger drive. Adler gave up the concept of drive in favor of "masculine protest" and "striving" because he considered the concept to be too mechanistic. Protest and striving are more appropriate human concepts; to humans, machines neither protest nor strive.

Related entry: BEHAVIORAL COUNSELING.

References

Ansbacher, H. L. (1983). Individual psychology. In R. J. Corsini & A. J. Marsella (Eds.), *Personality theories, research and assessment.* Itasca, IL: F. E. Peacock.

Arlow, J. A. (1989). Psychoanalysis. In R. J. Corsini & A. J. Marsella (Eds.), *Personality theories, research and assessment.* Itasca, IL: F. E. Peacock.

DUAL RELATIONSHIPS. A counselor has both a professional relationship and an administrative, instructional, supervisory, social, or sexual relationship with a client. Dual relationships can reduce counselor objectivity and, most important, place the client in a vulnerable position regarding freedom of consent.

The ethical guidelines of psychologists and counselors caution them to avoid dual relationships that could impair their professional judgment or increase the risk of exploitation. Such relationships include counseling employees, students, supervisees, close friends, or relatives. Sexual intimacies with clients are unethical. Marriage and family counselors are prohibited from establishing sexual relationships with former clients for a period of two years following the termination of professional relationships.

Related entry: ETHICS.

References

American Association for Counseling and Development (1988). *Ethical standards* (Rev. ed.). Alexandria, VA: American Association for Counseling and Development.

American Association for Marriage and Family Therapy (1988). *AAMFT code of ethical principles for marriage and family therapists.* Washington, DC: American Association for Marriage and Family Therapy.

American Psychological Association (1981). *Ethical principles of psychologists* (Rev. ed.). Washington, DC: American Psychological Association.

DYSFUNCTIONAL FAMILY. A family system that has responded to external or internal demands for change by stereotyping its functioning (Minuchin, 1974).

This is a condition in a family in which members are unable to attain the desired goals of closeness, self-expression, and meaning. As a consequence of the family members not meeting these needs, symptomatic behaviors develop (Foley, 1989).

The structure of dysfunctional families may become so rigid that it blocks any alternative transactional patterns. Often there is an individual in these families who is the identified patient. In structural family counseling the family's system of transactional rules is restructured so that members have available alternative ways of dealing with each other. Family members are released from stereotyped positions and functions. Once the family does not support unwanted behaviors and is able to sustain these changes in the face of family stressors, then counseling is no longer indicated.

Related entries: FAMILY COUNSELING; STRATEGIC PROBLEM-SOLVING COUNSELING.

References

Foley, V. O. (1989). Family therapy. In R. J. Corsini & D. Wedding (Eds.), *Current psychotherapies* (4th ed.). Itasca, IL: F. E. Peacock.

Minuchin, S. (1974). *Families and family therapy.* Cambridge, MA: Harvard University Press.

E

ECLECTIC COUNSELING. Approaches to counseling that attempt to utilize techniques and concepts from different theoretical models of the counseling process.

In the 1950s, Ohlsen (1955) described eclectic counseling as a means of integrating and using both directive and nondirective skills. Eclectic counselors would use the diagnostic skills of directive counselors and the response-to-feeling skills associated with nondirective counselors. Ohlsen described two styles of eclectic counseling that differed primarily in whether there were obvious shifts in roles and relationships during counseling. In one case, the eclectic counselor would try to integrate nondirective and directive techniques into a consistent approach, while in another case, the eclectic counselor would use either nondirective or directive techniques in response to specific client issues during a session.

Ponzo (1976) described an eclectic approach to counseling that included three phases: first is awareness, in which existential, client-centered, and Gestalt approaches are used to establish good relationships with clients; second is cognitive reorganization, in which cognitive approaches are used to help clients change maladaptive or nonproductive thinking; third is behavior change, in which behavioral approaches are used to help clients act differently and more productively.

Lazarus (1967) initially defined his multimodal approach to counseling as technical eclecticism. He proposed that a client's personality was organized into seven modes of functioning: behaviors, affective processes, sensations, images, cognitions, interpersonal relationships, and biological functions. He saw these human modes as interactional and as resulting in a firing order by which one mode influenced another. This approach to counseling is multifaceted and uses a variety of skills to influence the modes specific clients are experiencing the most difficulties with in resolving problems in their lives.

Surveys of clinical and counseling psychologists conducted in the 1970s and the 1980s reported that 30 to 50 percent of the respondents considered themselves to be eclectic in their practice of counseling and therapy (Messer, 1986). Garfield (1980) has advised counselors that given the present state of knowledge about counseling, it seems more justified to place one's confidence in empirical results and tenable hypotheses than to adhere to a single approach to counseling.

Related entry: MULTIMODAL APPROACH TO COUNSELING.

References

Garfield, S. L. (1980). *Psychotherapy: An eclectic approach.* New York: Wiley.

Lazarus, A. A. (1967). In support of technical eclecticism. *Psychological Reports, 21,* 415–416.

Messer, S. B. (1986). Eclecticism in psychotherapy: Underlying assumptions, problems and trade-offs. In J. C. Norcross (Ed.), *Handbook of eclectic psychotherapy* (pp. 379–397). New York: Brunner/Mazel.

Ohlsen, M. M. (1955). *Guidance: An introduction.* New York: Harcourt, Brace.

Ponzo, Z. (1976). Integrating techniques from five counseling theories. *Personnel and Guidance Journal, 54,* 415–419.

EDUCATIONAL COUNSELING. Diagnosis and counseling for clients with the following kinds of problems: (a) unwise selection of courses and curricula; (b) differential scholastic achievement; (c) insufficient general scholastic aptitude; (d) ineffective study habits; (e) reading disabilities; (f) insufficient scholastic motivation; (g) overachievement; (h) underachievement; and (i) special concerns of superior students (see Williamson, 1939).

Patterson, Schniedler, and Williamson (1938) said that educational problems, in most cases, were linked with vocational problems, which in turn often appeared as symptoms of difficulties in the emotional life. Problems overlapped in the same client. Thus, a concept of clients as individuals characterized by single problems was considered erroneous.

Counselors were to analyze their clients' present status and developmental history, help them to diagnose their educational problems, and then help them map out short-term and long-term plans of action. The counselors were to obtain a picture of the factors influencing their clients' educational problems, then they were to help them adjust to those problems and to plan wisely for the future.

Williamson (1939) argued that different types of students need different types of education if they are to be effective and avoid failure and frustration. Counselors are to identify those clients who may possibly fail to achieve their educational and occupational goals. Then they should try to counsel them toward other alternatives. In some cases, such clients will possess compensatory drives and skills. Their counselors would do well to encourage them, warn them that they may have to work harder than the average student, and advise them about subjects that may be more promising for them.

In his later book, *Counseling Adolescents,* Williamson (1950) criticized counselors because they often sought merely to adjust pupils to the educational system, and failed to make any attempts to modify the system itself. Still others, he pointed out, ignored the fact that students must achieve a happy balance of diverse and conflicting needs and interests. Students do not live by studies alone. Finally, he argued that educational counselors need to consider more than selection and guidance of qualified students, and they should not be indifferent to problems of morale and motivation that underlie many cases of educational failures.

Related entries: GUIDANCE; SCHOOL COUNSELING; TEACHER-COUNSELOR.

References

Patterson, O. G., Schniedler, G. G., & Williamson, E. G. (1938). *Student guidance techniques.* New York: McGraw-Hill.
Williamson, E. G. (1939). *How to counsel students.* New York: McGraw-Hill.
Williamson, E. G. (1950). *Counseling adolescents.* New York: McGraw-Hill.

EGO. A group of human functions that orient an individual toward the external world and mediate between it and the inner world. A process by which a person considers how the demands associated with his/her drives can be met in light of his/her conscience and the nature of reality (Arlow, 1989).

One of the major functions of the ego is to protect the mind from internal dangers such as conflict-laden impulses breaking through into consciousness. Anxiety is the warning signal to the ego, and it is usually followed by the use of a wide variety of defenses.

Analytical counseling views the ego as the center of consciousness or the experiential being of a person (Kaufmann, 1989). It is the sum total of a person's thoughts, ideas, feelings, memory, and sensory perceptions. At the moment of birth, ego and self appear as one. The first half of life is concerned with their separation. Then the process of individuation reverses itself as a person strives for realization of the self. A person needs to separate self from the collective and find his/her unique way.

Related entries: EGO STATES; EGOGRAM; ID.

References

Arlow, J. A. (1989). Psychoanalysis. In R. J. Corsini & D. Wedding (Eds.), *Current psychotherapies* (4th ed., pp. 19–64). Itasca, IL: F. E. Peacock.
Kaufmann, G. (1989). Analytical psychotherapy. In R. J. Corsini & D. Wedding (Eds.), *Current psychotherapies* (4th ed., pp. 119–154). Itasca, IL: F. E. Peacock.

EGO STATES. The three dynamic states that define important facets of the personality: parent, adult, and child (P.A.C.). According to transactional analysis, people constantly shift from one of these states to another, and their behavior at any one point in time is related by the ego state of the moment.

The parent ego state contains the attitudes and behaviors incorporated from external sources, primarily one's parents. This ego state is expressed as critical or nurturing behaviors toward others. Inwardly, it is experienced as parental messages, including "shoulds," "oughts," and other rules of living. The parent may be expressed as a positive ego state (the Nurturing Parent) or a negative one (the Critical Parent).

The adult ego is the objective part of our personality; it processes data, computes possibilities, and makes decisions on the basis of available data. The adult is oriented toward current reality. The child ego state consists of a person's feelings, impulses, and spontaneous actions. It includes the recordings of early experiences. The Natural Child is the spontaneous, impulsive, open, alive, and expressive part of our personality. The Adapted Child is that part of our person that has learned to conform to the expectations of others in order to gain acceptance and approval. The Adapted Child modifies behavior in order to get attention or other forms of "strokes."

In a transactional analysis group, participants are taught to recognize which of the three ego states they are functioning in at any given moment of time. The goal of these groups is to enable the members to decide whether another state would be more appropriate or useful. Mary and Robert Goulding (1979), leaders of the redecisional school of transactional analysis, describe ego state awareness: "As patients learn to be aware of the ego state they are in, they learn to better handle their feelings, to better recognize their position in their life script, to be more aware that they have been or are game playing. They become much more aware of their adaptive behavior, adaptive to their internal parent and to the outside world. After becoming aware, they can knowingly choose to adapt or not to adapt" (p. 26)."

Structural analysis is a tool used to help group members become aware of the content and functioning of their ego states of parent, adult, and child. With increased awareness, it should be possible for clients to discover what their options might be. Berne (1961) discussed two types of problems that may be uncovered by structural analysis. The first, exclusion, is manifested by a stereotyped attitude that is rigidly held to in threatening situations. Exclusion creates rigid ego states: the Constant Parent, the Constant Child, or the Constant Adult. Contamination exists when the boundary of one ego state overlaps that of another one. Either the parent or the child or both can contaminate the adult ego state. An example of the adult state being contaminated by the child is seen in statements such as "Nobody ever likes me," "Everybody always picks on me," or "I deserve whatever I want—immediately." An example of the adult being contaminated by the parent is found in statements like "Look out. People will take advantage of you," or "Keep with your own kind and never mix with people who are different."

Related entries: EGO; EGOGRAM.

References

Berne, E. (1961). *Transactional analysis in psychotherapy.* New York: Grove Press.
Goulding, M., & Goulding, R. (1979). *Changing lives through redecision therapy.* New York: Brunner/Mazel.

EGOGRAM. In transactional analysis the function and amount of energy placed within the parent, adult, and child ego states is exemplified in a bar graph format.

An egogram is constructed on a five-position bar graph that represents Critical Parent, Nurturing Parent, Adult, Free Child, and Adapted Child. The higher columns signify the greater amounts of time and energy expended in particular ego states.

The egogram operates with a constancy hypothesis, in that when one raises the time and energy in one ego state, another ego state will lose energy. A person's egogram will remain fixed and not change unless the person actively decides to change the energy balances in his or her ego states. A bell-shaped egogram implies that the personality has a well balanced energy system with psychological energy fairly evenly distributed.

The five functional ego states described in an egogram are as follows: (1) the Critical Parent is that part of one's personality that criticizes or finds fault; (2) the Nurturing Parent is empathetic and promotes growth; (3) the Adult engages in clear, rational thinking that is factual, nonemotional, and nonjudgmental; (4) the Free Child is spontaneous, curious, playful, fun, eager, and intuitive; (5) the Adapted Child is conforming, compromising, easy to get along with, and compliant.

Related entries: EGO; EGO STATES.

References

Dusay, J. (1977). *Egograms: How I see you and you see me.* New York: Harper and Row.

Dusay, J. M., & Dusay, K. M. (1989). Transactional analysis. In R. J. Corsini & D. Wedding (Eds.), *Current psychotherapies* (4th ed.). Itasca, IL: F. E. Peacock.

EIGENWELT. A mode of world discussed in existential counseling that refers to the "own world" or the relationship to one's self.

Our "own world" or Eigenwelt presupposes self-awareness and self-relatedness and is uniquely present in human beings. Eigenwelt asks, "What does the world mean to the individual observer?" A basic concept in existential counseling is called being-in-the-world. The three modes of world include Eigenwelt, Umwelt, or biological world, and Mitwelt, or the world of one's community. One implication of this analysis of modes of being-in-the-world is that it gives us a basis for understanding love. The importance of Eigenwelt to love has been stressed by existential philosophers, who insist that love presupposes that a person has become the "true individual" or the "solitary one" who has comprehended that to love another person one must be sufficient unto oneself.

Related entries: EXISTENTIAL COUNSELING; EXISTENTIALISM; MITWELT; UMWELT.

References

May, R., & Yalom, I. (1989). Existential therapy. In R. J. Corsini & D. Wedding (Eds.), *Current psychotherapies* (4th ed.). Itasca, IL: F. E. Peacock.

ELLIS, ALBERT (b. 1913). Albert Ellis is considered the founder of rational emotive therapy (RET) and a pioneer in cognitive approaches to counseling. Ellis argued that the basis for clients' emotional and behavioral difficulties lies in the ways that they subjectively respond to and interpret reality.

Albert Ellis was born on September 27, 1913, in Pittsburgh, Pennsylvania. He earned a business degree at City College of New York, followed by an M.A. and a Ph.D. in clinical psychology from Columbia University. He received training in psychoanalysis.

Ellis has held several clinical and teaching positions. He taught at Rutgers University and New York University. For a while, he was chief psychologist of the New Jersey State Diagnostic Center and also chief psychologist at the New Jersey Department of Institutions and Agencies.

In 1959 Albert Ellis founded the Institute for Rational Emotive Therapy and the Institute for Rational Living. The first is mainly a professional organization devoted to the training of psychotherapists. The second is a scientific and educational organization that is responsible for talks, seminars, and workshops, as well as the publication and sale of professional literature.

In 1962 he published *Reason and Emotion in Psychotherapy,* the first work on rational emotive therapy for professional counselors and therapists. His published works since 1957 have been more frequently cited than have his contemporaries in the fields of counseling and psychotherapy in major articles on counseling (Heesacker, Heppner, & Rogers, 1982). In 1985 he received the American Psychological Association Award for Distinguished Professional Contributions.

He quotes a saying attributed to Epictetus as a basis for his theory of personality therapy: ''It's never the things that happen to you that upset you; it's your view of them.''

Ellis employs active/directive techniques such as teaching, suggestion, persuasion, and homework assignments in a counseling context to overcome the indoctrination that results from irrational thinking. Change is assumed to come about mainly by clients making commitments to practice new behaviors that challenge ineffective behaviors.

Related entry: RATIONAL-EMOTIVE COUNSELING.

References

Ellis, A. (1962). *Reason and emotion in psychotherapy.* New York: Lyle Stuart.
Heesacker, M., Heppner, P. P., & Rogers, M. E. (1982). Classics and emerging classics in counseling psychology. *Journal of Counseling Psychology, 29,* 400–405.

EMOTIONAL FLOODING APPROACHES. Directly stimulating, intense emotional experiences such as rage are characteristic of these approaches to counseling.

They may use manipulation of the body, bodily exercises, reliving painful childhood memories, and/or fantastic forms of imagery to stimulate strong emotions. The major assumption is that emotional disorders can best be treated by encouraging the direct release of blocked emotions. Character analysis, bio-energetics, primal therapy, and implosive therapy are examples of emotional flooding approaches to counseling (see Prochaska, 1979, Chapter 9).

Related entry: BEHAVIORAL COUNSELING.

Reference

Prochaska, J. O. (1979). *Systems of psychotherapy: A transtheoretical analysis* (Chapter 9). Homewood, IL: Dorsey.

EMPATHY. Rogers defined empathy as

> entering the private perceptual world of the other and becoming thoroughly at home in it. It involves being sensitive, moment to moment, to the changing felt meanings which flow in this other person, to the fear or rage or tenderness or confusion or whatever that he or she is experiencing. It means temporarily living in his or her life, moving about in it delicately without making judgments, sensing meanings of which he or she is scarcely aware, but not trying to uncover feelings of which the person is totally unaware, since this would be too threatening. It includes communicating your sensings of his or her world as you look with fresh and unfrightened eyes at elements of which the individual is fearful. (Rogers, 1975, p. 4)

Egan (1975) defined two types of empathy. The first, known as primary empathy, is directly parallel to the above ideas about empathy presented by Rogers. The second type of empathy, advanced accurate empathy, goes beyond primary empathy skills. It involves the counselor's use of influencing skills such as self-disclosures, directives, and interpretations.

Egan (1990), in a later edition of the same book, described the technology of primary empathy as those communication skills which allow counselors to translate their understanding of their clients' experiences, behaviors, and feelings into responses in which they are able to share these understandings with their clients. In order to respond empathically, counselors must ask themselves, What are the core messages being expressed in terms of feelings and the experiences and behaviors that underlie those feelings? Primary empathy is both a human value regarding how counselors should treat clients and a communication skill that counselors learn and then use to help clients better manage problem situations and developmental opportunities.

Advanced empathic listening deals with what clients may be hinting, implying, or saying in confused ways. The most basic form of advanced empathy communication skills is when counselors are able to give expression to what clients may only imply; it differs from primary empathy communication skills, in which counselors reflect an accurate grasp of the content and feelings expressed by clients. Advanced empathy may sometimes include helping clients to identify and explore behavioral and emotional themes in problems and opportunities, especially self-defeating patterns of behaviors and emotions. Counselors may also use advanced empathy communication skills to make connections or build bridges that can help clients link their experiences, feelings, and behaviors.

Empathy can be described as the ability to understand people from their frame of reference rather than your own. When a counselor responds empathically to a client, it is an attempt to think with, rather than for or about, the client. Current concepts about empathy suggest that it is more than a single concept or skill. Rather, empathy is a multistage process consisting of multiple elements. Gladstein (1983) pointed out that affective and cognitive empathy can be helpful in certain stages of counseling with certain clients and for certain goals. At other times, empathy may interfere with achieving positive outcomes from counseling.

Related entry: CLIENT-CENTERED COUNSELING.

References

Egan, G. (1975). *The skilled helper.* Monterey, CA: Brooks/Cole.
Egan, G. (1990). *The skilled helper* (4th ed.). Monterey, CA: Brooks/Cole.
Gladstein, G. (1983). Understanding empathy: Integrating counseling, developmental and social psychological perspectives. *Journal of Counseling Psychology, 30,* 467–482.
Rogers, C. R. (1975). Empathic: An unappreciated way of being. *The Counseling Psychologist, 5,* 2–10.

EMPTY CHAIR TECHNIQUE. This technique is used in Gestalt counseling to give persons an opportunity to take ownership of opposing forces within themselves.

Gestalt counselors pay close attention to splits in personality that are rooted in the mechanism of introjection or the incorporating of aspects of others into your personality. The empty chair technique is one way of getting clients to externalize those traits and values of others that have been uncritically accepted as their own. In this technique the counselor might use two chairs, asking a client to sit in one chair and act fully as the ''top dog'' and then shift to the other chair and become the ''underdog'' in his personality conflict. This is a role playing technique in which all parts are played by the client. The idea is for the conflict to be experienced fully and to allow clients to get in touch with the feelings that they may be denying to themselves. The dialogues that are carried out through the empty chair technique are thought to help promote personality integration.

Related entries: EXPERIMENTS; GESTALT COUNSELING.

Reference

Corey, G. (1991). *Theory and practice of counseling and psychotherapy* (Chapter 8). Pacific Grove, CA: Brooks/Cole.

ENCOUNTER GROUPS. Personal growth groups that were developed in the 1960s and 1970s were called encounter groups.

In 1970 Rogers identified among the processes that occur in person-centered groups a condition called the basic encounter. At this point in the group, members are able to achieve close contact with one another and experience how meaningful their relationships can be when there is a commitment to work toward a common goal and a sense of community.

The encounter group emerged as an attempt to create a group that could increase an individual's capacity for enriched experience and personal involvement. The goals of encounter groups were to promote growth and change, new behavioral directions, heightened self-awareness, and a richer perception of one's circumstances as well as the circumstances of others (Stoller, 1970). These groups for normal persons emphasized the emotional aspects of individual living and utilized techniques to increase awareness of feelings and their impact on behavior. Encounter groups can vary from those that are minimally structured, such as those described by Carl Rogers (1970), to groups that are highly structured and open-ended (see Schutz, 1971).

Related entry: GROUP COUNSELING.

References

Rogers, C. R. (1970). *Carl Rogers on encounter groups.* New York: Harper and Row.
Schutz, W. (1971). *Here comes everybody: Body, mind and encounter culture.* New York: Harper and Row.
Stoller, F. H. (1970). A stage for trust. In A. Burton (Ed.), *Encounter.* San Francisco: Jossey-Bass.

ETHICAL GUIDELINES FOR GROUP COUNSELORS. The Association for Specialists in Group Work (ASGW) developed its first set of ethical guidelines for group counselors in 1980. These were revised and expanded in 1989.

In 1991 ASGW revised and expanded its Professional Standards for the Training of Group Workers. The standards provide that all professional counselors should possess basic knowledge and basic skills in group work. Other professional organizations in counseling psychology and social welfare, as well as some state licensure laws, contain ethical guidelines regarding group counseling.

The ASGW *Ethical Guidelines* (1989) clarify the group leader's responsibility for providing information about services to prospective clients. Informed consent requires that leaders make the members aware of their rights and responsibilities before they make a commitment to become part of any group. Member preparation should include a discussion of the values and limitations of groups, the risks involved in group participation, and any possible misconceptions that people may have about groups.

The ethical, legal, and professional aspects of confidentiality have different implications in group counseling situations. The legal concept of privileged communication generally does not apply in a group setting. The group counselor is responsible for informing the members about the ethical need for confidentiality and the absence of legal privilege concerning what is shared in a group (Hopkins & Anderson, 1990). Only a few states grant privileged communication in group marital and family therapy when third parties are present if the persons are instrumental in treatment (Van de Creek, Knapp, & Herzog, 1988). Because members cannot assume that anything they say or hear in a group will remain confidential, they should be able to make an informed choice about how much to reveal.

Group counselors are to avoid dual relationships with clients that could either impair the professional judgment of counselors or compromise the members' ability to participate fully in the group. Professional counseling relationships should not be used to further personal interests. It is important to remember that a goal of group counseling is to help members make their own decisions and function autonomously. Consequently, the tone in group counseling should be invitational so that members are always given the freedom not to participate in any specific group activities.

Related entry: GROUP COUNSELING.

References

Association for Specialists in Group Work (1989). *Ethical guidelines for group counselors.* Alexandria, VA: Association for Specialists in Group Work.

Association for Specialists in Group Work (1991, Fall). *Professional standards for the training of group workers.* Alexandria, VA: Association for Specialists in Group Work.

Hopkins, B. R., & Anderson, B. S. (1990). *The counselor and the law* (3rd ed.). Alexandria, VA: AACD Press.

Van de Creek, L., Knapp, S., & Herzog, C. (1988). Privileged communications for social workers. *Social Casework: The Journal of Contemporary Social Work, 69,* 28–34.

ETHICS. A branch of study in philosophy that concerns how people ought to act toward each other, pronouncing judgments of value about those actions, and developing rules of ethical justification. Ethics in counseling is concerned with two questions: How should counselors act? How should counselors justify holding one set of values rather than another?

Ethics in counseling involves the study and evaluation of moral beliefs and actions of counselors within certain professional domains. The terms *moral* and *ethical* are frequently used interchangeably in describing counselors' beliefs about how they act and as an evaluation of those beliefs or actions. However, morals are part of the human belief structure of counselors and can be studied as they are and as they ought to be. Morals are what counselors believe about what is right and wrong and good and bad character and conduct, while ethics involves making judgments of value about moral beliefs and actions (Kitchener, 1984a).

Ethics involves the study of the "individual good" and the "collective good" and as such is important to professional counselors who need to make decisions about what is desirable, good, and right for themselves, their clients, and their profession. Public trust in professional counselors is based on the belief that they as a group have a code of behavior that is designed to protect the public welfare.

If counseling is to be considered a profession, it has to have two mechanisms of self-regulation: self-generated codes of ethics, and collective statements regarding standards of professional practice (Jacobs, 1976). Two professional organizations that provide ethical guidelines for counselors are the American Psychological Association, particularly Division 17 or Counseling Psychology, and the American Counseling Association. Both organizations have developed codes of ethics, and the American Psychological Association also has published a statement of generic standards of practice for psychologists and specialty guidelines for counseling psychologists.

Counselors are ethically bound to respect the integrity and protect the welfare of people and groups with whom they work (APA 1981a, Principle 6). However, in many cases counselors must balance the rights of their clients against the rights of others in society. In such instances, they may need to employ ethical principles that are more general and fundamental than the moral rules found in professional codes of ethics. Kitchener (1984b) has suggested that the ethical principles of autonomy, beneficence, nonmaleficence, fidelity, and justice constitute the foundations for making such critical, evaluative ethical decisions.

Biggs and Blocher (1987) provide a model for describing ethical behavior of counselors that is based on Rest's model of morality (1984). The first step in ethical behavior is to recognize that an ethical problem exists. The counselor must identify how his or her behaviors can impact the welfare of others. Who? How? When? To what extent? The second step is for the counselor to think about and consider the probable consequences of his or her actions. What courses of action are open to the counselor? What principles and values should be used to define obligations and to choose among the alternatives? The choice of these principles, values, and outcomes in an ethical situation is very often a matter left to the professional judgment of individual counselors. The third step in the ethical behavior of counselors has to do with choosing plans or strategies to implement ethical principles and moral values. Finally, the fourth step is concerned with "acting" and "doing" and may require strength of character and firm resolve.

Related entries: AMERICAN ASSOCIATION FOR COUNSELING (AAC); AMERICAN ASSOCIATION FOR MARRIAGE AND FAMILY THERAPY (AAMFT); AMERICAN PSYCHOLOGICAL ASSOCIATION DIVISION 17— COUNSELING PSYCHOLOGY; DUAL RELATIONSHIPS; LIABILITY (COUNSELORS).

References

American Association for Counseling and Development (1988). *Ethical standards.* Alexandria, VA: American Association for Counseling and Development.
American Psychological Association (1977). *Standards for providers of psychological services* (Rev. ed.). Washington, DC: American Psychological Association.

American Psychological Association (1981a). *Ethical principles of psychologists.* Washington, DC: American Psychological Association.

American Psychological Association (1981b). Specialty guidelines for the delivery of services by counseling psychologists. *American Psychologist, 36,* 652–663.

Biggs, D., & Blocher, D. (1987). *Foundations of ethical counseling.* New York: Springer.

Jacobs, O. F. (1976). Standards for psychologists. In H. Dorkin & Associates (Eds.), *The professional psychologist today: New developments in law, health insurance and health practice* (pp. 19–32). San Francisco: Jossey-Bass.

Kitchener, K. S. (1984a). Guest editor's introduction. *The Counseling Psychologist, 12*(3), 15–18.

Kitchener, K. S. (1984b). Intuition, critical evaluation and ethical principles: The foundation for ethical decisions in counseling psychology. *The Counseling Psychologist, 12*(3), 43–56.

Rest, J. R. (1984). Research on moral development: Implications for training counseling psychologists. *The Counseling Psychologist, 12*(3), 19–30.

EXISTENTIAL COUNSELING. The emphasis in existential counseling is on the importance of developing high levels of awareness concerning life as a series of decisions, the future as opposed to the past, what is possibility and what is facticity, and the nature of one's fundamental project (Maddi, 1985).

It is an approach to counseling that strives to produce a microcosm of the conditions for ideal early development. Once hardiness is learned, clients will be more able to choose the future and tolerate failures sufficiently well to learn from them. Counseling should provide guidance for a client as he or she tries out future-oriented decision making, encountering failures and successes and growing in the process.

The crucial significance of the existential movement for counseling is that it reacts against the tendency to identify counseling with a specific set of techniques. Instead, existential counselors base their approach on an understanding of what makes men and women human beings. For them, anxiety is an inevitable part of the human condition and can be a potential source of growth. The purpose of counseling is not to "cure" clients of their anxieties but to help them become aware of what they are doing and to get them out of the victim roles. Counselors should challenge such clients to examine the manner in which they have answered life's existential questions and challenge them to revise these answers so that they can live more authentically (Corey, 1991).

Existence is best understood as being-in-the-world. To understand an individual it is necessary to understand the world as that person construes it. Persons exist in relationship to three levels of their worlds, called Unwelt, Mitwelt, and Eigenwelt. Unwelt describes a person's relationship to the biological and physical aspects of the world; Mitwelt refers to the social world; and Eigenwelt refers to the ways in which persons experience themselves. Personalities will differ in their ways of existing at each of these three levels of being.

Lying is the foundation of psychopathology. It is the only way that persons can flee from nonbeing and not allow existential anxiety into their lives. Lying leads to neurotic anxiety, which in turn leads to decisions to act on that anxiety and to development of symptoms of psychopathology. Neurotic anxiety is an inauthentic response to being; existential anxiety is an honest response to non-being. Lying can occur at any level of existence, but perhaps the most common level of lying is "for others." Honesty is the major solution for dissolving symptoms, and authenticity is a major goal of counseling. However, lying also leads people to a sense of objectification in which they are not aware of their ability to choose, so counseling must help clients experience themselves as capable of directing their own lives (Prochaska, 1979).

The counselor, by being authentic, may confront a client with information that is generated by the counselor's own genuine reactions to the client. Existential counselors may on occasion reveal their own experiences of clients and not just reflect their clients' experiences. Existential counseling qualifies in some ways as confrontational, and because of this, it differs from person-centered counseling with its primary emphasis on unconditional positive regard. Existential counselors are often willing to provoke pain in their clients and force them to reflect upon what they are thinking and doing in order to facilitate developmental processes.

A most dramatic technique used by existential counselors is that of paradoxical intention. Clients are helped to get control over their lives by outmaneuvering their symptoms and purposely exaggerating them. When you are out of control and worried, something that you can do in the short run to regain control is to try to lose control even further. It sounds paradoxical, but it may work for some clients (Maddi, 1985).

Related entries: EXPERIMENTS; MAY, ROLLO.

References

Corey, G. (1991). *Theory and practice of counseling and psychotherapy.* Pacific Grove, CA: Brooks/Cole.

Maddi, S. R. (1985). Existential psychotherapy. In S. J. Lynn & J. P. Garske (Eds.), *Contemporary psychotherapies: Models and methods* (pp. 191–220). Columbus, OH: Charles Merrill.

Prochaska, J. O. (1979). *Systems of psychotherapy: A transtheoretical analysis.* Homewood, IL: Dorsey.

EXISTENTIALISM. A philosophical movement which is primarily involved with the analysis of existence, specifically the existence of individual human beings. It is concerned with the nature of human problems such as freedom, exercise of the will, choice, and responsibility.

Existentialists hold that a person can take control of his/her life and shape it through active decision making. Authenticity is considered to be a form of human behavior which involves responsible exercise of the powers of awareness and decision making. The most complete existential philosophy, developed by Søren Kierkegaard (1813–1855), focused upon the subjective person and conceptualized life as a series of decisions. Persisting in the face of anxiety regardless of circumstances is considered a path to growth and development as an individual. According to Martin Heidegger (1889–1976), Dasein, or the ability to reach high levels of consciousness and uniqueness through reflection upon oneself, others, and the natural world, brings with it a sense of anxiety and confrontation with death. Dasein also mediates the kinds of caring actions that take into account the needs and resources of self, others, and the environment. Dasein analysis is an approach to counseling that emphasizes the human capabilities of giving meaning to existence.

Related entry: MAY, ROLLO.

References

Heidegger, M. (1962). *Being and time* (J. Macquarrie & E. S. Robinson, Trans.). New York: Harper and Row.

Kierkegaard, S. (1959). *Either/or* (D. Stevenson & L. Swenson, Trans.). Garden City, NY: Doubleday.

EXPERIMENTS. Gestalt techniques in which clients are able to confront the crises of their lives by playing out certain troubled relationships in the safety of a counseling setting.

Forms of Gestalt experiments include dramatizing a painful memory; imagining a dreaded encounter; playing one's parents; creating a dialogue between two parts within oneself; attending to an overlooked gesture; and exaggerating a certain posture. The counselor's task is to observe whether the client finds a particular experiment too safe or too risky. In some cases, counselors will need to invent experiments that are more in tune with their own personalities. For it is the counselor's capacity for establishing an authentic relationship with a client that is a basic requisite for using any Gestalt experiments effectively in the counseling process.

Related entries: EMPTY CHAIR TECHNIQUE; GESTALT COUNSELING.

References

Corey, G. (1990). *Theory and practice of group counseling* (3rd ed., pp. 318–353). Pacific Grove, CA: Brooks/Cole.

Polster, M. (1987). Gestalt therapy: Evolution and application. In J. K. Zeig (Ed.), *The evolution of psychotherapy* (pp. 312–325). New York: Brunner/Mazel.

F

FAMILY COUNSELING. The focus of family counseling is on the family as a whole. Interventions are attempts to modify the relationships in a family in order to achieve harmony.

Rules are frequently the cause of family problems; dysfunctional rules characterize dysfunctional families. The assumption is that a family system strives for homeostasis or equilibrium, and when this balance is threatened efforts are taken to restore equilibrium (Minuchin, 1984). For example, mechanisms within a family may be used to restrict the range of certain behaviors; disputes between children are not allowed to exceed certain limits and become physical. The regulation of autonomy in children is an instance of homeostatic functioning in the family system (Minuchin & Fishman, 1981). Homeostatic mechanisms within a family may also maintain equilibrium by reinstating rules to govern interpersonal relationships. Children's behavior problems viewed from a family systems perspective are seen as manifestations of family dysfunction. Family systems theory assumes that these problem behaviors are either the consequence of family dynamics or are reinforced by those dynamics.

Three basic concepts in family counseling are system, triangles, and feedback. The attention of the counselor focuses on the dysfunctional family system as the client. A family system has three important properties: wholeness, relationship, and equifinality.

Wholeness means that a family includes the people in it as well as the relationships among them. Relationship considers what is happening among the people in a family. The counselor asks, "What is the family doing?" and "What is going on between them?" Equifinality or self-perpetuation of structures means that family interventions should be made in the here and now. What perpetuates a problem is the current interactions within the family system.

Interlocking triangles are the basic building blocks of the family relationship system and are the means of increasing or reducing emotional intensity in the family system. Problem behaviors are viewed as tactics for gaining closeness or distance within the family system. Analyzing the various triangles in a family system and making interventions to change the system are important parts of family counseling. Family triangles may describe different generations, or they may describe a nuclear family of father, mother, and child.

Feedback in a family system refers to the adjustment processes. Negative feedback is a process whereby a problem in the family system is corrected so that the previous conditions in the family are restored. Positive feedback forces a family to change what is going on in the mutual lives of its members.

Family counseling is concerned with how family members interact and not with why they act as they do. Treatment focuses on the family as a system, not on the treatment of maladjusted individuals.

Virginia Satir's conjoint family therapy (1967), along with Bowen's family systems therapy (Bowen, 1978), laid the foundations for a systems approach to family counseling. Satir (1967) saw counseling as a process of facilitating effective communication in a relational context. The counselor was to be an observer of family interactions and a teacher of clear communication.

Problem-solving therapy concentrates on counseling families of triads or larger system structures (Haley, 1987). This approach focuses on behavior and its relational context and uses the concept of therapeutic directives. Haley describes analogic communication that is highly nonverbal, informal, and contextual as critical in human relationships in which family problems arise and maintain themselves.

Strategic problem-solving counseling involves giving directives and assessing responses. These directives are prescribed tasks that involve everyone in the family. Sessions are generally scheduled for about once a week; as problems are resolved the intervals between sessions are lengthened.

Structural family counseling is unique because of its emphasis on the structure of families. Organization and roles simply describe what is meant by the term *family structure*. Structure refers to those patterns of interaction that can be observed in a family within a therapeutic context. Minuchin's book *Families and Family Therapy* (1974) is a primary resource for structural family therapy. This approach is basically a process of helping families outgrow stereotyped patterns of which the presenting problem is a part. Essentially, the counselor attempts to join the family, enter into its interactive processes, and then affect its ways of operating.

Related entries: CONJOINT FAMILY COUNSELING; FAMILY CRISIS COUNSELING; STRATEGIC PROBLEM-SOLVING COUNSELING.

References

Bowen, M. (1978). *Family therapy in clinical practice.* New York: Jason Aronson.

Foley, V. D. (1989). Family therapy. In R. J. Corsini & D. Wedding (Eds.), *Current psychotherapies* (4th ed.). Itasca, IL: F. E. Peacock.

Haley, J. (1987). *Problem solving therapy* (2nd ed.). San Francisco, CA: Jossey-Bass.

Minuchin, S. (1974). *Families and family therapy.* Cambridge, MA: Harvard University Press.

Minuchin, S. (1984). *Family kaleidoscope.* Cambridge, MA: Harvard University Press.

Munuchin, S. & Fishman H. S. (1981). *Family Therapy Techniques.* Cambridge, MA: Harvard University Press.

Satir, V. (1967). *Conjoint family therapy.* Palo Alto, CA: Science and Behavior Books.

FAMILY CRISIS COUNSELING. The goals of crisis intervention in family counseling are to help the family resolve a crisis and if possible also to help the family member whose condition was critical to function at a more effective level of adaptation. Family crisis counseling is brief and immediate.

Donald G. Langsley and David Kaplan are credited with describing the first treatment for families in crisis at the Family Treatment Unit of Colorado Psychiatric Hospital in 1964. Crisis intervention with families is a team effort that involves brokering and helping people solve real problems in their lives. Langsley and Kaplan (1968) outlined family crisis treatment under seven main headings: immediate aid, defining the crisis as a family problem, focus on the current crisis, general prescription, specific prescription, identification of role conflicts, and renegotiation and management of future crises.

Related entries: CONJOINT FAMILY COUNSELING; FAMILY COUNSELING; STRATEGIC PROBLEM-SOLVING COUNSELING.

Reference

Langsley, D. G., & Kaplan, D. M. (1968). *The treatment of families in crisis.* New York: Grune and Stratton.

FEDERAL LEGISLATION AND COUNSELING. The federal government has played a significant role in defining counseling as an independent profession through a number of actions and laws.

Examples of federal legislation that have influenced the development of the profession of counseling include the following:

1938   The George Dean Act appropriated $14 million for vocational education. The Occupational Information and Guidance Service was established.

1939   The *Dictionary of Occupational Titles* was first published.

1944   The Veterans Administration established a nationwide network of guidance services for veterans.

1944   The United States Employment Service was developed to help citizens seeking employment.

1946   The George Barden Act was passed; it provided support for establishing training programs for counselors.

1958   The National Defense Education Act provided grants to schools to support counseling programs as well as contracts for counselor training to institutions of higher education.

1963   The Community Mental Health Centers Act provided for the development of mental health services, including counseling and outreach services.

1964   The National Defense Education Act amendment provided support for
       counselors in public schools.

1965   The Elementary and Secondary Education Act provided special funds for
       developing and expanding elementary school counseling.

1974   The Family Educational Rights and Privacy Act allowed students access
       to guidance and counseling records in public schools.

1975   The Education for All Handicapped Children Act identified specific pro-
       fessional tasks for school counselors who work with handicapped children.

Reference

Baruth, L. G., & Robins, E. H. III (1987). *An introduction to the counseling profession.*
       Englewood Cliffs, NJ: Prentice-Hall.

FEMINIST COUNSELING. An approach to counseling that uses such techniques as assertiveness training, modeling, and cognitive restructuring to
challenge and question attitudes toward women. Feminist counseling views
women's problems as inseparable from society's oppression of women.

These counselors state their values at the beginning of counseling and employ
those values for making interpretations and to model feminist behaviors and
attitudes (Okun, 1987). The goals of feminist counseling include (a) the development of androgyny, or the complementary existence of male and female characteristics within both males and females; (b) the development of equal power
relationships between men and women; (c) the acceptance of one's body image
"as is"; and (d) the choice of non–sex-biased careers (Cook, 1985; Dworkin,
1984).

Feminist counselors assume that women are socialized for inferior adult roles
in our culture (Broverman, Broverman, Clarkson, Rosenkrantz, & Vogel, 1970).
Consequently, counselors should include interventions that help women to overcome the handicaps and limitations associated with the negative socialization.
Strategies involve those that foster behavior changes, those that lead to cognitive
restructuring, and those that promote competence.

Klein (1975) identified nine feminist goals, which are stated in the form of
questions:

1. What is the connection between her pain, symptoms, and life situation? Is she
   reacting to role conflicts or frustrating, unsatisfying roles?

2. Are some of her pains "growing pains," consequences of her decision to
   change her life, break out of old patterns and take risks?

3. Is her self-esteem dependent on others' evaluations and reactions or based on
   her own judgments and values?

4. Are her ideals and role choices influenced by traditional sexist stereotypes?

5. Does her interpersonal style allow a full range of behavior, including direct
   expression of anger and power needs and a balance between autonomy and
   interdependence? Does she need to please others all the time or can she challenge and confront them as well?

6. Can she relate to both sexes as people? Does she feel good about herself and other women and draw support from shared experiences?

7. Is her role pattern her own free choice and personal blend, responsive to her needs, including her needs for competence and recognition?

8. Does she use and trust her own decision-making and problem-solving skills? Can she decide which problems are solvable and which are not without doubt and guilt?

9. Does she accept and like her body, enjoy her sensuality, and take responsibility for knowing and managing her sexual and reproductive life? (Pp. 15–16)

Related entry: SEX-ROLE STEREOTYPES.

References

Broverman, I., Broverman, D., Clarkson, F., Rosenkrantz, P., & Vogel, S. (1970). Sex role stereotypes and clinical judgments of mental health. *Journal of Consulting Psychology, 34,* 1–7.

Cook, E. P. (1985). Androgyny: A goal for counseling? *Journal of Counseling and Development, 63,* 567–572.

Dworkin, S. (1984). Traditionally defined client, meet feminist therapist: Feminist therapy as attitude change. *Personnel and Guidance Journal, 62,* 301–306.

Klein, M. (1975). Feminist concepts of therapy outcome. Cited in R. M. Whiteley & J. M. Whiteley (1978), *Sex bias in counseling theory: Counseling and human development.* Denver: Love Publishing.

Okun, B. F. (Ed.) (1987). *Effective helping: Interviewing and counseling techniques.* Monterey, CA: Brooks/Cole.

FREE ASSOCIATION. The fundamental procedure in the psychoanalytic approach to counseling is for clients to put all of their thoughts and feelings into words. Clients are not to choose what they will say or omit anything because they believe it to be trivial, irrelevant, nonsensical, painful, or embarrassing.

The client is supposed to let what is called the primary process dominate and suspend logical operations as much as possible so that his/her thinking will follow a more primitive course than it previously did. By practicing free association, the client relives infantile feelings. These reactions are then subject to logical scrutiny and reality testing.

If clients were able to let their minds go and associate without defending, then their associations would be expected to be dominated by instincts that are pressing to emerge into consciousness. They would free associate to the thoughts, feelings, fantasies, and wishes that express these instincts. However, since most clients have learned that the expression of instincts is dangerous and that the loosening of defenses could lead to terrifying pathology, they will express considerable resistance or defensiveness during their work at free association. To help the client continue to work at free association, the counselor must form a working alliance with the rational side of the person's ego, which wants to feel better and can understand how free association can help. The goal is to help clients become conscious of how primary process thinking and meanings contributed to the maladaptive behaviors and problems that brought them to their counselors.

Related entry: PSYCHOANALYTIC COUNSELING.

References

Giovacchini, P. L. (1983). Psychoanalysis. In R. J. Corsini & A. J. Marsella (Eds.), *Personality theories, research and assessment* (pp. 25–67). Itasca, IL: F. E. Peacock.
Prochaska, J. O. (1979). *Systems of psychotherapy: A transtheoretical analysis* (pp. 24–66). Homewood, IL: Dorsey.

FREUD, SIGMUND (1856–1939). Freud was both creative and productive; his collected works fill twenty-four volumes. He pioneered new techniques for understanding human behavior, which he referred to as dynamic analysis (commonly referred to as psychoanalysis).

He was born in Vienna into a family of three boys and five girls. The family had limited finances and lived in a crowded apartment. Four years after earning his medical degree from the University of Vienna, he attained a position there as a lecturer.

Freud believed that his outstanding attribute was his courage. He complained throughout his life about not having been given a better brain (Jones, 1955). During his lifetime he was critical of his own theories; but, he insisted, as the founder he alone had the right to decide what should be called psychoanalysis. In 1923 Freud published *The Ego and the Id,* in which he proposed a new and significantly different model for psychological structure and functioning. This model divided the mental apparatus into three distinct psychic structures: the id, the ego, and the superego. Neurotic symptoms were seen in terms of a conflict between a powerful id seeking immediate gratification of instinctual drives and an overpunitive and inhibitory superego. The conflict is exacerbated by ego defects that preclude the development of appropriate defense structures that would allow for acceptable tension reduction.

Related entries: GENITAL STAGE; OEDIPUS COMPLEX; ORAL STAGE; PHALLIC STAGE; PSYCHOANALYTIC COUNSELING; PSYCHOSEXUAL STATES OF DEVELOPMENT.

References

Freud, S. (1961). The ego and the id. In J. Strachey (Ed. and Trans.), *The standard edition of the complete psychological works of Sigmund Freud* (Vol. 19, pp. 3–66). London: Hogarth Press. (Original work published 1923)
Jones, E. (1953). *The life and works of Sigmund Freud* (Vol. 1). New York: Basic Books.
Jones, E. (1955). *The life and works of Sigmund Freud* (Vol. 2). New York: Basic Books.
Jones, E. (1957). *The life and works of Sigmund Freud* (Vol. 3). New York: Basic Books.

FUNCTIONAL ANALYSIS. A behavioral assessment strategy used for making a systematic and sequential operational diagnosis of problem behaviors. The goal is to understand the antecedent events leading up to a specific event, the resultant behaviors contained in the event, and finally the consequences resulting from this sequence.

A functional analysis ties together many pieces and issues underlying a specific complex interpersonal event and is sometimes referred to as the ABC model (Mahoney & Thoreson, 1974). In the assessment phase of behavioral counseling, a functional analysis enables the identification of those consequences of certain events that will maintain, increase, or decrease both desirable and undesirable behaviors related to the client's problem. It is important that antecedents, consequences, and components of a presenting problem are assessed and identified for each particular client. Two clients might complain of anxiety, while the functional analyses reveal different components of the problem behavior, different antecedents, and different consequences.

Any meaningful functional analysis examines the reinforcement patterns maintaining the system of an individual or a couple. The social reinforcers of attention and approval, including negative attention, are also considered in any functional analysis.

Related entries: BEHAVIORAL ASSESSMENT; BEHAVIORAL COUNSELING.

References

Ivey, A. E., & Downing, L. S. (1980). *Counseling and psychotherapy: Skills, theories and practice.* Englewood Cliffs, NJ: Prentice-Hall.

Mahoney, M. J., & Thoreson, C. E. (Eds.) (1974). *Self-control: Power to the person.* Pacific Grove, CA: Brooks/Cole.

Sulzer-Azaroff, B., & Mayer, G. (1977). *Applied behavioral analysis procedures with children and youth.* New York: Holt, Rinehart and Winston.

G

GAMES. An ongoing series of interpersonal transactions that ends with unpleasant negative feelings for at least one of the participants.

Games consist of three basic elements: a series of plausible, interpersonal transactions; an ulterior transaction that reflects a hidden agenda; and a negative payoff that concludes the game and is the real purpose of the game.

By engaging in game playing, people find evidence to support their present views of the world and collect bad feelings known as rackets. These reactions have much the same quality as did the feelings that clients had as children. Those clients who typically feel depressed, angry, or bored may be actively collecting these racket feelings and feeding them into long-standing feeling patterns that often lead to stereotypical ways of behaving. In other words, they choose games to play to maintain their racket feelings.

In group counseling, clients can become aware of the specific ways in which they choose game playing strategies as means of avoiding genuine contacts with others and how they also choose patterns of thinking/feeling/behaving that are self-defeating. Clients learn that the actual effect of games is to create distance between them and others.

Berne's (1964) *Games People Play* is an investigation of the defense strategies and gimmicks that people use to prevent intimacy and manipulate others to get what they want. Transactional analysis places considerable importance on helping clients recognize games, identify their roles in games, and learn to interrupt and avoid games.

Related entry: BERNE, ERIC.

References

Berne, E. (1964). *Games people play.* New York: Grove Press.
Corey, G. (1990). *Theory and practice of group counseling* (3rd ed.). Pacific Grove, CA: Brooks/Cole.

GAY AND LESBIAN COUNSELING. Homoerotic people may seek counseling in order to deal with identity issues related to "coming out." However, not all gay clients seek counseling because they are gay or want to address gay issues. Counselors will need to address the issues presented by gay clients and not make their sexual orientation the focus of counseling unless their clients agree.

Several coming out models provide a framework for understanding identity issues confronting gay clients (Cass, 1984; Sophie, 1987). The coming out process may occur at any age. Whenever gays come out they will be addressing an identity crisis and need assistance in dealing with the issues and in developing a positive sense of self. These clients may also need help in looking at both the positive and negative aspects of coming out before making this important decision.

In addition to issues of homophobia and coming out, gay clients bring issues to counseling that are no different than those presented by heterosexual clients. Contrary to popular stereotypes, a majority of gays and lesbians live with partners (Weinberg & Williams, 1974). As a consequence, they are apt to seek counseling because of relationship problems and the lack of role models in our society for same sex couples.

Drug and alcohol abuse may be the presenting problems for a significant percentage of gay clients. Research suggests that approximately 30 to 35 percent of the gay population are chemically dependent on alcohol or drugs (Lohrenz, Connely, Coyne, & Spare, 1978; Weinberg & Williams, 1974). Although the substance abuse may result from homophobia, counselors cannot help with this problem until the substance abuse has stopped. Counselors need to address sexual orientation issues of gay clients in a nonjudgmental manner as they concurrently try to deal with the issues of chemical abuse.

Another issue confronting gay clients is acquired immunodeficiency syndrome (AIDS). Few gay persons will not have had a friend who died from AIDS, and most must make difficult choices because of this serious epidemic in our society. Gay clients need accurate information about AIDS. Counselors may also need to be advocates for gay clients who suffer from AIDS.

References

Cass, V. C. (1984). Homosexual identity formation: A concept in need of definition. *Journal of Homosexuality, 10,* 105–126.

Lohrenz, L. J., Connely, J. C., Coyne, L., & Spare, K. E. (1978). Alcohol problems in several midwestern homosexual communities. *Journal of Studies in Alcohol, 39,* 1959–1963.

Sophie, J. (1987). Internalized homophobia and lesbian identity. *Journal of Homosexuality, 10,* 105–126.

Weinberg, G. (1973). *Society and the healthy homosexual.* Garden City, NY: Anchor Books.

Weinberg, M. S., & Williams, C. S. (1974). *Male homosexuals: Their problems and adaptations.* New York: Oxford.

GENITAL STAGE. In psychoanalytic theory, this is the final stage of psychosexual development; it is usually attained in late adolescence. This is a time when sexual gratification occurs through intercourse and is not limited to specific body areas.

In the genital stage, beginning after puberty, psychological identity is integrated and matures through the experience of sexual and interpersonal intimacy and the concurrent development of appropriate social values and attitudes. The healthy culmination of psychosexual development is expressed in terms of the individual's capacity for productive work and sexual orgasm.

Related entries: ORAL STAGE; PHALLIC STAGE; PSYCHOANALYTIC COUNSELING; PSYCHOSEXUAL STAGES OF DEVELOPMENT.

References

Baker, E. L. (1985). Psychoanalysis and psychoanalytic psychotherapy. In S. J. Lyman & J. P. Garske (Eds.), *Contemporary psychotherapies: Models and methods.* Columbus, OH: Charles Merrill.

Corsini, R. J., & Wedding, D. (Eds.) (1989). *Current psychotherapies* (4th ed., p. 594). Itasca, IL: F. E. Peacock.

GERONTOLOGICAL COUNSELING. Counseling that effects changes in orientation to processes of aging and helps elderly persons to face critical challenges when major losses occur or when adjustment is necessary to a changing environment (Fry, 1992).

Counseling of the elderly should not expect to implement a single solution to the vulnerabilities of old age. The path of successful aging varies from individual to individual, so that counselors need to help their clients chart their own approaches to dealing with the tasks that they may confront.

Corey (1990) proposes that counseling groups may be of particular value to elderly clients. Such groups can help older people to challenge myths or misconceptions about aging and help them deal with their developmental tasks.

References

Corey, G. (1990). *Theory and practice of group counseling* (3rd ed., p. 10). Pacific Grove, CA: Brooks/Cole.

Fry, P. S. (1992). Major social theories of aging and their implications for counseling concepts and practice: A critical review. *The Counseling Psychologist, 20,* 246–329.

Granikos, J. L., Grady, K. A., & Olson, J. B. (1979). *Counseling the aged: A training syllabus for educators.* Washington, DC: American Personnel and Guidance Association.

GESTALT COUNSELING. In Gestalt counseling the major goal is the promotion of self-awareness, including knowing the environment, responsibility for choices, self-knowledge, self-acceptance, and the ability to contact.

This approach is most useful for clients who know intellectually about themselves but still continue to create anxiety, depression, and other ills through rejecting themselves, alienating aspects of themselves, and deceiving themselves. In Gestalt counseling, the counselor and the client are present centered, emphasizing the direct experiences of both of them. The client reports his/her experiences, and the counselor acts as an observer of what is not in the client's awareness. In particular, there is a focus on what the client does and how it is done. Techniques used are experimental tasks that are attempts to expand direct experience. Awareness takes place now, in the present. Prior events may be the object of present awareness, but the awareness process itself is now.

Gestalt counseling is provided individually, in groups, in workshops, for families and couples, and for children. In all these cases, the basic goal remains the same: to challenge persons to become aware of how they are avoiding responsibility for their awareness and to encourage them to look for internal rather than external forms of support. Clients learn not to be dependent upon others and discover that they can do much more than they think they can.

Zinker (1980) described the following individual goals for Gestalt counseling:

—integrating polarities within oneself

—achieving contact with self and others

—learning to provide self-support instead of looking to others

—becoming aware of what one is doing in the present

—defining one's boundaries with clarity

—translating insights into actions

—being willing to learn about oneself by engaging in creative experiments

Gestalt counselors ask what and how questions but rarely ask why questions. The focus is on what clients experience in the immediate situation and how they experience it. The core elements involve issues of now and how. Now is the basis of awareness; how covers behavior and what is involved in the ongoing processes. Clients are to assume responsibility for whatever they are experiencing and doing rather than placing blame on others for who and what they are now. Techniques used to promote client focusing are aspects of the question, "What are you (the client) aware of now?" and the instruction "Try this experiment and see what you become aware of." Counselors often respond to a client's report of awareness with the instruction, "Stay with it." The idea is to encourage a client to continue experiencing certain feelings and to deepen and work through these feelings to completion.

The competent practice of Gestalt counseling requires that a counselor have background knowledge in psychodiagnosis, personality theory, and psychodynamic theory, as well as appropriate clinical training in Gestalt counseling. Gestalt counseling can be inappropriate or harmful with some client populations and may be most effective with overly socialized, restrained, constricted individuals whose level of functioning is primarily a result of internal restrictions. These individuals usually show a minimal enjoyment of living (Yontef & Simkin, 1989).

Related entries: AWARENESS; EMPTY CHAIR TECHNIQUE; EXPERI-
MENTS; PERLS, FREDERICK S.

References

Perls, F. S. (1973). *The Gestalt approach.* Palo Alto, CA: Science and Behavior Books.
Yontef, G. M., & Simkin, J. (1989). Gestalt therapy. In R. J. Corsini & D. Wedding
    (Eds.), *Current psychotherapies* (4th ed., pp. 323–359). Itasca, IL: F. E. Peacock.
Zinker, J. (1980). The developmental process of a Gestalt therapy group. In B. Feder &
    R. Ronall (Eds.), *Beyond the hot seat: Gestalt approaches to group.* New York:
    Brunner/Mazel.

GLASSER, WILLIAM (b. 1925). The founder of reality therapy, he was ed-
ucated in Cleveland, Ohio, and finished medical school at Case Western University in 1953.

In 1956 he became a consulting psychiatrist at the Ventura School for Girls,
a California facility for the treatment of delinquent adolescents. In 1961 Glasser
published his first book, *Mental Health or Mental Illness?,* in which he laid the
foundation for reality therapy. In his book entitled *Reality Therapy,* published
in 1965, he argued that we are all responsible for what we choose to do with
our lives and that people can learn to lead more responsible lives in a warm,
accepting, and nonpunitive therapeutic environment.

In 1972 he published *The Identity Society,* in which he laid the groundwork
for control theory. Although the ideas of control theory were not original with
Glasser, he applied these ideas to systems, and in particular to education.

Related entry: REALITY COUNSELING.

References

Glasser, W. (1961). *Mental health or mental illness?* New York: Harper and Row.
Glasser, W. (1965). *Reality therapy: A new approach to psychiatry.* New York: Harper
    and Row.
Glasser, W. (1972). *The identity society.* New York: Harper and Row.

GRIEF COUNSELING. Grief counseling involves dealing with loss, the resolution of ambivalence, and confrontation with death.

Grief has a very different tone depending upon the person's relationship with
the person who has died. The death of parents confronts us with our own vulnerability, while the death of a spouse can confront us with our fear of existential
isolation. Children try many methods of dealing with death anxiety, one of the
most common being the personification of death as a monster or a bogeyman.
Counselors working with bereaved clients often must deal with their death anxiety. Existential counselors recommend trying to alleviate but not eliminate anxiety about death. For them, death cannot be faced without anxiety (see May &
Yalom, 1989).

A most significant work on grief crisis and on dealing with death as a part
of life was done by Elisabeth Kübler-Ross, whose book *On Death and Dying*
(1969) paved the way for much of the subsequent research on the topic. She

dealt with the grief crisis as experienced by the dying person while in the process of dying. She delineated a five-stage process by which persons adjust to the idea of death: denial, anger, bargaining, depression, and acceptance. Rubin (1981) proposed a two-track model of bereavement that deals with the bereaved's emotional bond with the deceased and personality changes that have occurred in the bereaved as a result of the grief.

Weisman (1973) differentiates three kinds of untimely death—premature, unexpected, and calamitous—and suggests that they may require different kinds of counseling strategies.

Related entries: EXISTENTIAL COUNSELING.

References

Kübler-Ross, E. (1969). *On death and dying.* New York: Macmillan.
May, R., & Yalom, I. (1989). Existential psychotherapy. In R. J. Corsini & D. Wedding (Eds.), *Current psychotherapies* (4th ed., pp. 363–402). Itasca, IL: F. E. Peacock.
Rubin, S. (1981). A two track model of bereavement: Theory and application in research. *American Journal of Orthopsychiatry, 51*(1), 101–109.
Weisman, A. D. (1973). Coping with untimely death. *Psychiatry, 36,* 366–378.

GROUP COUNSELING. A counseling group has a specific focus, which may be educational, vocational, social, or personal. The interpersonal processes in group counseling stress conscious thoughts, feelings, and behaviors (Corey, 1990).

Counseling groups are problem oriented; their content and focus are determined largely by the members, who are basically well-functioning individuals. Their mutual concerns usually relate to the developmental tasks of the life span. In some cases, members of counseling groups may be facing situational crises and temporary conflicts, or they may be trying to change self-defeating behaviors.

Group counselors use verbal and nonverbal techniques as well as structured exercises. They facilitate interaction among the members, help them learn from one another, and assist them in setting personal goals. Counselors encourage members to translate their insights into concrete plans and take action outside of the group. They perform their role in a group by teaching members to focus on the here and now and to identify the concerns that they wish to explore in the group.

Members of a group set the goals for their mutual experiences. They may explore their styles of relating with others and learn more effective social skills. They may discuss their perceptions of one another and receive feedback. Group counseling is especially suited for adolescents because it gives them a place to express conflicting feelings, explore self-doubts, and come to the realization that they share these concerns with their peers. Counseling groups can also be valuable to the elderly in many of the same ways that they are of value to adolescents.

The major difference between group counseling and group therapy has to do with their goals. Therapy groups focus on remediation and treatment, while counseling groups emphasize growth, development, and prevention.

Related entry: ETHICAL GUIDELINES FOR GROUP COUNSELORS.

References

Corey, G. (1990). *Theory and practice of group counseling* (3rd ed.). Pacific Grove, CA: Brooks/Cole.
George, R. L., & Dustin, D. (1988). *Group counseling: Theory and practice.* Englewood Cliffs, NJ: Prentice-Hall.

GUIDANCE. A point of view in education that emphasizes the total development of individual students and promotes instructional as well as counseling services to achieve this goal. The basic attitude in guidance should be that the individual is of central importance (Humphreys & Traxler, 1954).

Historically, the term *guidance* was used in the field of education to designate assistance given to students in the solutions of problems that lay outside of classroom teaching situations. Early guidance services mainly dealt with vocational problems, but later these services were expanded to include social, personal, and educational problems. The goal was to assist individual students to grow in self-understanding, to make wise decisions, and to do effective planning. Ohlsen (1955) said that guidance was a cooperative enterprise in which many people working together helped students to solve their problems and to develop their potentialities. In 1986 Tyler wrote that guidance was a concept in counseling that "had gone the way of consumption in medicine" (Tyler, 1986, p. 153).

The major features of a guidance program in schools are as follows:

1. It is based on a study of the needs of the children in the particular school.

2. It includes organized groups of teachers who perform most guidance functions.

3. It includes guidance specialists who provide consultation to teachers and accept referrals from them.

4. It involves school administrators who support guidance as necessary to the education of students.

5. It reflects a high level of cooperation among teachers, administrators, and specialists who are committed to achieving the goals of the guidance program. (See Ohlsen, 1955)

Gladding (1988) makes a distinction between guidance and counseling. The former focuses on helping individuals make important choices, whereas the latter is concerned with helping people make changes in their lives. The relationship in guidance is between a "more experienced" person and a "less experienced" person. He considers guidance to be a part of professional counseling.

Related entries: EDUCATIONAL COUNSELING; SCHOOL COUNSELING; TEACHER-COUNSELOR; VOCATIONAL GUIDANCE.

References

Gladding, S. T. (1988). *Counseling: A comprehensive profession.* Columbus, OH: Charles Merrill.

Humphreys, J. A., & Traxler, A. E. (1954). *Guidance services.* Chicago: Science Research Associates.

Ohlsen, M. M. (1955). *Guidance: An introduction.* New York: Harcourt, Brace.

Tyler, L. E. (1986). Farewell to guidance. *Journal of Counseling and Human Service Professions, 1,* 152–155.

H

HANDICAPPED CHILDREN AND ADOLESCENTS (COUNSELING). An important component of counseling with handicapped clients is providing basic information about their handicapping conditions. However, these clients also may need help to recognize that their handicaps represent only one aspect of their personalities.

Counselors need to accommodate their approaches to the special needs of different handicapped clients. For example, the use of role playing and behavioral rehearsal may be particularly appropriate for retarded clients who are trying to improve their social skills.

Neely (1982) has listed four issues that commonly arise in the counseling of handicapped children: self-other relationships, self-conflict, socially maladaptive behaviors, and vocational concerns. DeBlassie and Cowan (1976) point out that mentally handicapped clients often face a greater number of personal frustrations, feel misunderstood, confront rejection from others, and have difficulties developing a sense of competence and self-esteem. Counselors must be prepared to help their handicapped clients to develop skills that allow them to see themselves as capable persons who are more than their handicaps or other people's stereotypes of them.

Related entry: COUNSELING.

References

Cobb, H. C., & Brown D. T. (1983). Counseling and psychotherapy with handicapped children and adolescents. In H. T. Prout & D. T. Brown (Eds.), *Counseling and psychotherapy with children and adolescents: Theory and practice for school and clinic settings.* Tampa, FL: Mariner Publishing Co.

DeBlassie, R. R., & Cowan, M. A. (1976). Counseling with the mentally handicapped child. *Elementary School Guidance and Counseling, 10,* 246–253.

Neely, M. A. (1982). *Counseling and guidance practices with special education students.* Homewood, IL: Dorsey Press.

HELPING MODEL (CARKHUFF, 1987). This model involves helping to facilitate insight and encouraging helpees to act on their problems and reach their goals. The helping process moves from insight to action.

The helper's responding skills, including empathy, respect, and sometimes concreteness or specificity in focusing the helpee's experiences, are used to facilitate insight. Their initiating skills, including genuineness, self-disclosure, concreteness in problem solving and program development, and, under specifiable conditions, helper confrontations of discrepancies in helpee behaviors, are used to promote planning and action behaviors.

Together, helpers and helpees interact to facilitate their mutual processing—exploring, understanding, acting—of the helpee's problems and goals. The focus in the helping is on the facilitation of the intrapersonal human processing skills of helpees. They are helped to explore their experiences, define their problems, understand their goals, and then develop programs to achieve them. Helpers will use their interpersonal processing skills to (a) see the world through the helpee's eyes, (b) respond accurately to those experiences, (c) personalize the helpee's problems and goals, and (d) initiate a course of action to resolve the problems and achieve goals.

Helper skills include (a) attending skills that promote involvement in the helping process; (b) responding skills that facilitate exploration of experiences; (c) personalizing skills that facilitate understanding by the helpees; and (d) initiating skills that stimulate acting by the helpees. After getting feedback from actions, the phases of helping may need to be recycled.

Carkhuff (1984) has used his model of helping to design lay training and treatment programs. He concluded from this research that, first, laypersons can be trained to function at minimally facilitative levels of conditions related to constructive client change in relatively short periods of time; and, second, that lay counselors can effect significant constructive changes in clients.

Related entry: COUNSELING.

References

Carkhuff, R. R. (1969). *Helping and human relations.* New York: Holt, Rinehart and Winston.
Carkhuff, R. R. (1984). *Helping and human relations: Vol. 1. Selection and training.* Amherst, MA: Human Resource Development Press.
Carkhuff, R. R. (1987). *The art of helping VI.* Amherst, MA: Human Resource Development Press.

HELPING MODEL (EGAN, 1986, 1990). This model of the helping process emphasizes helping clients to be better able to manage their problems and opportunities in living. Helping is viewed as an educational process which increases the options available to clients.

In this approach, helping is seen as a collaborative activity between helper and helpee that allows helpees to better handle problem situations and develop unused or underused opportunities and potentials. Egan (1990) calls this orientation a flexible, broadly based problem management and opportunity development framework for helping. It provides guidance and a structure for identifying the steps or phases in the helping process. In some ways this framework could be seen as a generic model of the counseling process.

The three stages of the helping process are as follows: (1) describing the present scenario—helping clients identify, explore, and clarify their problem situations and unused opportunities; (2) describing the preferred scenario—helping clients develop goals, objectives, or agendas based on an action-oriented understanding of the problem situation; (3) identifying strategies for getting there—helping clients develop action strategies for accomplishing goals. Throughout this process, counselors are to help clients act on what they have learned within the helping sessions and in their real day-to-day worlds.

Each stage of the helping model has three steps. In the first stage, counselors help clients tell their stories, identify and challenge blind spots, and identify and work on issues that will make a difference. These three steps are the cognitive part of stage one, which in turn must be linked to client actions in counseling and outside of counseling. In the second stage, counselors help clients develop a range of possibilities for the future, translate them into viable agendas, and identify incentives that enable them to make commitments to these agendas. During the final stage in the helping process, clients will brainstorm a range of strategies for implementing their agendas, choose the best strategies, and formulate a step-by-step procedure for accomplishing each goal of the preferred scenario.

The model of the helping process described by Egan (1986, 1990) provides basic principles, not formulas. The literature about this model suggests that the helping process in counseling is neither linear nor "neat and clean." However, this particular model can provide structure and direction for the helping process in counseling.

Related entry: COUNSELING.

References

Egan, G. (1986). *The skilled helper* (3rd ed.). Pacific Grove, CA: Brooks/Cole.
Egan, G. (1990). *The skilled helper* (4th ed.). Pacific Grove, CA: Brooks/Cole.

HISPANIC/LATINO AMERICANS. The term *Hispanic/Latino* is used here as a generic label to refer to those persons with a Spanish background whose origins are in Latin America or the Caribbean Islands.

Two prominent features of the Hispanic culture, the extended family structure and sex roles, should be of interest to counselors who work with Hispanic clients. The extended family structure includes (a) formalized kinship relations such as the *compadrazzo* (godfather) system, and (b) loyalty to family that takes precedence over loyalty to other social institutions. In addition, sex roles are traditionally more rigid and demarcated more clearly. Males are granted greater independence and at an earlier age than females, and there are greater expectations for achievement outside the home for males (see Padilla, 1981). However, it should be pointed out that the characteristics of the Hispanic/Latino culture are very complex; counselors should be cautious in making generalizations about persons from these cultural backgrounds.

Levine and Padilla (1980) identified characteristics of Anglo and Hispanic counselors effective with Hispanic clients. First, good counselors exhibited personableness, projecting warmth and empathy. Hispanic clients were found to seek counselors who were sensitive to their feelings, who did not overgeneralize, and who were accepting and nonprejudicial. Second, effective counselors were skillful at labeling problems in terms of the client's world view. With some Hispanic clients it may be effective to incorporate folk beliefs in defining their problems. A third characteristic of effective counselors was their ability to raise their clients' expectations for change.

Family counseling may be particularly effective with Hispanic clients. For example, when working with Hispanic/Latino youth and their families, counselors may find the technique of "cultural reframe" useful. This technique allows the counselors to shift the focus of blame from individuals to the acculturation process, which places different demands on the parent and adolescent generations (see Inclan & Herron, 1989).

In the 1985 U. S. Census, the second largest subgroup of Hispanics was Puerto Ricans (1.6 million). They live in every state, and approximately 75 percent of them live in urban areas. The highest concentrations are found in New York and New Jersey. In New York State, they were found to represent 59.4 percent of the state's Hispanic population of 1.7 million (Governors Advisory Committee for Hispanic Affairs, 1985).

First generation migrants from Puerto Rico exhibit predominantly traditional values, including machismo, a virtue that encompasses courage and romanticism, and *personalismo*, a virtue that calls for the development of inner qualities to attain self-respect and the respect of others. Second and third generations must cope with and adapt to the language, culture, and values of their new environments. These efforts on their part may lead to stress, unhappiness, and feelings of alienation. Many Puerto Rican families and youth seen by counselors are in the process of dealing with problems of acculturation and generational clashes (see Inclan & Herron, 1989). Although there is disagreement in the professional literature about the prevalence of psychiatric symptoms in the Puerto Rican community, there is general agreement that this population underutilizes mental health services (Daykin, 1980).

Related entries: CULTURE; MEXICAN AMERICANS; MULTICULTURAL COUNSELING.

References

Casas, J. M., & Vasquez Melbu, J. T. (1989). Counseling the Hispanic client: A theoretical and applied perspective. In P. Pedersen, J. G. Draguns, W. Lonner, & J. Trimble (Eds.), *Counseling across cultures* (3rd ed., pp. 153–175). Honolulu: University of Hawaii Press.

Daykin, O. S. (1980). *Social and community support systems in Hispanic neighborhoods in New York City: A public policy analysis* (Mental Health Policy Monograph Series No. 3). Nashville, TN: Vanderbilt University, Center for the Study of Families and Children, Institute for Public Policy Studies.

Governor's Advisory Committee for Hispanic Affairs (1985). *New York State Hispanics: A challenging minority.* Albany: Governor's Advisory Committee for Hispanic Affairs.

Inclan, J. (1985). Variations in value orientations in mental health work with Puerto Ricans. *Psychotherapy, 22*(25), 324–334.

Inclan, J. E., & Herron O. G. (1989). Puerto Rican adolescents. In J. T. Gibbs, L. N. Huang, and Associates (Eds.), *Children of color: Psychological interventions with minority youth* (pp. 251–277).

Levine, E. S., & Padilla, A. M. (1980). *Crossing cultures in therapy: Pluralistic counseling for the Hispanic.* Monterey, CA: Brooks/Cole.

Padilla, A. M. (1981). Pluralistic counseling and psychotherapy for Hispanic Americans. In A. J. Marsella & P. B. Pedersen (Eds.), *Cross cultural counseling and psychotherapy* (pp. 195–227). New York: Pergamon.

U. S. Bureau of Census (1985). *Persons of Spanish Origin in the United States: March 1985* (Advance Report) (Current Population Reports, Population Characteristics Series P-20, No. 403). Washington, DC: U.S. Government Printing Office.

HOLLAND'S THEORY OF VOCATIONAL CHOICE. This theory assumes that persons and environments resemble, to different degrees, one of six personality types: realistic, investigative, artistic, social, enterprising, and conventional. People are seen as searching for congruent environments that will allow them to exercise their skills and abilities, express their attitudes and values, and take on agreeable problems and roles.

The identification of a person's personality type and environment can provide information about the appropriateness of vocational choices. Holland (1966) originally thought that persons could be characterized as resembling one of the six personality types. However, later, in 1973, he argued that while one type usually predominated, individuals will use some coping strategies that may fall within the boundaries of two or more types. The personal characteristics associated with the different types included both likes and dislikes or tendencies to approach and avoid certain activities.

Holland developed the Vocational Preference Inventory (1977a) to assess types by asking subjects to select job titles which appealed to them. The Self-Directed Search was later designed to provide vocational guidance by expanding the number of vocational alternatives that persons considered when making educational and career decisions. The Kuder DD (Kuder, 1976) and the Strong-Campbell Interest Inventory (Campbell, 1977) also allow clients to assess their resemblance to the Holland personality types.

Related entries: CAREER DEVELOPMENT; SELF-DIRECTED SEARCH; VOCATIONAL GUIDANCE.

References

Campbell, D. B. (1977). *Strong-Campbell interest inventory manual.* Stanford, CA: Stanford University Press.

Holland, J. L. (1966). *The psychology of vocational choice.* Waltham, MA: Blaisdell.

Holland, J. L. (1973). *Making vocational choices: A theory of careers.* Englewood Cliffs, NJ: Prentice-Hall.

Holland, J. L. (1977a). *The vocational preference inventory.* Palo Alto, CA: Consulting Psychologists Press.

Holland, J. L. (1977b). *The self directed search.* Palo Alto, CA: Consulting Psychologists Press.

Kuder, F. (1976). *Kuder Form DD occupational interest survey.* Chicago: Science Research Associates.

HOMEOSTASIS. The tendency of a body to maintain balance; to have a constant level of water, salt, and other elements. Needs arise, and when met the organism restores a condition of balance or homeostasis. This concept also refers to how marital and sibling subsystems interact and create a condition of homeostasis or balance in a family.

Gestalt counselors assume that the organism/environment interaction is regulated according to the principle of homeostasis (Carmer & Rouzer, 1974). From a relative stage of equilibrium, needs arise which must be met to restore balance. Healthy persons are able to meet their needs by accommodating their perceptions accordingly. They are able to differentiate between important and unimportant aspects of their environment and are flexible in their interactions with the environment.

In family counseling, the behavior patterns in the family are seen as balance mechanisms more than individual characteristics of family members. The counselor might view alcoholism as a property of the family system that performs a role in the family by maintaining its homeostasis. In what ways does the family system need the alcoholic behaviors of one of its members? The goal of family counseling is to change the system and create a new homeostasis or new ways of relating among members. A family may resist changing their old ways of relating to each other. Dell (1982) states that the term *homeostasis* is superfluous because an interactional system is a result of the individuals who compose it and not of any "homeostatic mechanism" or "family rules" (p. 37). He suggests using the term *coherence* rather than homeostasis.

In transactional approaches to counseling, homeostasis is considered from the perspective of an energy system using an egogram. Resistance from clients is seen as protecting the homeostasis of the ego systems in their personalities. A stronger ego state force is holding down a lower force in order to prevent personal changes.

Related entries: ACTUALIZING TENDENCY; CLIENT-CENTERED COUNSELING.

References

Carmer, J. C., & Rouzer, D. L. (1974). Healthy functioning from the Gestalt perspective. *Counseling Psychologist, 4*(4), 20–23.

Dell, P. (1982). Beyond homeostasis: Toward a concept of coherence. *Family Process, 21,* 21–41.

Dusay, J. M., & Dusay, K. M. (1989). Transactional analysis. In R. J. Corsini & D. Wedding (Eds.), *Current psychotherapies* (4th ed.). Itasca, IL: F. E. Peacock.

Foley, V. D. (1989). Family therapy. In R. J. Corsini & D. Wedding (Eds.), *Current psychotherapies* (4th ed.). Itasca, IL: F. E. Peacock.

HUMANISTIC APPROACHES TO COUNSELING. Under this heading have traditionally been grouped person-centered and Gestalt counseling (Corey, 1991). However, Ellis (1973, 1985) has discussed the rational-emotive perspective as an approach to humanistic psychotherapy, while Mahoney and Thoresen (1974) have proposed that the cognitive-behavioral model is a humanistic approach to counseling. Clearly, all counselors are concerned with counseling humans. These modes of counseling are assumed to share a respect for their clients' experiences and a trust in their clients' capacities to make positive and constructive choices in their lives.

Humanists in counseling also assume that clients have within themselves the potential through which they can find meaning in their lives. Corey (1991) describes humanists as different from existentialists, who hold that clients are faced with the anxiety of choosing to create a never secure identity in a world that lacks intrinsic meaning. According to Corey (1991), the underlying assumption of the humanistic philosophy in counseling is captured by the illustration of "how an acorn, if provided with the appropriate nurturing conditions, will automatically grow in positive ways, pushed naturally toward its actualization as an oak" (p. 206).

The humanistic philosophy in counseling, as exemplified by the person-centered approach, is expressed in the view that counseling is primarily a growth-producing climate that is reflected in the attitudes and behaviors of the participants. Clients are to be empowered and to develop their capacities to make personal and social transformations. In this approach to counseling, clients are not viewed as sick, unstable, deficient individuals, but from their psychological perspectives and reference points. Concepts of mental illness are not considered objective criteria of a client's condition. Instead, these criteria are understood as reflecting specific and relative social/ethical contexts and values.

Related entries: AFFECTIVELY ORIENTED APPROACHES TO COUNSELING; AWARENESS; CLIENT-CENTERED COUNSELING; GESTALT COUNSELING.

References

Belkin, G. (1988). *Introduction to counseling* (3rd ed.). Dubuque, IA: W. C. Brown.

Corey, G. (1991). *Theory and practice of counseling and psychotherapy* (4th ed.). Pacific Grove, CA: Brooks/Cole.

Ellis, A. (1973). *Humanistic psychotherapy: The rational emotive approach.* New York: McGraw-Hill.

Ellis, A. (1985). Two forms of humanistic psychology: Rational emotive therapy vs transpersonal psychology. *Free Inquiry, 15,* 14–21.

Mahoney, M. J., & Thoresen, C. E. (1974). *Self control: Power to the person.* Pacific Grove, CA: Brooks/Cole.

HYPNOSIS OR HYPNOSUGGESTIVE PROCEDURES. Giving suggestions to clients or guiding clients to give themselves suggestions to increase relaxation and calmness, to enhance self-esteem and positive attitudes, and to promote certain expectations toward oneself. Suggestions may be used to reduce or crowd out negative self-suggestions that clients may be continually giving to themselves.

Some hypnosuggestive procedures include suggestions of the type commonly included in hypnotic induction procedures, such as suggestions for deep relaxation, calmness, drowsiness, and letting go of extraneous concerns. A counselor can define most hypnosuggestive procedures as either hypnosis or self-hypnosis. However, counselors are encouraged to label these procedures as self-hypnosis because this term reduces the fear of being under the control of another person, revealing secrets, or becoming unconscious (Barber, 1985). Defining the goal as self-hypnosis also places responsibility on the client to experience calmness and to try to make the suggestions come true. In other words, a client's belief in the power of hypnosis can itself become a self-fulfilling prophecy in making hypnosis effective for them.

Research suggests that hypnosuggestive procedures may be useful in working with clients who suffer from asthma, migraine, and addictive behaviors such as overeating or smoking. However, the generalizability of such research findings is limited because no two counselors necessarily use hypnosuggestions in exactly the same ways. More needs to be known about how effects of hypnosuggestive procedures differ from counselor to counselor and from client to client. An individual's response to hypnosuggestions seems to depend less on the formal induction procedures than on the quality of the interpersonal relationship between the client and the counselor, the client's ability to imagine, his or her expectations, how problems were defined by the counselor, and how the client interprets the meaning of the suggestions.

Related entry: SUGGESTION.

References

Barber, J. X. (1985). Hypnosuggestive procedures as catalysts for psychotherapies. In S. J. Lynn & J. P. Garske (Eds.), *Contemporary psychotherapies: Models and methods* (pp. 333–375). Columbus, OH: Charles Merrill.

Erickson, M. H., & Rossi, E. L. (1981). *Experiencing hypnosis: Therapeutic approaches to altered states.* New York: Irvington.

I

ID. A term used in psychoanalytic theory to describe the sum total of biological instincts, including the sexual and aggressive impulses of an individual. At birth, the id represents the total personality.

The id is that part of personality present at birth that is blind, demanding, and insistent. Its function is to discharge tension so as to return the person to a homeostatic condition of balance.

The id corresponds to the unconscious. The id reacts to contacts with the outer world as impingements and constructs a protective outer core against potentially disruptive stimulation. The progressive structuralization of this core leads to the formation of the ego.

Related entries: EGO; OEDIPUS COMPLEX; PSYCHOANALYTIC COUNSELING; PSYCHOSEXUAL STAGES OF DEVELOPMENT.

References

Arlow, J. A. (1989). Psychoanalysis. In R. J. Corsini & D. Wedding (Eds.), *Current psychotherapies* (4th ed., pp. 19–62). Itasca, IL: F. E. Peacock.

Giovacchini, P. L. (1983). Psychoanalysis. In R. J. Corsini & A. J. Marsella (Eds.), *Personality theories, research and assessment*. Itasca, IL: F. E. Peacock.

IDENTITY. The sense of oneself as a unique person; a definition of who you are, where you are going, and how you will get there. Erikson (1968) described a crisis of adolescence—the identity crisis—and how it was related to both childhood and adult stages of human development.

The characteristic behaviors of people who have a clear sense of identity include (a) a stable self-concept, (b) a clear sense of goals, (c) less susceptibility than others to peer pressure, (d) acceptance of self, (e) ability to make decisions without vacillating, (f) a sense of responsibility for what happens to them, and

(g) an ability to be physically and emotionally close to selected individuals without losing themselves (Hamachek, 1988).

Erikson's view of identity assumed that the ego develops through a series of eight stages. The ego is that component of the self that is in contact with the outside world through such human processes as thinking, perceiving, remembering, reasoning, and attending. During adolescence, the major tasks for the ego are to deal with issues of separation and to renegotiate relationships with parents, and to engage in both personal and environmental exploration before making important personal decisions for oneself.

A basic assumption in reality counseling is that persons have a "growth force" that impels them to strive for a "success identity." Glasser and Tunin (1979) describe how each individual has a health or growth force, and how people want to be content and enjoy a success identity that includes responsible behavior and meaningful interpersonal relationships. According to the reality approach to counseling, people are motivated by the need for identity. Glasser (1965) urges reality counselors to help clients fulfill their basic psychological needs, which include the need to love and be loved and the need to feel worthwhile to themselves and to others. In so doing, counselors will be able to help their clients develop a success identity. The key to clients developing a success identity is their responsible behavior; irresponsible behaviors will result in the formation of a failure identity.

Related entries: ADOLESCENCE; BLACK RACIAL IDENTITY DEVELOPMENT.

References

Erikson, E. H. (1968). *Identity: Youth and crisis.* New York: Norton.

Glasser, W. (1965). *Reality therapy.* New York: Harper and Row.

Glasser, W., & Tunin, L. M. (1979). Reality therapy. In R. Corsini (Ed.), *Current psychotherapies* (2nd ed., pp. 302–328). Itasca, IL: F. E. Peacock.

Hamachek, D. F. (1988). Evaluating self-concept and ego development within Erikson's psychosocial framework: A formulation. *Journal of Counseling and Development, 66,* 354–360.

IMPLOSIVE COUNSELING. A form of behavioral counseling in which the client is taught to imagine vividly the thing that he or she most fears through a process called flooding; as a result, the client becomes desensitized to a previously feared stimulus.

The theory underlying implosive counseling combines the effects of extinction with elements of classical conditioning. When the negative or neurotic behavior is not reinforced, the tendency of the client to continue that behavior will decrease. By concentrating intensely on the fearful stimulus, the client is taught to associate neutral stimuli with the anxiety-provoking ones. Implosive counseling is based on the "two factor model of avoidance learning" (Stampfl, 1970). Emotional symptoms are seen as avoidance responses that are learned and perpetuated on the basis of anxiety reduction. Anxiety needs to be extinguished if the client's symptoms are to be eliminated. This will occur if the conditioned stimuli that elicit anxiety are present in the absence of primary reinforcement. This kind of counseling may be used wherever some form of neurotic avoidance behavior is the symptom, typically in the case of phobias.

Related entries: BEHAVIORAL COUNSELING; EMOTIONAL FLOODING APPROACHES.

References

London, P. (1964). *Modes and morals of psychotherapy.* New York: Holt, Rinehart and Winston.

Stampfl, T. G. (1970). Implosive therapy: An emphasis on covert stimulation. In D. J. Levis (Ed.), *Learning approaches to therapeutic behavior change.* Chicago: Aldine.

INDIVIDUAL PSYCHOLOGY. An approach to understanding human behavior that sees each person as a unique, whole entity who is constantly becoming and whose development can be understood only within a societal context.

The name of this approach is derived from the Latin word *individuum,* which means "undivided" or "indivisible" (Dinkmeyer, Dinkmeyer, & Sperry, 1987). This view takes a holistic approach to understanding personality. All actions of an individual are seen in reference to the person's chosen style of life.

The Adlerian approach to counseling is based on the principles of individual psychology. The client is seen as a dynamic unified organism moving through life in definite patterns toward a goal. For a counselor to be effective, the meaning of a client's behavior must be clear in regard to its unity and central function. The way clients organize themselves as whole persons influences their perceptions of life and their relationships with others.

The major tenet of individual psychology is that all human behavior has a purpose and is goal directed in nature. Instead of looking at a client's history to identify causes of present behaviors, individual psychology would look to future goals for "causes."

Related entries: ADLER, ALFRED; ADLERIAN COUNSELING; DREIKURS, RUDOLPH.

References

Ansbach, H. L. (1983). Individual psychology. In R. J. Corsini & A. J. Marsella (Eds.), *Personality theories, research and assessment.* Itasca, IL: F. E. Peacock.

Dinkmeyer, O. C., Dinkmeyer, D. C., & Sperry, L. (1987). *Adlerian counseling and psychotherapy* (2nd ed.). Columbus, OH: Charles Merrill.

INSIGHT. Understanding the individual and environmental factors that are influencing behaviors. The process by which persons comprehend their motives, fears, and hopes and the way in which they have evolved in the course of their development.

Insight is considered in most approaches to counseling to be a significant factor that can influence changes in client behaviors. It may be viewed as a sign or a cause of changes in a client's condition. For example, insight in Adlerian counseling is seen as understanding translated into constructive actions. It reflects the client's understanding of the purposive nature of behavior and mistaken apperceptions as well as an understanding of the role both play in life movement. For an Adlerian counselor, intellectual insight merely reflects a client's desire to play the game of counseling. Instead, during the insight phase of counseling, clients are helped to become aware of why they choose to function as they do. Adlerians do not believe that clients should defer dealing with problems while seeking to develop insight.

Analytical counselors assume that basic changes in clients must be preceded by insight. Freud argued for the necessity of making the unconscious conscious, and supporting the conscious rational secondary processes in the client. Conscious understanding of the impact of developmental experiences on the present problem situation was considered insight and was considered a crucial element in psychoanalytic counseling.

Rational-emotive counselors assert that insights often do not lead to major changes in a client's condition. They merely allow clients to see that they have emotional problems which have dynamic antecedents in childhood experiences. In rational-emotive counseling, clients are led to gain insight into how their own beliefs and expectations related to antecedent events in their lives have had dysfunctional emotional consequences for them. Clients are also helped to gain insight into how they make themselves upset because they keep indoctrinating themselves with irrational beliefs. Finally, clients gain insight into the fact that they will have to work hard and practice in order to correct the irrational beliefs in their lives that are contributing to their problems.

A goal of Gestalt counseling is to increase awareness or insight. "Insight is a patterning of the perceptual field in such a way that the significant realities are apparent; it is the formation of a gestalt in which the relevant factors fall into place with respect to the whole" (Heidbreder, 1993, p. 335). There is a clear understanding of the structure of a situation. For instance, a special concern in Gestalt counseling concerns how the counselor and the client experience their relationship. The client learns how to become aware of awareness through focused awareness and experimentation.

Related entry: PSYCHOTHERAPY.

References

Dinkmeyer, D., & Dinkmeyer, D., Jr. (1985). Adlerian psychotherapy and counseling. In S. J. Lynn & J. P. Garske (Eds.), *Contemporary psychotherapies: Models and methods.* Columbus, OH: Charles Merrill.

Ellis, A. (1989). Rational emotive therapy. In R. J. Corsini & D. Wedding (Eds.), *Current psychotherapies* (4th ed.). Itasca, IL: F. E. Peacock.

Heidbreder, E. (1993). *Seven psychologies.* New York: Century.

Prochaska, J. (1979). *Systems of psychotherapy: A transtheoretical analysis.* Homewood, IL: Dorsey.

Yontef, G. M., & Simkin, J. S. (1989). Gestalt therapy. In R. J. Corsini & D. Wedding (Eds.), *Current psychotherapies* (4th ed., pp. 323–361). Itasca, IL: F. E. Peacock.

INSTINCTS. Instincts are defined as the psychological representations of a stimulus from within the body. The sources of instincts are biological (Freud, 1923/1961).

Energy is stored in the body and released because of a psychological excitation within some organ or tissue of the body. The excitory process is called a need, while its psychological manifestation is called a wish.

Even in the absence of satisfaction, instincts function constantly, although their intensity may vary. The aim of the instincts is to remove their sources or bodily needs. Instincts cause persons to seek objects or events to achieve a state of reduced tension.

Freud described the existence of self-preservative instincts or sexual instincts that are required for the maintenance of life. Their energy is called the libido. Freud also described aggressive or destructive instincts that are in opposition to the sexual instincts. He considered the id to be that part of the psyche that contains instincts, the unconscious, and pleasure demands.

Related entries: ID; PSYCHOANALYTIC COUNSELING.

References

Abeles, N. (1979). Psychodynamic theory. In H. M. Burks, Jr., & B. Stefflre (Eds.), *Theories of counseling* (3rd ed.). New York: McGraw-Hill.

Freud, S. (1961). Repression. In J. Strachey (Ed. and Trans.), *The standard edition of the complete psychological works of Sigmund Freud* (Vol. 14). London: Hogarth Press. (Original work published 1923)

INSTRUCTIONAL COUNSELING. The counselor is considered first and foremost an instructor who possesses expert knowledge and conceptual, organizational, and practical educational skills. Effective counseling depends upon whether the counselor's use of his/her knowledge and skills in instruction-learning interactions is capable of promoting client changes.

This approach to counseling has three components. First is the structural component, or the basic counseling skills intended to produce changes in client behaviors, cognitions, emotional reactions, attitudes, and perceptions. Second is the intentional component, or the purposeful nature of counselor activities. Third is the functional component; client changes must occur if it is to be said that instruction has taken place in counseling (Martin & Heibert, 1985).

The instructional counseling process has five more specific characteristics: (1) general goals toward which learning is directed; (2) preassessment of current client capabilities and characteristics in relation to these general goals; (3) objectives that transform general goals into specific statements or personal learning outcomes; (4) instructional activities aimed at facilitating changes toward these objectives; and (5) evaluation of client changes in relation to goals and objectives.

Counseling skills in instructional counseling include:

Structuring instruction (e.g., giving overviews, stating objectives, using set induction, giving examples, maximizing the physical arrangement of the counseling setting, modeling or demonstrating, summarizing and reviewing counseling activities, focusing by means of rhetorical questions, stating clear transitions from one counseling activity to another, using verbal markers of importance).

Soliciting client activities (asking probing questions, prompting client responses, redirecting questions from one client to another, controlling the pace of instruction, giving clear directions, using post-question wait time).

Reacting to client activities (giving informational feedback, reflecting meaning and affect, describing inconsistencies, maintaining active listening postures, suggesting alternatives, giving descriptive praise).

Reference

Martin, J., & Heibert, B. (1985). *Instructional counseling: A method for counselors.* Pittsburgh: University of Pittsburgh Press.

INTAKE INTERVIEW. A structured interpersonal session with clients in which the goal is to elicit information about their background as it relates to current problems or complaints. In many settings, history taking occurs during these intake interviews.

The intake interview has to do with gathering information and may or may not be conducted by the counselor who is assigned to see a client. Generally, the interviewer begins with the least threatening topics and proceeds systematically to ask questions about more sensitive areas.

Information solicited during intake interviews includes:

1. Identifying information about the client
2. General appearance and demeanor
3. History related to presenting problems
4. Past psychiatric and/or counseling history
5. Educational and job history
6. Health history
7. Social/developmental history
8. Family, marital, sexual history
9. Assessment of client communication patterns

In addition to or in lieu of asking the client to give a history during a session, the counselor may give the client a written history questionnaire or form to complete as homework before another scheduled session. If, after conducting an intake interview, the counselor is in doubt about a client's psychiatric status or the possibility of an organic brain disorder, the counselor may conduct or refer the client for a mental-status examination. This kind of interview allows the counselor to classify and describe the areas of mental functioning that are involved in making diagnostic decisions.

The interview is a common behavioral assessment instrument. Nelson (1983) observed that the interview was the one assessment strategy used more consistently than any other procedure—perhaps because of its practicality in applied settings and its potential efficiency. However, as Morganstern (1986) commented, little research has been conducted on the effects of interview procedures.

References

Cormier, W. H., & Cormier, L. S. (1991). *Interviewing strategies for helpers: Fundamental skills and cognitive behavioral interventions* (3rd ed.). Pacific Grove, CA: Brooks/Cole.

Morganstern, K. P. (1986). Behavioral interviewing. In A. S. Bellack & M. Hersen (Eds.), *Behavioral assessment: A practical handbook* (3rd ed.). New York: Pergamon.

Nelson, R. O. (1983). Behavioral assessment: Past, present and future. *Behavioral Assessment, 5,* 195–206.

INTELLIGENCE TESTS. These instruments are designed to measure an individual's aptitude for scholastic work or for occupations requiring abstract reasoning as well as his or her verbal and numerical skills (Aiken, 1979). Many intelligence tests are validated against measures of academic achievement (Anastasi, 1982).

The Stanford-Binet Intelligence Scale, a revision of the Binet-Simon scales, was published in 1916. L. M. Terman was the author of this scale, which yielded both a mental age score and an intelligence quotient based on the relationship between chronological age and mental age. The Stanford-Binet IV, the most recent version, is a norm referenced measure of general intelligence for persons between 2 and 23 years of age. This fourth edition of the Stanford-Binet eliminates mental age scores and uses standard scores. Fifteen subtests have been grouped into four areas: verbal reasoning, quantitative reasoning, abstract/visual reasoning, and short-term memory. The Stanford-Binet IV provides a profile of subtest and area scores (see Thorndike, Hagen, & Sattler, 1986).

In 1939 David Wechsler published the Wechsler Bellevue Intelligence Scale, an individual intelligence test for adults. He published his first revision in 1955 and his second revision in 1981. He also developed a preschool scale and a children's scale. All of his tests were developed without relying on any specific, clear-cut theory of intelligence. The Wechsler tests have subtests that are assigned either to a verbal scale yielding a verbal scale IQ or to a performance scale yielding a performance scale IQ and a full-scale IQ (Wechsler, 1981).

Related entries: ACHIEVEMENT TEST; APTITUDE TEST; TRAIT AND FACTOR COUNSELING.

References

Aiken, R., Jr. (1979). *Psychological testing and assessment* (3rd ed.). Boston: Allyn and Bacon.

Anastasi, A. (1982). *Psychological testing* (5th ed.). New York: Macmillan.

Thorndike, R. L., Hagen, E. P., & Sattler, J. M. (1986). *Guide for administering and scoring the fourth edition: Stanford-Binet intelligence scale.* Chicago: Riverside.

Wechsler, D. (1981). *Manual: Wechsler adult intelligence scale—revised.* New York: Psychological Corporation.

INTENTIONAL COUNSELING. This approach to counseling is concerned with the development of intentionality or purpose through the expansion of alternatives for living that are available to clients.

Clients who act with intentionality have a sense of capability, can generate alternative behaviors, and can approach problems from different vantage points (Ivey & Simek-Downing, 1980). Intentional living occurs in a cultural context, and implies three major abilities on the part of clients: the ability to generate a maximum number of verbal and nonverbal sentences to communicate with self and others within a given culture; the ability to generate a maximum number of sentences to communicate with a variety of diverse groups within a culture; and the ability to formulate plans, act on many possibilities existing in a culture, and reflect on these actions.

Within this counseling model, helping is defined as a general framework in which one person offers another person or group assistance, usually in the form of interviewing, counseling, or psychotherapy. Helpers and their clients may or may not enter into one of these three types of relationships through mutual consent. Interviews are the systematic methods and procedures for gathering information; counseling provides assistance to normal people to achieve their goals or to function more effectively; psychotherapy is restricted to clients with pathological problems, and may involve providing assistance in making major changes in the client's personality structure.

The central purposes of helping are to produce a more creative and generative client, and to increase response capacity and the ability to create new behaviors and thoughts. The counselor's task is to help produce alternatives, to aid clients in loosening and breaking old patterns, to facilitate their decision-making process, and to help them to find viable solutions to problems.

The approach to decision making in this model of counseling starts with a definition of the problem, continues with the generation of alternatives, and concludes with the selection of one alternative and implementation of that choice. Intentional counselors want their clients to have at least three alternatives to choose from; they will then help them select among these alternatives and implement a choice.

Three phases in decision making provide a structure for counseling: the problem definition phase, the work phase, and the decision for action phase. The first stage in counseling includes defining the problem, consideration of alternative definitions of the problem, and commitment to the most suitable definition of the problem. The second involves getting more specific facts about a problem situation, including a client's relevant thoughts and feelings about what is occurring in his/her life. At this stage, the counselor considers alternative counseling approaches that might be used to help clients. They choose one or more of these approaches to then examine the definition of the problem, to generate new ways of looking at the relevant issues, and to develop new issues for further discussion. The third stage of counseling is concerned with increasing the number of alternative solutions available to the client, reflecting on their advantages and disadvantages, deciding on an appropriate solution, and testing it out in the home environment.

Intentional counseling assumes that environmental factors as well as individual factors may underlie client problems. The former include such environmental influences as ageism, racism, sexism, and economic injustice, which may in turn precipitate or cause specific problems for clients. Sometimes clients do not need to change themselves, but instead need help from counselors in making appropriate changes in their environments.

The process of identification and selection of specific skills of counseling is termed the microskills approach. The basic microskills are the attending and influencing behaviors of counselors. The former involve eye contact, appropriate body language, and verbal following. They are a means of enabling clients to talk more freely about themselves and to participate actively in the counseling process. Attending skills such as reflection of feeling, questioning, and paraphrasing are focused on facilitating clients' exploration of their needs, wishes, thoughts, and feelings. Influencing skills allow the counselor to become directly involved in the process of counseling by sharing himself or herself.

Examples of influencing skills are directives, expressions of feelings, expressions of content, self-disclosures, interpretations, and direct mutual communications. The content of any counselor's microskills is determined by his or her experiences and theoretical orientation.

References

Ivey, A., & Authier, J. (1978). *Microcounseling: Innovation in interviewing, counseling psychotherapy and psychoeducation* (2nd ed.). Springfield, IL: Charles C Thomas.
Ivey, A. E., & Simek-Downing, L. (1980). *Counseling and psychotherapy: Skills, theories and practice.* Englewood Cliffs, NJ: Prentice-Hall.

INTERACTIONAL COUNSELING. This point of view in counseling assumes that behavior is simultaneously influenced by a person's view of the world and by the behavior of others with regard to the person.

The impact of each set of variables is linked to the other so that counseling interventions targeted at either will have an impact on both.

The interaction of views assumes that transactions between persons in relationships as well as larger social systems can influence behavior. The goals of interactional counseling range from increasing a client's observation and communication skills to changing the relationship or system within which the client's symptoms function. Change strategies are of three types:

1. Strategies that promote client awareness of interactional issues;

2. Strategies that provide feedback regarding interpersonal skills; and

3. Strategies that alter the functioning of client relationships and systems.

Through creating a therapeutic paradox, the counselor simultaneously encourages the client's symptoms and strips them of their interpersonal effects in the relationship with the counselor.

References

Claiborn, C. D., & Lichtenberg, J. W. (1989). Interactional counseling. *The Counseling Psychologist, 17,* 355–453.
Lichtenberg, J. W., & Barke, K. H. (1981). Investigation of transactional communication patterns in counseling. *Journal of Counseling Psychology, 28,* 471–481.

INTERESTS. A psychological concept that is primarily affective in nature and describes the objects or activities that stimulate individuals to react with feelings.

Interests are inferred through observations of behaviors involving choices, attention, and persistence. Interests are directed toward certain objects or processes, and their relative strength is observed by the preferential ordering of these objects or processes.

Interpretations of interests are based on verbal expressions of preferences, observations of participation in certain activities, tested knowledge or competencies, and inventories pertaining to objects, processes, and activities which a person responds to in terms of liking, preference, or choice. Interests involve individual differences in perception and evaluation.

E. K. Strong, the author of an early interest inventory, thought that we learn to like those things that we do well. However, it may be that differences in our self-concepts also are an important factor that influences the development of interests. Research over the years suggests that interests have more to do with motivational and personality variables than with ability variables. Still, certain interests may develop because talents reflected by ability are reinforced by our culture and are reflected by learned preferences of individuals in response to such reinforcement. Darley and Hagenah (1955) concluded that occupational interests, the development of vocational maturity, and the process of career development primarily reflect the value systems, needs, motivation, and personality of individuals.

Since the 1920s, interest inventories have been used to measure subjective interests. They were originally developed as aids in personnel selection. Standardized interest inventories allowed individuals to make social comparisons of their interests. An early attempt to deal specifically with studying interests was reported by E. L. Thorndike in the *Popular Science Monthly* of 1921.

Work by C. S. Yoakum and his colleagues at the Carnegie Institute of Technology starting about 1919 laid the groundwork for interest inventories as they are known today (see Campbell, 1971). One of the first inventories was done by Bruce Moore, who formulated a twenty-item instrument to differentiate between sales and design engineers. He correctly identified 78 percent of the sales engineers and 82 percent of the design engineers with his inventory. In 1926 J. B. Miner attempted to differentiate four groups of students who wanted to be involved in teaching, engineering, law, and medicine, and a random group of 570 students. He was able to demonstrate that the four groups of students with stated occupational goals could be differentiated from the random group on the basis of their inventoried interests. The first forms of the Strong Vocational Blank were constructed in 1927 and used items from those developed at the Carnegie Institute of Technology.

Related entries: KUDER GENERAL INTEREST SURVEY (FORM E); KUDER OCCUPATIONAL INTEREST SURVEY (FORM D-1956 AND FORM D-1966); SELF-DIRECTED SEARCH; STRONG-CAMPBELL INTEREST INVENTORY (STRONG VOCATIONAL INTEREST BLANK); VOCATIONAL GUIDANCE.

References

Campbell, D. P. (1971). *Handbook of the Strong vocational interest blank.* Stanford, CA: Stanford University Press.

Darley, J. G., & Hagenah, T. (1955). *Vocational interest measurement.* Minneapolis: University of Minnesota Press.

Roe, A. (1956). *The psychology of occupations.* New York: Wiley.

Thorndike, E. L. (1921). The permanence of interests and their relation to abilities. *Popular Science Monthly, 18,* 449–451.

INTERPERSONAL INFLUENCE MODEL OF COUNSELING. In this two-stage model of counseling, counselors are to first enhance their perceived expertness, attractiveness, and trustworthiness and the client's involvement in counseling. Second, they use their influence to maximize opinion or behavioral changes in clients.

In this model of counseling, it is assumed that the extent to which counselors are perceived as expert, attractive, and trustworthy reduces the likelihood of their being discredited by clients. By enhancing client involvement in counseling, counselors reduce the likelihood of clients discrediting the issues or problems being discussed.

Counselors attempt to change behaviors or opinions, and they precipitate dissonance in their clients. In turn, their clients then will attempt to reduce this dissonance by (a) changing the directions advocated by counselors, (b) discrediting the counselors, (c) discrediting the issues, (d) attempting to change counselors' opinions, or (e) seeking others who agree with or support their present positions. Strong (1968) proposed that counselors will increase the likelihood that the first alternative will occur if they reduce the likelihood of the second and third.

It is the client's perceptions of counselor expertness, attractiveness, and trustworthiness that determine counselor ability to exert influence over client opinions and behaviors. Counselors' actual and relevant experiences and knowledge are seen as less important influence factors in counseling than are clients' perceptions of their counselors' relevant competencies.

Perceived expertness of counselors was attributed to three primary points: visible evidence of expertness, reputation, and interview behaviors. Perceptions of counselor attractiveness were attributed to similarity to, compatibility with, and liking of the counselor. Client perceptions of both expertness and attractiveness seem to be most influenced by counselor interview behaviors. Finally, perceived trustworthiness of counselors was assumed to be based on (a) reputation for honesty, (b) social role, (c) sincerity and openness, and (d) lack of motivation for personal gain. Corrigan, Dell, Lewis, and Schmidt (1980) reported that much less research had been done on perceived trustworthiness than on attractiveness or expertness.

References

Corrigan, J. D., Dell, D. M., Lewis, K. N., & Schmidt, L. D. (1980). Counseling as social influence process: A review. *Journal of Counseling Psychology Monograph, 27,* 295–343.

Strong, S. R. (1968). Counseling: An interpersonal influence process. *Journal of Counseling Psychology, 15,* 215–224.

Strong, S. R., & Schmidt, L. D. (1970). Trustworthiness and influence in counseling. *Journal of Counseling Psychology, 17,* 197–204.

INTERPRETATION. The process by which counselors suggest possible meanings for client behaviors. Brammer and Shostrom (1977) defined interpretation as presenting to clients for consideration a set of hypotheses regarding the meanings of their behaviors.

The goal of interpretations is to make sense out of clients' experiences, both those of which they are aware and those of which they are unaware. Brammer and Shostrom (1977) suggest that counselors make more specific interpretations during middle stages of counseling and more general interpretations during later stages. When interpreting the client's behaviors, counselors should state the ideas or thoughts most clearly associated with the client's emotional and behavioral problem conditions and then identify possible motivations, intentions, and functions of these problem conditions. It should be noted that interpretations may increase client awareness of strengths as well as deficits.

Johnson (1986, p. 154) says that interpretation can lead to insight, better psychological living, and effective changes in behavior. Interpretations often deal with the implicit part of a client's message; as a result the counselor's statements are apt to verbalize issues that clients may have felt only vaguely. Interpretation can identify causal relations between clients' explicit and implicit messages and behaviors and help clients view their actions from an alternative point of view.

Research by Claiborn, Ward, and Strong (1981) suggests that highly discrepant interpretations are more likely to be rejected by clients, while congruent or slightly discrepant interpretations are most likely to facilitate client changes.

References

Brammer, L., & Shostrom, E. (1977). *Therapeutic psychology* (3rd ed.). Englewood Cliffs, NJ: Prentice-Hall.

Claiborn, C. D., Ward, S. R., & Strong, S. R. (1981). Effects of congruence between counselor interpretations and client beliefs. *Journal of Counseling Psychology, 28,* 101–109.

Johnson, D. W. (1986). *Reaching out: Interpersonal effectiveness and self-actualization* (3rd ed.). Englewood Cliffs, NJ: Prentice-Hall.

INVOLUNTARY CLIENTS. Clients who are under pressure to engage in the counseling process; they are likely to demonstrate resistance or reluctance and not be cooperative, at least initially.

These clients may feel forced to see a counselor and present themselves as not needing help. Reluctant clients are those who do not want to participate in counseling; they are usually not self-referred. They are apt to find counseling less satisfactory, improve less than do those who were not reluctant, and tend to terminate the counseling process prematurely (Paradise & Wilder, 1979). Resistant clients often seek counseling willingly but are unable to become fully involved in the counseling process.

Reluctance and resistance in nonvoluntary clients can be viewed as forms of avoidance. These clients need to recognize incentives for engaging in counseling and learning how better to manage problem situations in their lives. It is sometimes helpful for counselors to discuss openly the pressures that may have resulted in a client's involuntary referral. Involuntary clients are quite likely to present themselves as resistant or defensive.

In family counseling, resistance results from a need to keep the family homeostatic or stable (Jackson, 1968). It is usually not the desire for change that leads families to seek counseling, but rather changes which they do not like or have not adjusted to.

Related entry: CORRECTIONAL COUNSELING.

References

Cormier, W. H., & Cormier, L. S. (1991). *Interview strategies for helpers* (3rd ed.). Pacific Grove, CA: Brooks/Cole.

Egan, G. (1990). *The skilled helper: A systematic approach to effective helping* (4th ed.). Pacific Grove, CA: Brooks/Cole.

Harris, G. A., & Watkins, D. (1987). *Counseling the involuntary and resistant client.* College Park, MD: American Correctional Association.

Jackson, D. (1968). *Therapy, communication and change.* Palo Alto, CA: Science and Behavior Books.

Paradise, L. V., & Wilder, O. H. (1979). The relationship between client reluctance and counseling effectiveness. *Counselor Education and Supervision, 19,* 35–41.

IRRATIONAL BELIEFS. Unreasonable convictions that produce emotional disturbances for a person. For example, a person may insist that the world should be or must be different from what it actually is known to be.

In the rational-emotive approach to counseling, it is assumed that the main reason that people overreact or underreact to obnoxious stimuli is because of some dogmatic, irrational, unexamined beliefs that have not been objectively scrutinized. Emotional upsets, as distinguished from feelings of sorrow, regret, annoyance, and frustration, are caused by irrational beliefs. They generally take the form of the statement, "Because I want something, it is not only desirable or preferable that it exist, but it absolutely should, and it is awful when it doesn't."

Some irrational ideas lead to self-condemnation or anger; others lead to a low tolerance for frustration. The rational-emotive counselor helps clients identify which irrational ideas are evidenced through their belief systems and emotional reactions.

Ten major irrational ideas are as follows:

1. It is a dire necessity to be approved of by every significant person in your community.
2. One needs to be competent in all possible respects if one is to consider oneself worthwhile.
3. Human unhappiness is externally caused, and people have little or no control over sorrows and emotional disturbances.
4. One's past history will indefinitely determine one's present behaviors.
5. It is catastrophic if the perfect solution to human problems is not found.
6. A person should be concerned and dwell on the possibility that dangerous or fearsome events may occur.
7. Bad and wicked people should be severely punished and blamed for their villainy.
8. It is awful when things are not the way that one would like them to be.
9. It is easier to avoid than to face life difficulties and self-responsibilities.
10. A person should get upset over other people's problems and disturbances. (Ellis, 1974).

Related entries: A-B-C THEORY; MUSTURBATION; RATIONAL-EMOTIVE COUNSELING.

References

Ellis, A. (1974). *Humanistic psychotherapy.* New York: McGraw-Hill.
Ellis, A. (1984). *Rational emotive therapy and cognitive behavior therapy.* New York: Springer.

J

JOURNALS (PROFESSIONAL). The American Counseling Association publishes the following journals:

Career Development Quarterly

Counseling and Values

Counselor Education and Supervision

Elementary School Guidance and Counseling

The Family Journal: Counseling and Therapy for Couples and Families

Journal for Specialists in Group Work

Journal of Addictions and Offenders Counseling

Journal of Counseling and Development

Journal of Employment Counseling

Journal of Humanistic Education and Development

Journal of Multicultural Counseling and Development

Measurement and Evaluation in Counseling and Development

Rehabilitation Counseling Bulletin

The School Counselor

The American Counseling Association also publishes a newspaper entitled *Guidepost,* and a magazine entitled *American Counselor.*

The American Psychological Association publishes the *Counseling Psychologist* and the *Journal of Counseling Psychology.*

The American Association of Mental Health Counselors publishes the *Journal of Mental Health Counseling.*

Related entries: AMERICAN ASSOCIATION FOR COUNSELING (AAC); AMERICAN ASSOCIATION FOR MARRIAGE AND FAMILY THERAPY

(AAMFT); AMERICAN PSYCHOLOGICAL ASSOCIATION DIVISION 17—COUNSELING PSYCHOLOGY.

References

American Association of Mental Health Counselors, 5999 Stevenson Avenue, Alexandria, VA 22304.

American Counseling Association, 5999 Stevenson Avenue, Alexandria, VA 22304.

American Psychological Association, 750 First Street NE, Washington, DC 20002-4242.

JUNG, CARL (1875–1961). Carl Jung is considered the founder of the Jungian or analytical approach to counseling and psychotherapy.

Jung was born in Kesswill, Switzerland, and received most of his education in Basel. He had formulated some of his major ideas before he came to know Freud. His medical thesis was on the so-called occult phenomena (Jung, 1902/1957). An exchange of letters led to a meeting with Freud in 1907 in Vienna. Jung was later appointed the first president of the International Psychoanalytic Association.

By identifying main themes in psychological material and amplifying them with parallel motifs from mythology, comparative religion, and literature, Jung forged a new way of looking at clinical material. He viewed symbols as the language of communication between consciousness and the unconscious.

Related entries: ANALYTICAL COUNSELING; ANIMA; ANIMUS; ARCHETYPES.

References

Jung, C. G. (1957). On the psychology and pathology of so-called occult phenomena. *Psychiatric studies, Collected works: Vol. 1* (Bollingen Series 20). Princeton, NJ: Princeton University Press. (Originally published 1902)

Kaufmann, Y. (1989). Analytical psychotherapy. In R. J. Corsini & D. Wedding (Eds.), *Current psychotherapies* (4th ed., pp. 119–152). Itasca, IL: F. E. Peacock.

McCullough, L. (1993). Interest in Carl Jung's ideas is growing. *The Guidepost/American Counseling Association, 36*(1), 12–13.

K

KELLY, GEORGE ALEXANDER (1905–1967). Kelly's major contributions to counseling are found in the two-volume work *The Psychology of Personal Constructs,* published in 1955. His theory of personal constructs is a pioneer cognitive approach to counseling that emphasizes looking at how clients construe their lives.

George Kelly was born in Kansas and grew up there. He attended Friends University in Wichita and later, in 1926, received a B. A. degree in physics and mathematics from Park College. In 1928 he completed an M. A. with a major in educational sociology at the University of Kansas. In 1929 he spent a year at the University of Edinburgh and studied under Sir Godfrey Thomson, the eminent statistician and educator. In 1931 he was awarded a Ph.D. from the State University of Iowa. His dissertation was on the common factors in speech and reading disabilities. He spent the major part of his career as a professor at Ohio State University.

Related entry: PSYCHOLOGY OF PERSONAL CONSTRUCTS.

References

Kelly, G. A. (1955). *The psychology of personal constructs* (2 vols.). New York: Norton.
Maher, B. (1969) (Ed.). *Clinical psychology and personality: The selected papers of George Kelly.* New York: John Wiley.

KUDER GENERAL INTEREST SURVEY (FORM E). This measure has 168 items and 10 interest scales—outdoor, mechanical, computational, scientific, persuasive, artistic, literary, musical, social service, and clerical—as well as a verification scale. It is designed for use in grades six through twelve and has a sixth grade reading level.

The Kuder General Interest Survey has evolved from a series of Kuder vocational interest inventories published over a period of more than forty years.

The first Kuder Vocational Preference Record, or Form A, published in 1939, had the following scales: literary, scientific, artistic, persuasive, social service, musical, and computational. There were forty items. An item consisted of five activities that a person was to rank in order of preference. In Form B of this test, a triad item format was introduced, and a person was to indicate which activity was most liked and which was least liked.

The Kuder General Interest Survey is a revision and downward extension of the Kuder Vocational Preference Record for grades six through twelve. It can be used in counseling junior high and high school students about their educational decisions.

Related entries: INTERESTS; SELF-DIRECTED SEARCH; STRONG-CAMPBELL INTEREST INVENTORY (STRONG VOCATIONAL INTEREST BLANK).

References

Harmon, L. W. (1978). Review of Kuder preference record-vocational. In O. K. Buros (Ed.), *The eighth mental measurements yearbook.*

Kuder, G. F. (1975). *General interest survey (Form E) manual.* Chicago: Science Research Associates.

KUDER OCCUPATIONAL INTEREST SURVEY (FORM D-1956 AND FORM DD-1966). This test reports similarities between a person's responses to the interest items and the responses of selected occupational groups. It indicates whether a person's interests are, for example, more like those that are typical of physicians than of chemists, or more like those of pharmaceutical salespersons than bookstore managers. This test also has college major criterion group scales. In 1985, ten vocational interest scales were added to the Kuder Occupational Interest Survey.

Related entries: INTERESTS; SELF-DIRECTED SEARCH; STRONG-CAMPBELL INTEREST INVENTORY (STRONG VOCATIONAL INTEREST BLANK).

Reference

Kuder, F., & Zytowski, D. G. (1991). *Kuder Occupational Interest Survey Form DD general manual.* Monterey, CA: California Test Bureau.

L

LATENCY STAGE. The period of mid-childhood in psychosexual development, which follows the phallic stage and lasts until puberty.

At this stage, children direct their interests to the larger world and the process of formal education. The sexual drive is sublimated, to some extent, to activities in school, hobbies, sports, and friendships with members of the same sex.

This period is described by Erikson (1963) as marked by a need to resolve the conflict between industry and inferiority. Erikson thought the central task of middle childhood was to achieve a sense of industry, which was associated with creating goals that were personally meaningful and then achieving them.

Related entries: ANAL STAGE; GENITAL STAGE; ORAL STAGE; PHALLIC STAGE; PSYCHOANALYTIC COUNSELING; PSYCHOSEXUAL STAGES OF DEVELOPMENT.

References

Arlow, J. A. (1989). Psychoanalysis. In R. J. Corsini & D. Wedding (Eds.), *Current psychotherapies* (4th ed., pp. 19–62). Itasca, IL: F. E. Peacock.

Erikson, E. H. (1963). *Childhood and society* (2nd ed.). New York: Norton.

LEGAL FOUNDATIONS OF COUNSELING PRACTICE. In 1971 Iowa legally recognized counselors as professionals who provided personal as well as vocational and educational counseling. In Weldon vs. Virginia State Board of Psychologists Examiners in 1974, a judgment was rendered that counseling was a profession distinct from psychology. The U.S. House of Representatives in HR 3270 (94th Congress, 1976) defined counseling as a process through which a trained counselor assisted an individual or group to make satisfactory and responsible decisions concerning personal, educational, and career development (see Gladding, 1988).

The first state law regulating counseling was passed in Virginia in 1976; it described counseling as a generic profession with specialties. After this time, many states defined and regulated the practice of professional counseling, primarily through certification (protection of title) and/or licensure (protection of practice). By 1989, thirty-two states had passed counselor licensure laws.

Four types of counselor credentialing procedures are as follows:

1. Inspection, or a process in which a state agency periodically examines the professional activities of counselors to determine if their practices are consistent with public safety, health, and welfare.

2. Registration, or a process in which counselors submit information to the state concerning the nature of their professional practice. Those who meet the defined standards are qualified as registered counselors. In some cases, they use the title registered practicing counselor.

3. Certification is when a state board or department issues a certificate indicating that a person has minimal competencies and no known character defects which would interfere with the professional practice of counseling. Candidates may need to pass an examination and provide letters of reference in order to obtain such a certificate.

4. Licensure, or "title protection," assures that individuals do not engage in the professional practice of counseling without a license. Special state boards usually oversee the issue of such licenses (see Swanson, 1983).

Related entry: LIABILITY (COUNSELORS).

References

Gladding, S. T. (1988). *Counseling: A comprehensive profession* (pp. 243–246). Columbus, OH: Charles Merrill.

Swanson, C. D. (1983). The law and the counselor. In J. A. Brown & R. H. Pate, Jr. (Eds.), *Being a counselor* (pp. 26–44). Monterey, CA: Brooks/Cole.

LIABILITY (COUNSELORS). Malpractice litigation is based on the following four conditions: (1) a client/counselor relationship was established; (2) the counselor acted in a negligent or improper manner; (3) an actual injury was sustained by the client; and (4) the counselor's conduct caused the injury (Lovett & Lovett, 1988). Civil liability of counselors means that they can be sued for not doing right or for doing wrong to their clients.

Malpractice is the failure to render proper counseling services through ignorance or negligence, resulting in injuries or losses to clients. Negligence means that a counselor has not followed commonly accepted standards of the profession and that due care was not being exercised.

Causes of counselor malpractice include using techniques that are not within the realm of accepted practices; using techniques without proper training; not explaining consequences of certain techniques to a client; and failing to follow procedures that might have been more helpful for a client's condition (Lovett & Lovett, 1988). Recent court decisions have held counselors liable when clients follow their advice and suffer damages as a consequence. The best defense against being charged with malpractice may be to routinely obtain informed consent from clients. Proper records are also crucial if counselors are ever involved in a malpractice suit.

Related entry: LEGAL FOUNDATIONS OF COUNSELING PRACTICE.

References

Corey, G. (1991). *Theory and practice of counseling and psychotherapy* (4th ed.). Pacific Grove, CA: Brooks/Cole.

Lovett, T., & Lovett, C. J. (1988). *Suggestions for continuing legal education units in counselor training.* Paper presented at the annual meeting of the American Association for Counseling and Development, Chicago.

LIFE CAREER DEVELOPMENT. A perspective on career development that includes how individuals during their lifetime integrate roles, settings, and events to establish a life career.

Career development is viewed as more than an occupational choice. Super and Bohn (1970) make a distinction between an occupation, or what one does, and a career, or the course of life decisions over a period of time. Jordaan (1974) said that new concepts of career development should emphasize vocational histories and career criteria rather than static life conditions and occupational criteria. In the 1970s, these counselors and others wanted to go beyond a work-focused definition of career and instead emphasize how career development included all aspects of people's lives. Work roles and settings should not be viewed in isolation from other important life roles, settings, and events and should be considered in the context of the total span of human development.

Jones and others (1972) proposed that the concept of career should encompass patterns of personal choices and their relationship to the person's life style; components of career need to include occupation, education, personal and social behaviors, learning how to learn, citizenship, and leisure time activities.

Related entries: CAREER DEVELOPMENT; SUPER, DONALD E.

References

Jones, G. B., Hamilton, J. A., Granchow, L. H., Helliwell, C. B., & Wolff, J. M. (1972). *Planning, developing and field testing career guidance programs.* Palo Alto, CA: American Institutes for Research.

Jordaan, J. P. (1974). Life stages as organizing modes of career development. In E. L. Herr (Ed.), *Vocational guidance and human development.* Boston: Houghton Mifflin.

Super, D. E., & Bohn, M. J., Jr. (1970). *Occupational psychology.* Belmont, CA: Wadsworth.

M

MANIA. A mood disorder typically involving a variety of symptoms but most characteristically an elevated, euphoric mood ranging in severity from relatively normal states of happiness or pleasure to "delirious" mania in which the sufferer experiences paranoid delusions and is likely to respond aggressively toward other people or property (Klerman, 1978, p. 259).

According to the *Diagnostic and Statistical Manual of Mental Disorders* (Third Edition, Revised [DSM-III-R]) of the American Psychiatric Association, the presence of a manic episode or a less virulent hypomanic episode is the essential feature of mood disturbance identified as bipolar disorder. Bipolar disorder involves a history of at least one episode of mania (or hypomania) and one or more major depressive episodes. The DSM-III-R defines a manic episode as a distinct period during which the predominant mood is either elevated, expansive, or irritable. The disturbance is sufficiently severe to cause marked impairment in occupational functioning or in usual social activities or relationships with others, or to require hospitalization to prevent harm to self or others. The associated symptoms include inflated self-esteem or grandiosity (which may be delusional), decreased need for sleep, pressure of speech, flight of ideas, distractibility, increased involvement in goal-directed activity, psychomotor agitation, and excessive involvement in pleasurable activities which have a high potential for painful consequences that the person often does not recognize (pp. 214–215).

Related entries: DEPRESSION; *DIAGNOSTIC AND STATISTICAL MANUAL OF MENTAL DISORDERS*—THIRD EDITION, REVISED.

References

American Psychiatric Association (1987). *Diagnostic and statistical manual of mental disorders* (3rd ed., revised). Washington, DC: American Psychiatric Association.

Klerman, G. (1978). Affective disorders. In A. Nicholi (Ed.), *Harvard guide to modern psychiatry* (pp. 253–281). Cambridge, MA: Belknap Press.

MANN'S TIME-LIMITED PSYCHOTHERAPY. A form of short-term psychoanalytically oriented psychotherapy developed by James Mann (1973).

After two to four evaluative sessions to determine the suitability of psychotherapy, Mann recommends that clients be seen for twelve weeks. There is normally only one forty-five to fifty minute session each week. Mann considers the fixed and limited number of sessions in itself to be a curative factor. Because of the limited time for therapy, clients must have high ego strength and the ability to work through a central issue. Although Mann's approach incorporates traditional psychoanalytic methods, the goal is to resolve some acute problem in the client's life by directly cultivating insight rather than focusing on transference, interpretation, or extensive analysis of ego defenses to cultivate insight.

Related entry: PSYCHOANALYTIC COUNSELING.

References

Mann, J. (1973). *Time-limited psychotherapy.* Cambridge, MA: Harvard University Press.
Mann, J., & Goldman, R. (1982). *A casebook in time-limited psychotherapy.* New York: McGraw-Hill.
Sifneos, P. (1978). Patient management. In A. Nicholi (Ed.), *Harvard guide to modern psychiatry* (pp. 481–494). Cambridge, MA: Belknap Press.
Ursano, R., & Silberman, E. (1988). Individual psychotherapies. In J. Talbott, R. Hales, & S. Yudofsky (Eds.), *Textbook of psychiatry* (pp. 855–890). Washington, DC: American Psychiatric Press.

MARATHON. A form of encounter group that meets for an extended period of time (usually twelve to forty-eight hours) without interruption to facilitate the lowering of group participants' defenses.

A group counseling approach that was very popular in the 1960s, its goal is to penetrate defenses to a more honest and genuine level. The marathon encounter is more a technique than an approach. It is feasible to use any number of counseling approaches in the marathon setting, but Fritz Perl's Gestalt therapy has probably been most frequently used in this context. Critics charge that marathon sessions do not give group members sufficient time to assimilate their insights or to integrate their newfound understanding into enduring benefits.

Related entries: ENCOUNTER GROUPS; GROUP COUNSELING.

Reference

Rosenbaum, M. (1976). Group psychotherapies. In B. Wolman (Ed.), *Therapist's handbook: Treatment methods of mental disorders* (pp. 163–183). New York: Van Nostrand Reinhold.

MARRIAGE COUNSELING. Conjoint marital counseling involves counseling both spouses together, while concurrent marital counseling involves separate counseling for each spouse.

A marital schism is a situation in a marriage that results in poor relationships and psychological separation, usually due to the inability of one of the marital partners to break a tie with the parental home. Another problem dealt with in marriage counseling is a marital skew or a marital relationship characterized by one spouse's excessive dominance.

Rational emotive therapy (RET) is used extensively in marriage counseling. Usually marital partners are seen together. The counselor listens to their complaints and tries to show them that even if the complaints are justified, upsetness is not. The marital partners learn to apply RET principles so as to minimize incompatibilities and maximize compatibilities (Ellis, 1975; Ellis & Dryden, 1987).

Marriage counseling also includes those who use Adlerian approaches (Pew & Pew, 1972). Married couples' group therapy and married couples' study groups provide two settings for marriage counseling. Phillips and Corsini (1982) have written a self-help book to be used by couples who are experiencing difficulties in their marital relationships.

The central focus in behavioral approaches to marriage counseling is to help partners learn more positive and productive means of achieving desired behavioral changes in one another (Jacobson & Margolin, 1979).

For evaluating marital counseling, Lazarus (1981) has developed a twelve-term marital satisfaction questionnaire that pinpoints areas of distress. He recommends using this instrument to assess improvements in marital happiness.

Related entries: AMERICAN ASSOCIATION FOR MARRIAGE AND FAMILY THERAPY (AAMFT); DYSFUNCTIONAL FAMILY; FAMILY COUNSELING.

References

Ellis, A. (1975). *How to live with a neurotic* (Rev. ed.). North Hollywood, CA: Wilshire Books.

Ellis, A., & Dryden, W. (1987). *The practice of rational emotive therapy.* New York: Springer.

Jacobson, N., & Margolin, G. (1979). *Marital therapy.* New York: Brunner/Mazel.

Lazarus, A. A. (1981). *The practice of multimodal therapy.* Baltimore: Johns Hopkins University Press.

Pew, M. L., & Pew, W. (1972). Adlerian marriage counseling. *Journal of Individual Psychology, 298,* 192–202.

Phillips, C. E., & Corsini, R. J. (1982). *Give in or give up.* Chicago: Nelson Hall.

MASLOW, ABRAHAM (1908–1970). In many respects, Maslow literally developed the field of humanistic psychology. Although he did not coin the terms *self-actualization* or *humanistic psychology,* he did a great deal to popularize them.

He was born in Brooklyn, New York, and received a Ph.D. in comparative psychology at the University of Wisconsin. From 1951 until 1970 he was Chair of the Psychology Department at Brandeis University. In 1968 he was elected President of the American Psychological Association.

Among his books are *Motivation and Personality* (1954), *Toward a Psy-*

chology of Being (1962), *Religions, Values and Peak Experiences* (1964), and *The Farther Reaches of Human Nature* (1971).

In contrast to those of many other psychologists, Maslow's conclusions about human nature were based on the study of "normal" and "supernormal" personalities.

Related entry: HUMANISTIC APPROACHES TO COUNSELING.

References

Maslow, A. (1954, 1970). *Motivation and personality.* New York: Harper and Row.
Maslow, A. (1971). *The farther reaches of human nature.* New York: Viking.

MASOCHISM. Generally masochism refers to pleasure derived from the experience of pain. Most commonly conceived in sexual terms as sexual masochism.

Defined in the *Diagnostic and Statistical Manual of Mental Disorders* (Third Edition—Revised [DSM-III-R]) as "recurrent intense sexual urges and sexually arousing fantasies involving the act (real, not simulated) of being humiliated, beaten, bound, or otherwise made to suffer" (p. 287). To be diagnosed, a person must either act on these urges or at least feel "marked distress" over them for a minimum period of six months.

Freud considered masochism to be evidence of the death instinct, *thanatos.* Erich Fromm, a neo-Freudian, conceptualized masochism as the individual's neurotic attempt to build up a weak ego by inflicting pain and suffering on a figure perceived as authoritative and powerful (Meissner, 1978, p. 130)

Related entry: DEFENSE MECHANISMS.

References

American Psychiatric Association (1987). *Diagnostic and statistical manual of mental disorders* (3rd ed. revised). Washington, DC: American Psychiatric Association.
Meissner, W. M. (1978). Theories of personality. In M. Nicholi (Ed.), *Harvard guide to modern psychiatry* (pp. 115–145). Cambridge, MA: Harvard University Press.

MAY, ROLLO (b. 1909). He has championed the interdisciplinary nature of existentialism through his books, which include theological, philosophical, and clinical references.

Existential psychotherapy was introduced in the United States in 1958 with the publication of *Existence: A New Dimension in Psychiatry and Psychology,* edited by Rollo May, Ernest Angel, and Henri Ellenberger.

He first lived in Ohio, and as a young child moved to Michigan with his five brothers and a sister. In 1938 he received a master of divinity degree from Union Theological Seminary, and in 1949 he received a Ph.D. in clinical psychology from Columbia University.

May believes that counseling should be aimed at helping people discover the meaning of their lives and the problems of being. His popular book *Love and*

Will (1969) reflected his own personal struggles with love and intimate relationships. He has authored or coauthored fourteen books.

Related entries: DASEIN ANALYSIS; EXISTENTIAL COUNSELING; EXISTENTIALISM.

References

May, R. (Ed.) (1961). *Existential psychology.* New York: Random House.
May, R., & Yalom, I. (1989). Existential psychotherapy. In R. J. Corsini & D. Wedding (Eds.), *Current psychotherapies* (4th ed., pp. 363–402). Itasca, IL: F. E. Peacock.

MEDIATION. The process by which a counselor facilitates an agreement between two or more disputing parties (Witty, 1980). This is a cooperative approach to conflict resolution that emphasizes "Where do we go from here?" rather than finding fault.

Mediation processes focus on self-disclosure, empathy, self-imposed decisions, and creating alternatives. Chandler (1985) described several principles upon which mediation should be based:

1. Participants must be willing to discuss their concerns with each other.

2. Participants should be willing to express their personal wants and needs.

3. The process should stress mutual agreements and emphasize the importance of maintaining the relationship between the participants.

4. The relationship between the participants should be relatively egalitarian.

5. Agreements should be written in the participants' own words and accurately as well as specifically note the specific items about which they have agreed upon.

6. The process should involve joint advocacy, enhance self-worth of the participants, and allow for responsible self-determination.

Mediators must be perceived as credible and competent by the participants in the process. Generally, they should structure the mediation process by establishing a cooperative tone, setting the rules, obtaining commitments to the process, and providing an overview of the stages in the process. During the early stages of mediation, or the "forum phase," the mediator explores the issues and determines whether the conflict can be handled appropriately through mediation (Chandler, 1985). After this, the mediator begins information gathering activities which might involve both parties at the same time or meetings with one party at a time.

In the strategic planning phase of mediation, all information and facts are reviewed. The history of the conflict is also reviewed. If some issues are unclear to the mediator, the participants may be asked to clarify or provide additional information. Toward the end of this phase, the mediator begins to develop a plan of action through active consultation with the participants.

The problem-solving phase, according to Chandler (1985), involves defining potential solutions to the conflict. The resulting agreements should be written documents that the participants develop for themselves and the content of which is their responsibility.

Related entry: CONSULTATION.

References

Chandler, S. M. (1985). Mediation: Conjoint problem-solving. *Social Work,* July–August, 346–349.

Hershenson, D. B., & Power, P. W. (1987). *Mental health counseling: Theory and practice.* New York: Pergamon.

Witty, C. (1980). *Mediation and society: Conflict management in Lebanon.* New York: Academic.

MEDITATION. A form of mental exercise involving the intentional focus of attention or emptying the mind; it produces such beneficial effects as improved mental and physical health and fosters spiritual development.

The techniques and form of meditation vary so dramatically that Smith (1975) refers to meditation as "a family of mental exercises" and notes diverse techniques such as "sitting still and counting breaths, attending to a repeated thought, or focusing on virtually any simple external or internal stimulus" (p. 558).

Traditionally, meditation has been regarded by religious traditions as a method of deepening and enhancing spiritual insight. Perhaps Charles Tart's (1975) work provides the richest psychological theory on meditative states and their relationship to ordinary consciousness. He regards meditation and meditative states as forms of altered states of consciousness (ASCs). Each unique state of consciousness (SOC) can be considered a discrete state of consciousness (d-SOC), and if the d-SOC differs markedly from our ordinary awareness then it can be regarded as a discrete altered state of consciousness (d-ASC). Thus, meditation can be thought of as a variety of techniques for systematically inducing specific d-ASCs (Tart, 1975, p. 14).

Related entry: RELIGION.

References

Smith, J. (1975). Meditation as psychotherapy: A review of the literature. *Psychological Bulletin, 82,* 558–564.

Tart, C. (1975). Science, states of consciousness, and spiritual experiences: The need for state-specific sciences. In C. Tart (Ed.), *Transpersonal psychologies* (pp. 9–58). New York: Harper and Row.

MENTAL AGE. An age-equivalent score that was used in the Binet-Simon scales. This developmental index of cognitive functioning was also used later in scoring the 1916 and 1937 versions of the Stanford-Binet. The mental age (MA) typically reflects the raw score for the majority of a particular age group on a test. A ratio IQ was determined by dividing the MA by the subject's chronological age (CA) and multiplying the result by 100.

Some psychometricians regard the MA as a better measure of intellectual functioning than standard score IQs. However, the MA as a measure of mental ability cannot be easily interpreted in a straightforward manner because the variability of these scores differs at different ages. In most developmental tasks, there will be greater unit differences between 4 and 6 year olds than between 14 and 16 year equivalent scores. Two children with the same MA may have the same raw score on the test, but these children are probably different in their actual strengths and weaknesses. Diagnostically, the pattern of responses is more meaningful than MA or age-equivalent scores.

Related entry: INTELLIGENCE TESTS.

References

Anastasi, A. (1976). *Psychological testing* (4th ed.). New York: Macmillan.
Sattler, J. (1990). *Assessment of children* (3rd ed.). San Diego: Jerome M. Sattler.

MENTAL HEALTH COUNSELING. The provision of professional counseling services, involving the principles of psychotherapy, human development, learning theory, group dynamics, and the etiology of mental illness and dysfunctional behavior, to individuals, couples, families, and groups for the purposes of treating psychopathology and promoting optimal mental health (NACMHC Board, 1985).

Mental health counselors often deal with adult clients, although some do work with children and adolescents. Many of them also espouse a developmental rather than a disease perspective and focus on assessing client strengths and on using psychoeducational approaches to helping clients overcome their deficits. Mental health counselors work closely with health care providers and frequently consult with physicians regarding medication or even hospitalization of clients.

When the American Mental Health Counseling Association was founded in 1976, many members worked in community mental health centers. However, by 1989 approximately 46 percent of the members were employed as private practitioners.

In 1986 the American Mental Health Counseling Association had 10,000 members. A major goal of this group since its inception has been to allow mental health counselors to be viewed as service providers. A critical step in trying to achieve their goal was the development of a professional certification process. In February 1979 the National Academy of Certified Clinical Mental Health Counselors first administered a certificate examination for mental health counselors. Later, they developed a more elaborate set of criteria, including a taped sample of clinical work accompanied by a critique.

In 1981 Florida passed a counselor licensure law that used the title "licensed mental health counselor" rather than "licensed professional counselor" as being protected by law. In 1989 seven of the thirty-two states with counselor licensure laws also used as the protected title "licensed mental health counselor."

References

Brooks, D. K., Jr. (1991). Mental health counseling. In D. Capuzzi & D. R. Gross (Eds.), *Introduction to counseling: Perspectives for the 1990s* (pp. 250–270). Boston: Allyn and Bacon.

National Academy of Certified Mental Health Counselors (1985). *Definition of mental health counseling*. Alexandria, VA: National Academy of Certified Mental Health Counselors.

META-COGNITION. A person's awareness, knowledge, and ability to apply his/her cognitive skills to the various processes of human cognition, including memory, learning, thought, and problem solving.

Campione, Brown, and Ferrara (1982) identify two aspects of meta-cognition. The first consists of knowledge about the cognitive processes needed to solve a particular task. Problem solvers must have conscious awareness of their executive functions as evidenced by their ability to verbalize their knowledge. The second aspect of meta-cognition is the ability of problem solvers intentionally to regulate or guide their skills, such as planning, monitoring, checking, and so on, to perform a specific task effectively.

Related entries: RATIONAL-EMOTIVE COUNSELING; SELF-INSTRUCTIONAL TRAINING.

References

Bourne, L., Dominowski, R., & Loftus, E. (1979). *Cognitive processes*. Englewood Cliffs, NJ: Prentice-Hall.

Campione, J., Brown, A., & Ferrara, R. (1982). Mental retardation and intelligence. In R. J. Sternberg (Ed.), *Handbook of human intelligence* (pp. 392–490). New York: Cambridge University Press.

MEXICAN AMERICANS. Counselors should be aware of certain characteristics of verbal and nonverbal communication when counseling Mexican American clients individually or in families.

Mexican Americans have a concept of *personalismo* that denotes a preference for personal contact and individualized attention in their social relationships. They expect less physical distance and more frequent physical contact than do Anglos (see LeVine & Padilla, 1980). Counselors may want to stand close to Mexican American clients, exchange warm handshakes, and perhaps even place a hand on their client's shoulder in order to reduce anxiety. Counselors also need to be sensitive to the tendency of Mexican American clients to want to disclose personal information very slowly. Falicov (1982) suggests that client self-disclosure may be facilitated when the counselor becomes a philosopher of life through storytelling, anecdotes, humor, analogies, and proverbs.

In family counseling, the counselor may want to search for strengths and praise the family's dignity in order to develop a positive therapeutic alliance. Interpretations of dysfunction or direct confrontations may tend to increase insecurity and be seen as disapproval rather than as a stimulus for change. In the early stages of counseling, a focus on parent-child interactions may be more readily accepted than a focus on marital issues or on issues concerning the parents' families of origin.

Related entries: CULTURE; MULTICULTURAL COUNSELING; NATIVE AMERICANS; PREJUDICE.

References

Falicov, C. J. (1982). Mexican families. In M. McGoldrick, J. K. Pearce, & J. Giordana (Eds.), *Ethnicity and family therapy.* New York: Guilford.

LeVine, E. S., & Padilla, A. M. (1980). *Crossing cultures in therapy: Pluralistic counseling for the Hispanic.* Pacific Grove, CA: Brooks/Cole.

Ramirez, O. (1989). Mexican American children and adolescents. In J. T. Gibbs, L. N. Huang, & Associates (Eds.), *Children of color: Psychological interventions with minority youth* (pp. 224–250). San Francisco: Jossey-Bass.

MILIEU THERAPY. A counseling approach designed for the treatment of the severely mentally ill in institutional settings such as hospital-based psychiatric wards, state hospitals, or private psychiatric facilities.

This approach seeks to build on the therapeutic opportunities generated by interpersonal interaction and community involvement. Milieu therapy was first conceived in 1929 by Ernst Simmell, who sought to create a supportive institutionally based intervention for schizophrenics that contrasted with their home environments. H. S. Sullivan, however, was the first to set up a milieu program, in Baltimore in 1931. After World War II, the approach became widespread, largely in response to the perceived neglect of the state hospital system.

Milieu therapy stressed open communication and power sharing among patients and staff. Every effort was made to deepen patients' insight into their problems through extensive analysis of individual and group interactions. Patients were encouraged to assume responsibility for themselves and to take an active role in the life of the community. A wide variety of activities, both recreational and therapeutic, is provided to facilitate participation. Most communities also encourage patient governance, although the basic rules and expectations are initially established by staff. Since the development of psychotropic medication, most programs have an open door policy where patients voluntarily participate in treatment.

Black, Yates and Andreasen (1988) describe a number of therapeutic conditions that research suggests will maximize the effectiveness of Milieu treatments. These factors include: small units, short length of stay, a high staff-to-patient ratio, low staff turnover, a low percentage of psychotic patients, democratic decision making with clear lines of authority, low levels of perceived anger and aggression, high perceived levels of support, and the use of a practical problem-solving approach.

References

Black, D., Yates, W., & Andreasen, N. (1988). Schizophrenia, schizophreniform disorder, and delusional (paranoid) disorder. In J. Talbott, R. Hales, & S. Yudofsky (Eds.),

Textbook of psychiatry (pp. 357–402). Washington, DC: American Psychiatric Press.

Day, M., & Semrad, E. (1978). Schizophrenic reactions. In A. Nicholi (Ed.), *Harvard guide to modern psychiatry* (pp. 199–252). Cambridge, MA: Belknap Press.

Schwartz, A., & Swartzburb, M. (1976). Hospital care. In B. Wolman (Ed.), *Therapist's handbook: Treatment methods of mental disorders* (pp. 199–226). New York: Van Nostrand Reinhold.

MINNESOTA MULTIPHASIC PERSONALITY INVENTORY (MMPI). This test was first published in 1943 as an objective personality inventory that would provide an efficient way of making a psychodiagnostic evaluation.

The test utilized empirical methods to identify items that differentiated criterion groups of normal persons and clinical subjects or psychiatric patients. This procedure yielded an inventory with four validity scales and ten basic clinical or personality scales. Starke Hathaway and Jovian McKinley accumulated a collection of self-reference statements from textbooks, psychological reports, and personality tests and questionnaires. They administered this original set of items to the following clinical groups: hypochondriasis, depression, hysteria, psychopathic deviant, paranoia, psychasthenia, schizophrenia, and hypomania, and then did item analyses to determine those statements that differentiated members of a particular clinical group from samples of normals. Later the Masculinity-Femininity Scale was developed to distinguish heterosexual and homosexual males, and the Social Introversion Scale was developed to distinguish socially retiring females from those who were quite active in extracurricular collegiate activities. This scale was subsequently generalized to males.

This test may be administered at a computer terminal, and the results, including an interpretation of the protocol, are quickly available to the counselor. Raw scores on the MMPI are transformed to T scores with a mean of 50 and a standard deviation of 10. Profiles may be referred to as a two-point code indicating the scales with the two highest T scores. Generally, this test is used with persons having a sixth grade reading level who are 16 years of age or older. With adolescents, it is important to remember that both their normal and abnormal profiles differ from those of adults on the MMPI.

Related entries: PERSONALITY THEORY; TRAIT AND FACTOR COUNSELING.

References

Graham, J. R. (1987). *The MMPI: A practical guide* (2nd ed.). New York: Oxford University Press.

Hathaway, S., & McKinley, J. (1967). *The Minnesota Multiphasic Personality Inventory manual.* New York: Psychological Corporation.

Hathaway, S. R., & McKinley, J. C. (1983). *The Minnesota Multiphasic Personality Inventory manual.* New York: Psychological Corporation.

MITWELT. This term refers to the manner in which a person relates to the world socially and through dealing with others.

The term, used in existential counseling, may also apply to the age that people live in, their times, their generation, and their contemporaries. From the view of existential counseling, it is necessary to understand the phenomenological world of the client, which involves community or the world of other humans.

Related entries: EIGENWELT; EXISTENTIAL COUNSELING; UMWELT.

Reference

May, R., & Yalom, I. (1989). Existential psychotherapy. In R. J. Corsini & D. Wedding (Eds.), *Current psychotherapies* (4th ed., pp. 363–402). Itasca, IL: F. E. Peacock.

MULTICULTURAL COUNSELING. Two or more persons with different ways of perceiving their environment working together in a helping relationship (Pedersen, 1988). The assumption is that all counseling can be considered multicultural because cultural differences in world views can and do influence the processes and outcomes of communication with any client (Pedersen, 1988).

Multicultural counseling has tended to emphasize issues that bear on the effectiveness of counseling clients who are not Anglo or white. However, Smith and Vasquez (1985) caution that it is important to distinguish individual and group differences that are tied to ethnic and cultural factors from those that are associated with deprived economic status. A failure to do so may lead counselors to mistakenly view their client's reaction to poverty and discrimination as a reflection of cultural and ethnic status.

About 50 percent of so-called minority group members who initiate counseling terminate after one session (Sue & Sue, 1981). Shipp (1983) has argued that the tendency for African American clients to terminate early can be attributed to the culturally insensitive treatment that they receive. A primary concern in multicultural counseling in the United States has to do with the dominant white cultural values in society and the consequences for persons from the underrepresented populations (Katz, 1985). White culture in the United States is seen as a synthesis of beliefs, values, and norms that reflect white European ethnic traditions and does not recognize African American, Hispanic/Latino, Chicano, Native American, and Asian American contributions to the culture.

Sue (1978, 1981) identified the following guidelines for effective multicultural counseling:

1. Counselors need to recognize their own norms and values regarding acceptable and desirable behaviors and how these beliefs influence their attitudes toward clients who have different cultural perspectives.

2. Counselors need to be aware of cultural norms and even biases that are found in different approaches and theories of counseling.

3. Counselors need to understand the different environments in which clients have lived and how they bear upon their experiences.

4. Counselors need to understand the reasons that clients have different world views, and moreover why these divergent perspectives make sense to them.

5. Counselors should be able to frame counseling strategies in such ways that they are credible to clients with different cultural perspectives.

6. Counselors should possess a wide range of beliefs, attitudes, and skills that allow them to form therapeutic relationships with diverse clients.

Related entries: AFRICAN AMERICANS; BLACK RACIAL IDENTITY DEVELOPMENT; CHINESE AMERICANS; CULTURE; MEXICAN AMERICANS; PREJUDICE; SEX-ROLE STEREOTYPES.

References

Katz, J. H. (1985). The sociopolitical nature of counseling. *The Counseling Psychologist, 13,* 615–624.

Pedersen, P. (Ed.) (1985). *Handbook of cross cultural counseling and therapy.* Westport, CT: Greenwood Press.

Pedersen, P. (1988). *A handbook for developing multicultural awareness.* Alexandria, VA: American Association for Counseling and Development.

Shipp, P. L. (1983). Counseling blacks: A group approach. *Personnel and Guidance Journal, 62,* 108–111.

Smith, E. M. J., & Vasquez, M. J. T. (1985). Introduction. *The Counseling Psychologist, 13,* 531–536.

Sue, D. W. (1978). Eliminating cultural oppression in counseling: Toward a general theory. *Journal of Counseling Psychology, 25,* 419–428.

Sue, D. W. (1981). *Counseling the culturally different: Theory and practice.* New York: Wiley.

Sue, D. W., & Sue, D. (1981). Barriers to effective cross-cultural counseling. *Journal of Counseling Psychology, 24,* 420–429.

MULTIMODAL APPROACH TO COUNSELING. This approach uses a wide range of counseling techniques to treat problems across seven dimensions of personality: behavior, affect, sensation, imagery, cognition, interpersonal relationships, and biological factors.

Multimodal counseling assumes that few problems of clients have a single cause or a unitary cure. This approach is defined as technical eclecticism because the counselor uses many techniques drawn from different sources without adopting the theoretical perspectives that underlie them. The goal of multimodal counseling is to come up with the best methods for helping each client rather than to force all clients' problems into the same counseling framework. Counselors plan their treatments for clients after they have constructed individual modality profiles that identify problems and possible treatments, using the BASIC ID. This acronym provides a structure for describing personality in terms of ongoing behaviors, affective processes, sensations, images, cognitions, interpersonal relationships, and biological or somatic processes. Multimodal counseling treats client problems within a given modality as well as the interaction between a specific modality and each of the six others.

While modality profiles list specific problems in each dimension of the BASIC ID, structural profiles provide a quantitative self-rating of the client's tendencies in each of the seven modalities. Using a ten-point scale for each modality, clients rate the extent to which they perceive themselves as doing, feeling, sensing, imagining, thinking, and relating. They also rate their observation and/or practice of health habits. A high D score indicates a health-minded individual. In marriage counseling, spouses may construct their own profiles, estimates of how their spouse sees them, and profiles describing how they see their spouses.

Bridging is a procedure in which the counselor responds to a client in his or her dominant modality before branching off into other dimensions that may ultimately be more productive. This procedure contrasts with challenging or confronting clients who do respond in the preferred modality of the counselor. Tracking refers to the examination of the firing order of the client's different modalities. Some clients generate negative emotions by first dwelling on catastrophic ideas (cognitions), immediately followed by unpleasant mental pictures (images) that lead to tension and heart palpitations (sensations), culminating in withdrawal or avoidance (behavior). This sequence of cognitions, images, sensations, and behaviors (a CISB pattern) may call for different counseling strategies than does a sequence of sensations, cognitions, images, and behavior (an SCIB pattern). Multimodal counselors recommend that counseling techniques be administered in the same sequence as the client's firing order.

Related entry: BASIC ID.

References

Lazarus, A. A. (1985). *Casebook of multimodal therapy.* New York: Guilford.
Lazarus, A. A. (1989). Multimodal therapy. In R. J. Corsini & D. Wedding (Eds.), *Current psychotherapies* (4th ed.). Itasca, IL: F. E. Peacock.

MUSTURBATION. A comic term coined by Albert Ellis, founder of rational-emotive therapy (RET), referring to the irrational thought process of demandingness.

People may persist in the unfounded notion that they must have what they want or face disaster. They fail to recognize that while the desired outcome is desirable, it is usually not necessary. Ellis contended that irrational thought such as musturbation leads to emotional difficulties and life problems. Ellis identified several variations on the "must" theme: the assumptions that one must be successful, be approved of, be treated well, or have an easy life.

Related entries: IRRATIONAL BELIEFS; RATIONAL-EMOTIVE COUNSELING.

References

Ellis, A., & Grieger, R. (1977). *Handbook of rational-emotive therapy.* New York: Springer.

Grieger, R., & Boyd, J. (1989). Rational-emotive approaches. In D. Brown & H. Prout (Eds.), *Counseling and psychotherapy with children and adolescents* (2nd ed., pp. 301–362). Brandon, VT: CPPC.

N

NATIONAL BOARD OF CERTIFIED COUNSELORS. This professional organization administers the National Counselor Examination as part of a national counselor certification process. This examination is used by many state-level counselor credentialing agencies as part of their licensure or registry processes.

In 1982 the National Board of Certified Counselors was established by the American Association for Counseling and Development to develop a generic certification system for counselors. It has since become an independent nonprofit organization that has certified over 18,000 professional counselors.

The National Board of Certified Counselors grants two professional certificates—National Certified Counselor and National Certified Career Counselor. Certified counselors are expected to maintain and renew certification through continuing education, and they must also agree to abide by the Code of Ethics of the National Board of Certified Counselors.

National certified counselors usually hold at least a master's degree in counseling or a closely related field from a regionally accredited university. They must have two years' professional experience as well as supervised experience. They also must pass a written examination. National certified career counselors must hold the National Certified Counselor credential and must have coursework and experience related to career counseling.

Related entries: AMERICAN ASSOCIATION FOR COUNSELING (AAC); COUNSELING.

Reference

National Board of Certified Counselors (1988). *Your guide to the national counselor examination: How to prepare.* Alexandria, VA: National Board for Certified Counselors.

NATIVE AMERICANS. Tribal diversity makes it difficult to generalize about counseling Native Americans. In general, they may prefer to discuss their problems with friends and parents rather than counselors (see Dauphinais, La-Fromboise, & Rowe, 1980).

Problems of Native American high school students are similar to those of Anglo youth. They include concerns about the future, depression, apathy, ways of maintaining good grades, class scheduling problems, and making decisions about school and their future. However, many Native Americans are said to consider mental distress or illness to be an outcome of human weakness or an excuse to avoid the discipline needed to maintain their traditional cultural values.

In general, Native American youth are looking for counselors who understand the practical aspects of their culture and can give them sound advice about their lives. They do not seek counselors who reflect and restate their feelings for the purpose of analysis (Dauphinais, Dauphinais, & Rowe, 1981).

In many cases, counselors may not need to acquire conventional psychological training in order to work effectively with Native American clients. An important aspect of counseling with these youth is to incorporate Native American cultural practices and the social context into treatment.

Shangreaux, Pleskac, and Freeman (1987) have developed an excellent systems intervention program for Native American families. They recommend exercising patience, using self-disclosure to establish trust, allowing time for relationship building by using humor and small talk, and establishing credibility through genuine concern and caring. Drawing, storytelling, or using family models may elicit information about family structure and alliances without being threatening.

Manson, Walker, and Kivlahan (1987) suggest two Native American approaches to counseling that are based on traditional healing practices. The four circles intervention involves the symbolic organization of the important relationships in one's life. Four circles represent a symbolic search for balance in one's relationships. The talking circle intervention resembles conventional group counseling.

Related entries: AFRICAN AMERICANS; ATTNEAVE, CAROLYN; CHINESE AMERICANS; CULTURE; MULTICULTURAL COUNSELING.

References

Dauphinais, P., Dauphinais, L., & Rowe, W. (1981). Effects of race and communication style on Indian perceptions of counselor effectiveness. *Counselor Education and Supervision, 21,* 72–80.

Dauphinais, P., LaFromboise, T. D., & Rowe, W. (1980). Perceived problems and sources of help for American Indian students. *Counselor Education and Supervision, 20,* 37–44.

Manson, S. M., Walker, B. D., & Kivlahan, O. R. (1987). Psychiatric assessment and treatment of American Indians and Alaska Natives. *Hospital and Community Psychiatry, 38,* 165–173.

Shangreaux, V., Pleskac, D., & Freeman, W. (1987). *Strengthening Native American families: A family systems model curriculum.* Lincoln, NE: Lincoln Indian Center.

NEUROLINGUISTICS PROGRAMMING. A communication model that assumes that human experiences are encoded in an individualized series of representational systems that correspond to the visual, auditory, and kinesthetic modalities. Most persons are considered to have a preferred representational system or modality that they use for encoding their daily experiences.

A counselor's awareness of a client's preferred representational system is supposed to facilitate the development of rapport and trust and may even provide useful diagnostic and treatment information. The counselor identifies a client's preferred modality by: (a) listening for the client's uses of visual, auditory, and kinesthetic predicates, (b) monitoring the client's eye movements, and/or (c) asking the client's opinions regarding preferred modalities.

References

Bandler, R., & Grindner, J. (1975). *The structure of magic I.* Palo Alto, CA: Science and Behavior Books.

Bandler, R., & Grindner, J. (1976). *The structure of magic II.* Palo Alto, CA: Science and Behavior Books.

O

OCCUPATIONAL INFORMATION. The provision of relevant information about occupations in career counseling. The goal is to increase client knowledge of the world of work, including different job duties and tasks, employment opportunities, lines of advancement, and future employment trends.

If the client's problem is indecision or unrealism, then the presentation of occupational information may be appropriate. However, when clients are indecisive and anxious, then decision-making processes may become less effective with the presentation of new occupational information (Crites, 1981).

Three strategies may be used for imparting occupational information to clients:

1. Counselors can present the information to their clients in an interview;
2. Counselors can educate their clients regarding how to gather information outside the interview situation; and
3. Counselors can utilize a computerized occupational information system as an adjunct to career counseling.

In all three cases, it is necessary for clients to be able to discuss the meaning of occupational information for their own career decisions. The occupational information test of the Career Maturity Inventory can be used to assess clients' knowledge of the world of work (Crites, 1973, 1978).

Related entry: VOCATIONAL GUIDANCE.

References

Crites, J. O. (1973, 1978). *Theory and research handbook for the Career Maturity Inventory.* Monterey, CA: CTB/McGraw-Hill.

Crites, J. O. (1981). *Career counseling: Models, methods and materials.* New York: McGraw-Hill.

OEDIPUS COMPLEX. A proposition in psychoanalytic counseling that children from about three to six years of age desire sexual relations with the opposite-sex parent.

The desire is repressed and is part of the unconscious. In the case of females, this condition is called the Electra complex.

These sexual desires are evident during the phallic stage of psychosexual development. The conflict is over the object of children's sexual desires.

Related entries: DREIKURS, RUDOLPH; ID; PHALLIC STAGE; PSYCHO-ANALYTIC COUNSELING.

References

Baker, E. L. (1985). Psychoanalysis and psychoanalytic psychotherapy. In S. J. Lynn & J. P. Garske (Eds.), *Contemporary psychotherapies: Models and methods* (pp. 19–67). Columbus, OH: Charles Merrill.

Prochaska, J. O. (1979). *Systems of psychotherapy: A transactional analysis.* Homewood, IL: Dorsey.

ORAL STAGE. In psychoanalytic theory, it is the first stage of psychosexual development and extends from birth to about eighteen months. It is a time in which most libidinal gratification occurs through biting, sucking, and oral contacts.

With deprivation, a child can be fixated at the oral stage, with energies directed primarily toward finding oral gratification. In the case of overindulgence, a child can also be fixated at the oral stage, but with his or her energies directed toward trying to repeat and maintain such gratifying conditions. Fixation of either type can lead to the development of an oral personality that may include the following bipolar traits: optimism-pessimism, gullibility-suspiciousness, cockiness–self-belittlement, manipulativeness-passivity, and admiration-envy.

Related entries: PHALLIC STAGE; PSYCHOANALYTIC COUNSELING; PSYCHOSEXUAL STAGES OF DEVELOPMENT.

References

Arlow, J. A. (1989). Psychoanalysis. In R. J. Corsini & D. Wedding (Eds.), *Contemporary psychotherapies* (4th ed., pp. 19–62). Itasca, IL: F. E. Peacock.

Corsini, R. J., & Wedding, D. (Eds.) (1989). *Current psychotherapies* (4th ed., p. 596). Itasca, IL: F. E. Peacock.

ORGONE ENERGY. The primordial cosmic energy; universally present and demonstrable visually, thermically, electroscopically, and by means of Geiger-Müeller counters.

Wilhelm Reich believed that understanding the orgone or universal life energy was the key not only to psychiatry but to many of the physical sciences as well. He held that the goal of psychiatric treatment was mobilization of the orgone energy in the organism, and the liberation of biophysical emotions from muscular and character armorings. The goal was to establish, if possible, orgiastic potency, which was considered the capacity for total abandonment to the flow of orgone energy during orgasm, which Reich asserted was impossible for neurotic persons.

Although Reich died in the federal penitentiary in Lewisburg, Pennsylvania, in 1957 after being convicted of criminal contempt for refusing to defend himself against claims of quackery by the Food and Drug Administration, he had a long career as a distinguished psychoanalytic theoretician and therapist. Reich, who received his medical degree in 1922 from the University of Vienna, was one of the select group in Freud's Vienna Psychoanalytic Society. In 1933 Reich was forced to leave Germany with Hitler's assumption of power; by 1939 he had come to the United States, where he joined the faculty of the New School for Social Research in New York City. He founded both the Orgone Institute in New York and the Wilhelm Reich Foundation on a 200 acre farm in Maine named "Orgonon" (Reich, 1969, pp. 3–6).

Today only a small number of scientists embrace Reich's claims about orgone energy, but his contributions to psychoanalytic thought continue to be widely recognized. In particular, the Reichian notion of character structure and character analysis has been influential. Character armor was thought of as a defensive psychic structure that protected the ego internally from instinctive urges and externally from social-emotional pressures. Ultimately, the emotional armoring is reflected physically in rigid and inflexible posture that blocks the flow of orgone energy through the organism. Thus, neurotic individuals whose character armor is more rigid are more debilitated than normal persons, whose mental and physical armoring is flexible (Meissner, 1978, p. 127).

References

Meissner, W. (1978). Theories of personality. In A. Nicholi (Ed.), *Harvard guide to modern psychiatry* (pp. 115–146). Cambridge, MA: Belknap Press.

Reich, W. (1945). *Character-analysis: Principles and technique for psychoanalysts in practice and training.* New York: Orgone Institute Press.

Reich, W. (1969). *Wilhelm Reich: Selected writings: An introduction to orgonomy.* New York: Noonday Press.

P

PARAPROFESSIONALS. A category of mental health workers who provide direct services to clients (including counseling) to supplement the services of professional counselors.

Paraprofessionals receive special training related to counseling and client advocacy. They provide assistance to clients in the form of support, and they make referrals as deemed necessary. In all cases, paraprofessionals are expected to be under the supervision of professional counselors.

Reference

Macht, L. (1978). Community psychiatry. In A. Nicholi (Ed.), *Harvard guide to modern psychiatry* (pp. 627–649). Cambridge, MA: Belknap Press.

PARENT EGO STATE. The controlling, limit setting, and rule making part of the personality. The parent ego state contains "shoulds" and "oughts." It expresses one's value system and is nurturing as well as controlling.

Steiner (1974) differentiates between the Nurturing Parent and the Pig Parent. The Nurturing Parent acts out of genuine concern for others and provides support or protection when needed. The warm, fatherly, but firm policeman is an example of such a parent. The Pig Parent acts out of anger, fear of others, and an irrational need to control. This type of parent engenders fear and hatred in others.

The parent ego state is basically made up of behaviors and attitudes that are copied from parents or authority figures. When the parent is in control, people use controlling words like "should," "ought," "must," "better not," or "you will be sorry." They may point their fingers or stand impatiently with their hands on their hips. In ambiguous situations, the parent ego state may provide the best basis for decision making.

Related entries: ADULT EGO STATE; BERNE, ERIC; CHILD EGO STATE; EGO; EGO STATES; EGOGRAM; TRANSACTIONAL ANALYSIS.

References

Dusay, J. M., & Dusay, K. M. (1989). Transactional analysis. In R. J. Corsini & D. Wedding (Eds.), *Current psychotherapies* (4th ed., pp. 405–453). Itasca, IL: F. E. Peacock.
Steiner, C. (1974). *Scripts people live.* New York: Grove.

PARSONS, FRANK (1854–1908). Parsons is considered to have founded the guidance movement when he established the Boston Vocation Bureau in 1908.

Frank Parsons received his education in civil engineering at Cornell University in Ithaca, New York. Before taking a teaching position in the public schools, he was employed by the railroad. All during his lifetime he was a tireless social reformer. He argued the advantages of municipal ownership of utilities over private ownership, the necessity for government ownership of railroads, and the need for scientific approaches to matching persons and occupations.

Parsons promoted a philosophy of mutualism that held as a basic principle the concept of brotherly love or the ideal of mutual help. Society should evolve to a state where citizens work out of love for society. Parsons was also an advocate of rapid Americanization of immigrants. He believed that social progress would be impossible if the "heroic [Anglo-Saxon] blood" of America was diluted by the "fouled mixture of serfhood pouring in from Europe" (Parsons, 1894, p. 4).

For society to progress, industrial monopolies needed to be controlled and individuals had to be better prepared as workers. He spent a great deal of his life criticizing the free enterprise system and arguing for reform of the city. For him, the city was the major social problem of the future.

Parsons was also concerned about the fact that many unprepared individuals, mostly youth and immigrants, were taking factory jobs because the public school system was too academic and not relevant for the new urban, industrial society. In the Boston Vocation Bureau, Parsons developed "scientific" procedures to help individuals choose a vocation through self-study and learning about the demands of certain occupations. The Vocation Bureau, an adjunct to the Boston Civic Service House, was a settlement house designed to serve the needs of new Jewish, Italian, and Polish citizens.

The staff of the Vocation Bureau counseled anyone who sought their services. However, a majority of their clients were high school students and working boys and girls. Clients were given extensive occupational information, which they needed to study carefully before being advised by a staff counselor, who engaged them in an intensive self-analysis of traits and accomplishments.

Related entries: CAREER COUNSELING; CAREER DEVELOPMENT; *CHOOSING A VOCATION.*

References

Parsons, F. (1894). *Our country's need.* Boston: Privately printed.
Parsons, F. (1909). *Choosing a vocation.* Boston: Houghton Mifflin.
Stephens, W. R. (1970). *Social reform and the origins of vocational guidance.* Washington, DC: National Vocational Guidance Association.

PASTORAL COUNSELING. The application of insights, theories, and techniques of contemporary counseling psychology to pastoral problems. The pastoral counselor assumes that solving more obvious psychological problems of individuals is a prerequisite to solving spiritual problems and to a growth in holiness (Stafford, 1969).

Pastoral counseling is a specific kind of helping relationship within a religious context. Haas (1970) describes pastoral counseling as a helping relationship in which clients can experience themselves more completely and find solutions to their problems with the aid of a counselor who is willing to listen, who responds to feelings and perceptions of clients, and who is able to make interpretations and confront clients when necessary. Pastoral counseling usually involves a series of contacts with clients in which systematic attempts are made to alter the psychological conditions that may be producing distress or disrupted relationships, including those of a spiritual nature.

Pastoral counseling can help clients to increase their abilities to love God, their neighbors, and themselves more fully. This form of counseling is within the heritage of pastoral care or the Christian tradition of helping that is directed toward healing, sustaining, guiding, and reconciling persons whose troubles arise in the context of ultimate concerns. For this reason, pastoral counseling is often viewed as part of the pastoral care mission. Campbell (1966) describes pastoral counseling as "the utilization, by a minister, of a one-to-one or small group relationship to help people handle their problems more adequately and grow toward fulfilling their potentialities. This is achieved by helping them reduce their inner blocks which prevent them from relating in need satisfying ways" (p. 20). As a result of such counseling, clients will be able to handle their problems and responsibilities, continue toward fulfillment of their personhood, and develop constructive relationships. In particular, they will find that their relationships with God are increasingly meaningful and that they are able to be renewal agents in their families, communities, and churches.

Related entries: RELIGION; SPIRITUAL EMERGENCE/EMERGENCY.

References

Campbell, H. J., Jr. (1966). *Basic types of pastoral counseling.* Nashville, Tennessee: Abingdon Press.
Haas, H. J. (1970). *Pastoral counseling with people in distress.* St. Louis: Concordia Publishing.
Stafford, J. W. (1969). Pastoral counseling. In E. Weitzel (Ed.), *Contemporary pastoral counseling* (pp. 1–18). New York: Bruce Publishing.

PERLS, FREDERICK S. (1893–1970). In the 1940s, with Laura Perls, he founded the Gestalt approach to counseling, which teaches a phenomenological method of awareness.

After acquiring the M.D. degree from the University of Berlin in 1916, he served in the German army. He later received training in psychoanalysis in Vienna and practiced in Johannesburg, South Africa.

In 1947 he published his first book, *Ego Hunger and Aggression: A Revision of Freud's Theory and Method.* In 1951 he coauthored with Ralph Hefferline and Paul Goodman a major book entitled *Gestalt Therapy: Excitement and Growth in the Human Personality.*

He came to the United States in 1946 and founded the New York Institute for Gestalt Therapy in 1952. Later, he became associated with the Esalen Institute in Big Sur, California. Perls became the "in" therapist and counselor of the 1960s and early 1970s. His aphorism "You do your thing and I'll do mine" became part of sixties pop culture in the United States.

Related entry: GESTALT COUNSELING.

References

Perls, F. (1947). *Ego hunger and aggression: A revision of Freud's theory and method.* New York: Random House.

Perls, F., Hefferline, R., & Goodman, P. (1951). *Gestalt therapy: Excitement and growth in the human personality.* New York: Julian Press.

PERSONALITY THEORY. Personality theory refers to systematic hypotheses about the nature of the human condition.

Personality theory includes observations of behaviors and theoretical constructs that account for these behaviors. Gordon Allport defined personality as the dynamic organization within an individual of those psychophysical systems that determine his or her unique adjustments to the environment. He stressed the dynamism of human interaction within the environment (see Leibert & Spiegler, 1974). In contrast, Hans Eysenck took a dispositional approach in defining personality. He viewed personality as a more or less stable and enduring organization of a person's character, temperament, intellect, and physique which determines that person's unique adjustment to the environment (see Leibert & Spiegler, 1974).

Rychlak (1973) said that a good theory of personality must answer four major questions. The first is, What is the structure of personality? The second involves motivation. How is the person motivated to action through the operation of the hypothesized structures? Next is the temporal question, How does the structure change over time? How this question is answered often becomes a developmental feature of the theory. Finally, there is the problem of individual differences. How does the theory account for the predictability of certain traits and the variation of individuals on these common traits?

Related entries: MINNESOTA MULTIPHASIC PERSONALITY INVEN-

TORY (MMPI); PROJECTIVE PERSONALITY TESTS; SIXTEEN PERSON-
ALITY FACTOR QUESTIONNAIRE.

References

Liebert, R., & Spiegler, M. (1974). *Personality: Strategies for the study of man* (Rev.
    ed.). Homewood, IL: Dorsey.
Rychlak, J. (1973). *Introduction to personality and psychotherapy: A theory-construction
    approach.* Boston: Houghton Mifflin.

PHALLIC STAGE. In psychoanalytic theory, this is the third stage of psychosexual development, extending from three to seven years of age. It is a time
in which libidinal gratification occurs through direct experience with the geni-
tals. There is a repressed desire to possess the parent of the opposite sex and to
replace the parent of the same sex.

In males this repressed desire is called the Oedipus complex. In females it is
called the Electra complex.

Overrejection and overindulgence can both lead to fixation at the phallic stage
and the development of a personality that includes the following bipolar traits:
vanity–self-hatred, pride-humility, stylishness-plainness, flirtatiousness-shyness,
gregariousness-isolation, and brashness-bashfulness. A major defense used by
these persons is apt to be repression.

Related entries: ANAL STAGE; GENITAL STAGE; ORAL STAGE;
PSYCHOANALYTIC COUNSELING; PSYCHOSEXUAL STAGES OF
DEVELOPMENT.

References

Arlow, J. A. (1989). Psychoanalysis. In R. J. Corsini & D. Wedding (Eds.), *Contempo-
    rary psychotherapies* (4th ed., pp. 19–62). Itasca, IL: F. E. Peacock.
Corsini, R. J., & Wedding, D. (Eds.) (1989). *Current psychotherapies* (4th ed., p. 597).
    Itasca, IL: F. E. Peacock.

PHENOMENOLOGY. A philosophical school founded by Edmund Husserl.
He argued that humans do not experience the objective world but instead construct a subjective or phenomenal world.

Husserl has been called the "father of phenomenology" despite the fact that
Georg Wilhelm Hegel was actually the first philosopher to take a position self-
described as phenomenological. The subjective or psychological was considered
the boundary between ourselves and the "real" world.

Phenomenology provides the philosophical and epistemological rationale for
person-centered counseling, existential counseling, Gestalt counseling, and the
psychology of personal constructs. Clients are assumed to have constructed
views of reality to which they respond. These humanistic approaches to counseling are primarily interested in reality as seen by their clients, rather than
reality as an objective condition.

Related entry: CLIENT-CENTERED COUNSELING.

References

Liebert, R., & Spiegler, M. (1974). *Personality: Strategies for the study of man* (Rev. ed.). Homewood, IL: Dorsey.

Rychlak, J. (1973). *Introduction to personality and psychotherapy: A theory-construction approach.* Boston: Houghton Mifflin.

PLAY THERAPY. The primary techniques or methods used in counseling with children younger than 12 years of age.

Virginia Axline (1947, 1964) did much to popularize the term *play therapy.* She thought that a counselor could help a child develop the trust necessary for a therapeutic alliance by following the child's lead in free-play activities, not intruding into these activities, and withholding interpretations. The child, through play, would give symbolic messages that later could be expressed verbally and interpreted.

Play techniques can be used in many ways for counseling children (Thompson & Rudolph, 1992):

1. Play can be used to establish rapport.
2. Play can help counselors understand children's relationships and ways of interacting in their environment.
3. Play can help children to reveal feelings that they are unable to verbalize.
4. Play can be used to act out feelings of anxiety or tension.
5. Play can be used to teach socialization skills.

Counselors may get involved in the play or observe the child during play. They may or may not choose to structure the play sessions.

Gestalt activities involving the seven processes of contact functioning—looking, listening, touching, talking, moving, smelling, tasting—may also be used with children. Children can become aware of their present actions and feelings by participating in activities that bring about contact functioning. Oaklander (1978) described several Gestalt techniques that were adapted for children.

Landreth (1987) suggested that play therapy is an essential tool for working with children. For example, James and Myer (1987) described the use of puppets, while Allan and Berry (1987) described how sandplay can be used by counselors who have basic skills in play therapy.

References

Allan, J., & Berry, P. (1987). Sandplay. *Elementary School Guidance and Counseling, 21,* 300–306.

Axline, V. (1947). *Play therapy.* Boston: Houghton Mifflin.

Axline, V. (1964). *Dibs: In search of self.* Boston: Houghton Mifflin.

James, R., & Myer, R. (1987). Puppets: The elementary school counselor's right or left arm. *Elementary School Guidance and Counseling, 21,* 292–299.

Landreth, G. (1987). Play therapy: Facilitative use of child's play in elementary school counseling. *Elementary School Guidance and Counseling, 21,* 253–261.

Oaklander, V. (1978). *Windows to our children.* Moab, UT: Real People Press.

Thompson, C. L., & Rudolph, L. B. (1992). *Counseling children* (3rd ed.). Pacific Grove, CA: Brooks/Cole.

POSITIVE REINFORCEMENT. Reinforcement that increases the occurrence of desired behavior.

Positive reinforcement refers to any contingency following a desired behavior that will increase the likelihood of that behavior recurring.

Related entry: BEHAVIORAL COUNSELING.

References

Gage, N., & Berliner, D. (1975). *Educational psychology.* Chicago: Rand McNally.
Wielkiewicz, R. (1986). *Behavior management in the schools: Principles and procedures.* New York: Pergamon.

PREJUDICE. A biased attitude toward another person or group based on preconceived mistaken or stereotypical beliefs.

Prejudice can be defined socially as either negative or positive but usually implies a negative bias and judgments based on unsound, inaccurate, or insufficient grounds (Axelson, 1985). Prejudice is often confused with discrimination but differs in that prejudice refers to unwarranted judgments or opinions, while discrimination is biased behavior toward another person or group (Deaux & Wrightson, 1984).

Related entries: BLACK RACIAL IDENTITY DEVELOPMENT; MULTICULTURAL COUNSELING.

References

Axelson, J. (1985). *Counseling and development in a multicultural society.* Monterey, CA: Brooks/Cole.
Cox, O. (1948). *Caste, class, and race.* New York: Doubleday.
Deaux, K., & Wrightson, L. (1984). *Social psychology in the Eighties* (4th ed.). Monterey, CA: Brooks/Cole.

PRIMARY PREVENTIVE COUNSELING. This approach to counseling emphasizes primary prevention.

The goal is to utilize a wide number of counseling methods to work with identified at-risk targets in order to divert future dysfunctions by maintaining healthy functioning and good coping skills (see Coyne, 1987). The overall purpose is that of primary prevention or reducing the incidence of dysfunctions in a designated collection of people.

Two major classes of methods are used to carry out strategies for system changes and personal changes. Direct services place the counselor in contact with the target. With indirect services, the counselor works with other people or through systems to help the target. The targets for primary preventive counseling include individuals, small groups, and systems involving families, work settings, schools, churches, synagogues, and community agencies. High risk situations are the targets for counselor interventions.

Related entry: CUBE MODEL OF COUNSELING.

References

Blocher, D., & Biggs, D. (1983). *Counseling psychology in community settings.* New York: Springer.
Coyne, R. K. (1987). *Primary preventive counseling.* Muncie, IN: Accelerated Development.
Morrill, W., Oetting, E., & Hurst, J. (1974). Dimensions of counselor functioning. *Personnel and Guidance Journal, 52,* 354–359.
Vincent, J., & Trickett, E. (1983). Primary preventions and the human context: Ecological approaches to environmental assessment and change. In R. Felner, L. Jason, J. Moutsugu, & S. Farber (Eds.), *Preventive psychology: Theory, research and practice* (pp. 67–86). New York: Pergamon.

PROJECTIVE PERSONALITY TESTS. A set of stimuli (e.g., inkblots, ambiguous pictures) to which the person creates a response such as a drawing or a story.

The projective principle is psychoanalytic in origin. It is a method of presenting a person with a stimulus situation to which the person responds according to what the situation means to him or her and how he/she feels.

Lindzey (1961) described a projective technique as an instrument that is particularly sensitive to covert or unconscious aspects of behavior. It encourages a wide variety of responses, is multidimensional, and evokes rich or profuse responses with a minimum of awareness. Obrzut and Cummings (1983) stated that the central assumption with projective techniques is that respondents will project or reflect their inner needs, desires, and/or conflicts when asked to impose meaning or order on ambiguous or unstructured stimuli. The Rorschach inkblots method and the Thematic Apperception Test are examples of recognized and widely used projective techniques.

Related entry: PERSONALITY THEORY.

References

Lindzey, G. (1961). *Projective techniques and cross-cultural research.* New York: Appleton-Century-Crofts.
Obrzut, J. E., & Cummings, J. A. (1983). The projective approach to personality assessment: An analysis of thematic picture techniques. *School Psychology Review, 12,* 414–420.

PSYCHOANALYTIC COUNSELING. The client expresses in words whatever thoughts, images, or feelings come to mind without censorship concerning the significance of any ideas. The client's thoughts are attributed to the dynamic internal pressure of his/her drives as organized in unconscious fantasies (see Arlow, 1989).

Traditional psychoanalysis is divided into four phases. The opening phase begins with the first contact with the client. During these initial interviews, the nature of the client's difficulty is ascertained and a decision is made regarding treatment. After a few face-to-face sessions, the client is asked to lie on the couch. During the opening phase, the counselor learns more about the client's history and development and tries to understand the nature of the client's unconscious conflicts. This phase of treatment could last from three to six months.

The next two phases of psychoanalysis are known as transference and working through. They represent the major focus of treatment. As the client begins to relate current difficulties to unconscious childhood conflicts, the counselor begins to assume a major significance in the life of the client. The client's perceptions and demands on the counselor become inappropriate and not realistic. As a result, the professional relationship becomes distorted as the client introduces personal considerations into the treatment context. Analysis of this transference condition is the central task in treatment; the process enables the client to understand how he or she misperceives, misinterprets, and relates to the present situation in terms of the past.

Working through involves the continued analysis of transference and its impact on the client's present life. This phase in treatment consists of repetition, elaboration, and amplification. Recall helps to illuminate the nature of transference.

The resolution of transference is the final phase of treatment. At this time, there may be a sudden and intense aggravation of the very symptoms for which the client originally sought counseling. This situation is interpreted as a last-ditch effort on the part of the client to convince the counselor that he or she is not ready to terminate the relationship. In this final phase of treatment, the client may also present new insights or findings that confirm or elaborate upon the interpretations that were made earlier in counseling (see Arlow, 1989).

The development and analysis of transference form the core of most forms of psychoanalysis. The task of the counselor is to facilitate the development of transference through maintenance of a nonintrusive and neutral stance. A major part of the counselor's task is to identify and analyze the client's resistance to reexperiencing these traumatic events and memories.

Another important aspect of psychoanalysis has been termed the therapeutic alliance (Applebaum, 1977). This refers to the real and contemporary aspects of the counseling relationship, which provide a sense of structure, support, and delimited gratification that can be curative and promote change.

The eventual goal of most psychoanalytic interventions in counseling is to deliver a properly timed and accurate interpretation that will result in insight. This process moves from listening and observation, to the clarification of particular themes and significant aspects of client material, to the confrontation of the client's efforts to avoid self-observation and understanding, and then to reflection of the important latent and manifest aspects of the client's communications during counseling. Eventually the themes presented in counseling are brought together and explained by means of an interpretation, the goal of which is to help the client understand the patterns and origin of present behaviors in terms of unconscious or historical experience and processes. Interpretation may be of two types, either contemporary or genetic (see Baker, 1985).

Baker (1985) differentiates classical psychoanalysis from psychoanalytic psychotherapy, which emphasizes problem resolution, enhanced adaptation, and support of ego functions with limited character change. In psychoanalytic psychotherapy, the client is typically seen face to face and the counselor assumes an active and directive stance.

Related entries: FREUD, SIGMUND; MANN'S TIME-LIMITED PSYCHOTHERAPY.

References

Applebaum, S. (1977). *The anatomy of change.* New York: Plenum.
Arlow, J. A. (1989). Psychoanalysis. In R. J. Corsini & D. Wedding (Eds.), *Current psychotherapies* (4th ed., pp. 19–62). Itasca, IL: F. E. Peacock.
Baker, E. L. (1985). Psychoanalysis and psychoanalytic psychotherapy. In S. J. Linn & J. B. Garske (Eds.), *Contemporary psychotherapies: Models and methods* (pp. 19–67). Columbus, OH: Charles Merrill.

PSYCHODRAMA. An approach to counseling in which clients are able to enact situations dramatically in individual, family, or group settings. Past, present, or future scenes, either imagined or real, are acted out in a counseling setting as if they were occurring at the moment.

Role playing is an activity in counseling that has its roots in psychodrama. However, role playing as used in psychodrama emphasizes an in-depth exploration of emotions, while generic role playing activities will more often focus on practicing effective behaviors.

Psychodrama was developed by Jacob Moreno, who was originally interested in better understanding children's make-believe play in the parks in Vienna. In 1921 he began the "Theater of Spontaneity," which is considered the beginning of psychodrama or the therapeutic approach to improvisational drama. Moreno was both a psychiatrist and a philosopher who also originated the self-help group, sociometry, and an early form of existentialism that coined such terms as *here and now* and *encounter.*

Moreno used psychodrama to help clients to develop role distance and a perspective that allowed them to consider alternatives to their present roles. In some cases they might be able to redefine their expectations for themselves and others. Psychodrama encourages individuals to expand their role repertoire and to learn to observe themselves in the process of enacting various roles.

Five elements in psychodrama are:

1. The directors, who orchestrate the enactments.

2. Protagonists, or the clients who are the focus of the psychodramas. They may play themselves, their parents, different parts of themselves, or even act as observers of various scenes.

3. Auxiliaries, who play supporting roles such as an employer, a sibling, a figure in a dream, or even an organization such as the government. Auxiliaries may take the role of protagonists when role reversal is being used in counseling.

4. The stage, a designated area for the enactment of a psychodrama, such as an area in a group counseling room that has been cleared of chairs. Some hospital settings have special stages for psychodrama.

5. The audience, whose roles may shift during psychodrama; some of them may be asked to be the protagonist or the auxiliaries.

A typical instruction given by counselors using psychodrama is "Don't tell us, show us." The key to successful psychodrama is spontaneity, which is fostered by warm-up techniques that generate group cohesion and involvement.

Related entry: GROUP COUNSELING.

References

Blatner, A. (1988). *Foundations of psychodrama: History, theory and practice.* New York: Springer.

Blatner, A. (1989). Psychodrama. In R. J. Corsini & D. Wedding (Eds.), *Current psychotherapies* (4th ed., pp. 561–572). Itasca, IL: F. E. Peacock.

PSYCHOEDUCATION. The counselor acts as a teacher rather than a therapist and may teach interpersonal skills and attitudes which the clients can use to solve present and future psychological problems and to enhance their satisfaction with life.

Psychoeducation usually involves prevention or development. It is mainly concerned with teaching individuals or groups those skills, understandings, and competencies that will help them manage their lives more intentionally. It may be contrasted with a remedial approach in which counselors seek to help clients solve problems that have already developed (Ivey & Simek-Downing, 1980).

Gordon's parent effectiveness training (1971) and Guerney's relationship enhancement (1977) are examples of psychoeducational interventions. The relationship enhancement program teaches basic communication skills that are selected and organized in such a way as to apply to family issues of communication. Exercises and structured techniques are used to instruct families or couples in these basic communication skills.

Related entry: DELIBERATE PSYCHOLOGICAL EDUCATION.

References

Gordon, T. (1971). *Parent effectiveness training.* New York: Wyden.

Guerney, B., Jr. (1977). *Relationship enhancement skill training programs for therapy, problem prevention and enrichment.* San Francisco: Jossey-Bass.

Ivey, A., & Simek-Downing, L. (1980). *Counseling and psychotherapy: Skills, theories and practice.* Englewood Cliffs, NJ: Prentice-Hall.

PSYCHOLOGY OF PERSONAL CONSTRUCTS. In a construct theory view, individuals are like scientists who are devising hypotheses that render events understandable and to some degree predictable. Humans are always in the process of attributing meaning to their experiences. The fundamental question is, What crucial prediction is the client testing with his or her behavior?

Personal constructs are the individual's conclusions, interpretations, or deductions about life. To construe means to interpret, to understand, to deduce, or to explain. Constructs refer to how things are seen as being alike and yet different from other things, and they represent the specific ways in which persons anticipate certain events. They are constructed by each person in order to predict and hence control the things that might happen in the future. Only after events have been interpreted in terms of their beginnings and endings and in terms of their similarities and contrasts does it become possible to try to anticipate them.

George Kelly (1955), in his theory of personality, which he called the psychology of personal constructs, argued that human beings are essentially interpretive. They are in the process of attributing meaning to their ongoing experiences. For Kelly, "a person anticipates events by construing their replications" (1955, p. 50). They are testing their beliefs about the future. In what ways that can be predicted will tomorrow replicate today? The inability of persons to revise their construing processes when their expectations are disconfirmed is considered a symptom of a psychological disturbance. Kelly (1955) notes, "We may define a disorder as any personal construction that is used repeatedly in spite of consistent invalidation" (p. 831).

People differ from each other in the approaches they take to anticipating the same events. How does a specific client phrase or punctuate events, and what are the major themes that are perceived in them?

A person's construction system is composed of a finite number of dichotomous constructs that are either-or in nature. When we hear a person say, "John is intelligent," the word *intelligent* implies both a similarity and a contrast. The person doing the construing has abstracted from the overall perception of John the characteristic of intelligence, which is seen as a replication of something seen before and hence a way in which John is similar to some other person or event. At the same time that a person construes John as intelligent, the person also implies a contrast. This contrast for one person might be "stupid," while for another the contrast might be "not intelligent." Any construct has two poles, one on each side of the dichotomy. Those elements abstracted by the constructs are like each other at each pole and unlike the elements at the opposite end. The range of convenience of a construct refers to the extent of or breadth of things for which it is considered useful. The focus of convenience refers to those things or events for which a construct is optimally useful.

Of the counseling techniques developed within personal construct theory, fixed role therapy is by far the most discussed in the literature. Instead of working on one problem at a time in counseling, the counselor may suggest that the client adopt an alternative personality structure by role playing a character somewhat different from the present self for a two-week period (Epting & Nazario, 1987).

Related entry: KELLY, GEORGE ALEXANDER.

References

Epting, F., & Nazario, A., Jr. (1987). Designing a fixed role therapy: Issues, techniques and modifications. In R. A. Neimeyer & G. J. Neimeyer (Eds.), *Personal construct therapy casebook.* New York: Springer.

Kelly, G. A. (1955). *The psychology of personal constructs: A theory of personality* (2 vols.). New York: Norton.

Sechrest, L. J. (1983). Personal constructs theory. In R. J. Corsini & A. J. Marsella (Eds.), *Personality theories, Research and assessment* (pp. 229–286). Itasca, IL: F. E. Peacock.

PSYCHOSEXUAL STAGES OF DEVELOPMENT. Freud described five stages from birth through adolescence in the development of libido: (1) the oral stage, the first year or so of life; (2) the anal stage, the second and third years; (3) the phallic stage, up to about age 6; (4) the latency stage, from 6 to 12 years of age; and (5) the genital stage, which occurs at puberty.

According to psychoanalytic approaches to counseling, neuroses can be traced to a fixation at one of the psychosexual stages. Some individuals will be fixated at the oral, anal, or phallic stage and demonstrate the related personality types. Others experience conflicts at each stage and demonstrate a mixed personality that is a combination of traits and defenses of each stage. No one develops a mature, genital character without undergoing a successful analysis (Prochaska, 1979). For Freud, the stages of life are determined primarily by the unfolding of sexuality in the oral, anal, phallic, and genital stages.

Related entries: ANAL STAGE; GENITAL STAGE; ORAL STAGE; PHALLIC STAGE; PSYCHOANALYTIC COUNSELING.

References

Hall, C. (1954). *A primer to Freudian psychology.* New York: Mentor Books.

Prochaska, J. O. (1979). *Systems of psychotherapy: A transtheoretical analysis* (pp. 23–66). Homewood, IL: Dorsey.

PSYCHOTHERAPY. A form of psychological treatment for problems of an emotional nature in which a trained person deliberately establishes a professional relationship with a patient with the object of removing, modifying, or retarding existing symptoms, of mediating disturbing patterns of behavior, and of promoting positive personality growth and development (see Wolberg, 1954, and Schofield, 1964, 1986).

The exact origin of the term *psychotherapy* is uncertain, but the term *psychotherapeutics* appears in publications around 1890. Schofield (1964, 1986) says that the origins of modern psychotherapy are to be found in the history of Freud's thought. The discovery within the context of psychoanalytic psychotherapy of the nature and importance of the patient-physician relationship has influenced every form of psychotherapy devised since Freud.

It is possible to identify at least thirty-six systems of psychotherapy as we approach the end of the twentieth century. Indeed, one writer (Parloff, 1976) described more than 130 different forms of psychotherapies, while another (Corsini, 1981) reported that there were 250 different types of psychotherapies.

Eysenck (1952) questioned the effectiveness of psychotherapy. He compared improvement in psychotherapy patients with improvement in comparable untreated patients. He reported that patients treated by psychoanalysis improved to the extent of 44 percent; patients treated eclectically improved to the extent of 64 percent; and patients treated custodially or by general practitioners improved to the extent of 72 percent. He concluded that there was an inverse correlation between recovery and psychotherapy. The more psychotherapy, the lower the recovery rate. Later research by Sloane, Staples, Cristol, Yorkston, and Whipple (1975) found more positive support for the effectiveness of behavioral and psychoanalytic psychotherapies.

References

Corsini, R. J. (Ed.) (1981). *Handbook of innovative psychotherapies.* New York: Wiley.

Eysenck, H. J. (1952). The effects of psychotherapy: An evaluation. *Journal of Consulting Psychology, 16,* 319–324.

Parloff, M. B. (1976, February 21). Shopping for the right therapy. *Saturday Review,* pp. 14–16.

Schofield W (1964). *Psychotherapy: The Purchase of Friendship.* Englewood Cliffs, NJ: Prentice-Hall.

Schofield, W. (1986). *Psychotherapy: The purchase of friendship.* (2nd Ed.). New Brunswick, NJ: Transaction Books.

Sloane, R. B., Staples, A. H., Cristol, N. J., Yorkston, N.J., Whipple, K. (1975). *Short term analytically oriented psychotherapy vs behavior therapy.* Cambridge, MA: Harvard University Press.

Wolberg, L. R. (1954). *The technique of psychotherapy.* New York: Grune and Stratton.

PUNISHMENT. Any contingency that has the effect of decreasing the future occurrence of some undesirable behavior.

There are two forms of punishment. Positive punishment occurs when the punisher imposes on the subject an aversive or otherwise undesirable stimulus following the occurrence of some unwanted target behavior with the intention of reducing the recurrence of that target behavior. Negative punishment occurs when the punisher removes from the subject some desired appetitive stimulus following the occurrence of a target behavior (Wielkiewicz, 1986).

Although reinforcement is preferable to punishment, sometimes reinforcement is either ineffective or unavailable in a particular situation. The behavior modification approach has developed a variety of punishment techniques to assist in the management of behavior, including response cost strategies, satiation (or negative practice), overcorrection, and time-out (Swanson & Reinhart, 1979).

Related entry: BEHAVIORAL COUNSELING.

References

Swanson, H., & Reinhart, H. (1979). *Teaching strategies for children in conflict.* St. Louis: C. V. Mosby.

Wielkiewicz, R. (1986). *Behavior modification in the schools: Principles and procedures.* New York: Pergamon.

R

RATING SCALES. An assessment technique used to evaluate subjects on the basis of the evaluator's observations of the subject (Anastasi, 1976).

Since some judgment or interpretation is necessarily involved, it is essential to operationalize each trait to be evaluated in clear and unambiguous terms. Human error introduces many different types of bias into the rating process. For example, the halo effect is the tendency of evaluators to be unduly biased by an irrelevant characteristic of the subject. The Hawthorne effect occurs when the act of singling out a subject for evaluation has the inadvertent effect of improving or otherwise biasing performance. When evaluators are unfamiliar with either the subject or the trait being rated, they may be inclined to rate subjects toward the middle of the scale. This is called central tendency error (Isaac & Michael, 1982).

Related entries: BEHAVIORAL ASSESSMENT; BEHAVIORAL COUNSELING; TRAIT AND FACTOR COUNSELING.

References

Anastasi, A. (1976). *Psychological testing* (4th ed.). New York: Macmillan.
Isaac, S., & Michael, W. (1982). *Handbook of research and evaluation* (2nd ed.). San Diego: Edits.

RATIONAL-EMOTIVE COUNSELING. A theory of personality and an approach to counseling that attributes emotional disturbances to a person's demands, insistences, and/or dictates.

Demandingness gets clients into their emotional troubles; counseling tries to help them to lessen the dictatorial, dogmatic, and absolutistic beliefs that underlie their distressful problem situations. Rational-emotive counseling teaches clients how to recognize their shoulds, oughts, and musts, how to differentiate rational and irrational beliefs, how to use the logico/empirical method of science to examine their problems, and how to accept the realities of their situations. Counselors try to help their clients sharpen their thinking and philosophize about their lives more effectively.

Rational-emotive counseling uses various means of dramatizing preferences and musts so that clients can learn to differentiate between the two. Role playing, modeling, humor, unconditional acceptance, and disputation all help to create a therapeutic environment in which clients may feel free to give up irrational thinking and adopt more effective modes of thought. Clients may also be encouraged to take risks in their interpersonal relationships with others and/or to take risks associated with getting in touch with their own feelings.

Rational-emotive counseling employs behavioral strategies to help clients change their dysfunctional symptoms, learn more effective ways of acting, and change their cognitions. Counselors may give assignments that force clients to confront the irrational nature of their "demands." Operant conditioning may be used to reinforce changes in behaviors or changes in irrational thinking about changing behaviors.

Rational-emotive counseling tries to minimize the effects of a client's self-defeating outlook and to help him/her acquire a more realistic, tolerant philosophy of life. These counselors often use a fairly rapid-fire active-directive-persuasive-philosophical style. They challenge clients, attack their basically irrational beliefs, and help them to identify more rational thought and how it can be applied to their problem.

Rational-emotive counseling evolves through four somewhat overlapping yet distinct stages (Greiger & Boyd, 1980). The first stage, rational-emotive psychodiagnosis and goal setting, consists of (a) separating environmental concerns or problems in living (A problems) from emotional and/or behavioral problems (C problems); (b) ascertaining the nature of irrational beliefs that create emotional disturbances; (c) determining whether or not a client is disturbed about the original disturbance or has developed a problem about the emotional problem itself; and (d) directing the client to focus on the emotional or behavioral problems as the prime arena for counseling rather than on any external or environmental problems.

In the second stage of counseling, rational-emotive insight and goal setting, the clients are helped to acknowledge their maladaptive feelings and behaviors and to assume responsibility for them as self-created. They are to acknowledge the cognitive basis of their symptoms and the following six insights: (1) maladaptive feelings and behaviors do exist; (2) through their thinking, they cause their emotional disturbances; (3) they can accept themselves even though they create their emotional problems; (4) their disturbances are caused by specific irrational ideas which they acknowledge; (5) it is acceptable and desirable to check out the validity of their beliefs; and (6) they can give up their irrational beliefs and adopt more effective ones. Following induction of these insights, counseling goals are agreed upon.

The third stage, rational-emotive working through, is the central core of rational-emotive counseling. Counselors help their clients through cognitive, emotive, and behavioral techniques to actively dispute their irrational beliefs. They also help clients to discriminate rational wants from irrational demands and to define terms so that cognitive distortions are recognized as fallacious (Ellis, 1977). During this stage, counselors encourage their clients to find alternative ideas that can withstand disputation and lead to more effective living.

The fourth stage in counseling, rational-emotive reeducation, focuses on trying to habituate clients to think in new rational ways or to come to believe automatically in these new ideas.

Related entries: A-B-C THEORY; AWFULIZING; ELLIS, ALBERT; IRRATIONAL BELIEFS; META-COGNITION; MUSTURBATION.

References

Ellis, A. (1977). Rational emotive therapy: Research data that support the clinical and personality hypotheses of RET and other modes of cognitive-behavior therapy. *The Counseling Psychologist, 7*, 2–42.

Ellis, A. (1989). Rational emotive therapy. In R. J. Corsini & D. Wedding (Eds.), *Current psychotherapies* (4th ed., pp. 197–240). Itasca, IL: F. E. Peacock.

Ellis, A., & Greiger, R. (1987). *Handbook of rational emotive therapy* (2 vols.). New York: Springer.

Greiger, R., & Boyd, J. (1980). *Rational emotive therapy: A skills based approach.* New York: Van Nostrand Reinhold.

REALITY COUNSELING. Clients are helped to evaluate whether their wants are realistic and whether their present behaviors are helping them. After they become aware of the ineffective behaviors that they are using to control the world, they can learn alternative ways of meeting their needs.

Glasser (1981) described control theory as a basis for his approach to counseling. The basic assumption of this theory is that persons create an inner world that satisfies their needs. This inner world reflects the way they perceive the world. Their behaviors are attempts to control their perceptions of the external world to fit this internal and need-satisfying world. Reality counselors hold that all behavior is generated within ourselves and that people have choices in what they do. Thus, they concentrate on what clients can do in their present situations to change the behaviors that are designed to fulfill their needs.

Clients decide if what they are doing is getting them what they want, and then they determine what, if any, changes they are willing to make in their behaviors. The counselor functions as a teacher by helping clients formulate specific plans of action and offering them behavioral choices. Clients learn how to create a success identity by recognizing and accepting responsibility for their chosen behaviors.

Before counseling can occur, a significant level of involvement needs to be established between counselor and client. In order to achieve this goal, counselors must have developed a style that is perceived as sincere and authentic by clients. They should be able to listen, talk about topics that are relevant to their clients, and express warmth, understanding, and acceptance. Only when counselors and clients have established such a level of involvement can counselors successfully confront clients with the reality and consequences of their current behaviors. Counselors hope to teach their clients to value the attitude of accepting responsibility for their actions or inactions. They need to be firm in their refusal to accept excuses and not give up their belief in the client's ability to live a more responsible life.

Clients are given the opportunity to explore various facets of their lives. They are allowed to articulate their expectations for counseling and to try to pinpoint what they want from life. The major task in reality counseling is for clients to make the following evaluation: Does your present behavior have a reasonable chance of getting you what you want now, and is it taking you in a direction that you want to go in your life? Counselors will encourage their clients to make value judgments by getting them to confront the consequences of their behaviors and judge the quality of their present lives. Only after such self-assessment will clients ever change. Then they are ready to explore other possible behaviors and formulate action plans.

The steps in reality therapy are essentially similar to the principles of reality therapy (Glasser & Zunin, 1973). The first step, involvement, refers to being personal and making friends with clients. They must believe that counselors are concerned about them. During this step, it is important to ascertain what the client wants. The second step emphasizes and focuses on the present behaviors of clients. The question for the client is, "What are you doing?" The third step is called value judgment. The question is, "Is what you are doing helping you?" The client is to make a judgment. Step four involves planning responsible behavior. Counselors now help their clients to make small, manageable, specific, and positive plans to do better. The goal in step five is to obtain a commitment to the client's plan to do better. It may be either oral or in writing. Step six is called Accept No Excuses. Excuses are seen as unacceptable because they allow clients to avoid responsibility and get themselves off the hook. Step seven is called Do Not Punish. The reason is that punishment is intended to cause pain. Instead, discipline, because it is about the natural consequences that follow certain actions, is considered appropriate. It is also important that the counselor not criticize a client. The last step is called Never Give Up. Counselors should not give up on clients no matter what they say or do.

Related entries: GLASSER, WILLIAM; SCHOOL COUNSELING.

References

Corey, G. (1991). *Theory and practice of counseling and psychotherapy* (4th ed., pp. 369–394). Pacific Grove, CA: Brooks/Cole.

Glasser, W. (1965). *Reality therapy: A new approach to psychiatry.* New York: Harper and Row.

Glasser, W. (1981). *Stations of the mind.* New York: Harper and Row.

Glasser, W., & Zunin, L. (1973). Reality therapy. In R. Corsini (Ed.), *Current psychotherapies.* Itasca, IL: F. E. Peacock.

RECREATIONAL COUNSELING. A form of counseling or rehabilitation that involves clients' learning how to use their leisure time constructively.

Recreational activities can be an effective adjunct to counseling and therapy by providing shared experiences for institutionalized clients to work through social-emotional issues with a "here and now" orientation (Schwartz & Swartzburg, 1976). Recreation programs give geriatric clients the opportunity to "restore or preserve creative function" and to "simply have fun" (Whanger & Busse, 1976). Dulcan (1988) notes that recreational programs are an especially important adjunct to treatment for children and adolescents. They provide socially incompetent youth with opportunities to develop effective social skills and build self-esteem within a structured or semistructured setting.

References

Dulcan, M. (1988). Treatment of children and adolescents. In J. Talbott, R. Hales, & S. Yudofsky (Eds.), *Textbook of psychiatry* (pp. 985–1020). Washington, DC: American Psychiatric Association.

Schwartz, A., & Swartzburg, M. (1976). Hospital care. In B. Wolman (Ed.), *Therapist's handbook: Treatment methods of mental disorders* (pp. 199–226). New York: Van Nostrand Reinhold.

Whanger, A., & Busse, E. (1976). Geriatrics. In B. Wolman (Ed.), *Therapist's handbook: Treatment methods of mental disorders* (pp. 287–324). New York: Van Nostrand Reinhold.

REFERRAL. A referral occurs when a counselor recommends that a client see another professional or source of help to meet some need the counselor is not able to address satisfactorily.

Hansen (Hansen, Stevic, & Warner, 1977) identifies three problem dimensions to the process of referral: the effect on the counselor, the effect on the client, and issues related to follow-up on the referral. Clients may resist a new counselor because of reluctance to enter a new and unknown counseling relationship. A counselor may be resistant to making referrals because of feelings of inadequacy or incompetence. It is necessary but sometimes difficult to follow up on a referral to be sure that the client has benefitted from the additional services.

Related entry: PARAPROFESSIONALS.

References

Cormier, W., & Cormier, L. (1979). *Interviewing strategies for helpers: A guide to assessment, treatment, and evaluation.* Monterey, CA: Brooks/Cole.

Hansen, J., Stevic, R., & Warner, R. (1977). *Counseling: Theory and process* (2nd ed.). Boston: Allyn and Bacon.

REFLECTION OF FEELINGS. A counseling technique intended to help a client become more consciously aware of her/his emotions related to a specific issue, person, or situation.

Reflection is a rephrasing of the client's feelings, or the affect part of the message. Usually part of the message reveals the client's feelings about the content. For example, a client may feel *discouraged* (affect) about not doing well in a class (content). Many clients have a tendency to focus on the content and attempt to deal with their problems on the instrumental level without attending to the feelings they have about the content. Reflection of feelings helps clients solve their problems by reestablishing their awareness of the emotions that are also affecting their decision making and behavior. Counselors need to observe a client's verbal and nonverbal behavior carefully to determine the emotionality implied by the client's demeanor.

Related entry: CLIENT-CENTERED COUNSELING.

References

Brammer, L., & Shostrom, E. (1977). *Therapeutic psychology: Fundamentals of counseling and psychotherapy* (3rd ed.). Englewood Cliffs, NJ: Prentice-Hall.

Cormier, W., & Cormier, L. (1979). *Interviewing strategies for helpers: A guide to assessment, treatment, and evaluation.* Monterey, CA: Brooks/Cole.

REHABILITATION COUNSELING. Rehabilitation counselors help handicapped and/or disabled persons to achieve the highest possible level of productive functioning. They assist their clients to better understand both their problems and their capabilities, and then they help them to use available resources to achieve their vocational, social, and personal goals.

Rehabilitation stresses reeducation of handicapped individuals who have previously lived independent lives. Habilitation focuses on educating handicapped clients who have been disabled from early life and who have never been self-sufficient (Bitter, 1979). Persons with disabilities have either a physical or a mental condition that limits their activities or functioning. A handicap is an observable or discernable limitation that is made so by the presence of various barriers. An example of a disabled person with a handicap is a quadriplegic individual assigned to a third floor apartment with no access to an elevator. Rehabilitation counselors help their clients overcome handicaps and effectively cope with their disabilities.

Rehabilitation counselors work with clients who are impaired and may have physical, mental, or behavioral disorders. They often focus their counseling efforts on helping clients to obtain employment and may in the course of counseling need to provide a range of supportive services.

Twelve major functions of rehabilitation counselors are:

1. Personal counseling
2. Case finding
3. Eligibility determination
4. Training
5. Provision or restoration
6. Support services
7. Job placement

8. Planning

9. Evaluation

10. Agency consultation

11. Public relations

12. Follow-along (Schumacher, 1983)

Rehabilitation counselors were among the first group of professional counselors to set up a system of certification—the Commission on Rehabilitation Counselor Certification (CRCC). The Council of Rehabilitation Education (CORE) accredits rehabilitation counseling programs. The majority of rehabilitation counselor education programs are accredited through the CORE process.

References

Bitter, I. A. (1979). *Introduction to rehabilitation.* St. Louis: C. V. Mosby.
Schumacher, B. (1983). Rehabilitation counseling. In M. M. Ohlsen (Ed.), *Introduction to counseling* (pp. 313–324). Itasca, IL: F. E. Peacock.

RELIABILITY. The consistency or generalizability of target behaviors such as responses to tests or treatments.

Reliability is a term that frequently refers to the degree to which test scores are consistent, dependable, or repeatable. Reliability is a function of the degree to which test scores are free from errors of measurement. These refer to factors that contribute to discrepancies between observed scores and true scores of individuals.

A person tested on two different occasions will score differently, even on the same test. The difference is caused by errors of measurement or factors that can cause changes in scores from one occasion to another. The standard error of measurement is used to estimate the score range in which a person's true score may fall.

Test manuals usually report a number of different types of reliability coefficients. These include (a) test-retest, (b) alternate forms, (c) split half reliability, and (d) other internal consistency methods. One of the factors influencing reliability is the length of tests. Others are the reliability of scoring, the range of individual differences in a group, and the difficulty of test items.

Related entry: VALIDITY.

References

American Educational Research Association, American Psychological Association, National Council on Measurement in Education (1985). *Standards for educational and psychological testing.* Washington, DC: American Psychological Association.
Cronback, L. J. (1984). *Essentials of psychological testing* (4th ed.). New York: Harper and Row.

RELIGION. Religious development is relatively predictable for children and is best described by stage theories of development. During and after adolescence, models of transition and crisis seem more appropriate for understanding religious development (see Worthington, 1989).

Pargament (1987) outlined a comprehensive theory of religion as a coping strategy for dealing with threatening life events. He identified three ways that religion might be involved in coping with a stressful transition in life. First, religion might be part of each aspect of the coping process. Second, religion could contribute to coping. Third, religion could be an outcome of coping with stress. Spilka, Shaver, and Kirkpatrick (1985) proposed a theory of attribution in religion that attempts to answer the question, ''Under what conditions is religious faith affected during life transitions?''

Allport (1950) proposed a three-stage model of the development of religious maturity. The first is called ''raw credulity'' or an authority based belief system. In the second, doubts flood the mind about the improbabilities of faith. With the third, persons are able to live with ambiguity, doubt, and faith alternating in their lives.

Fowler (1981) described religious faith as developing in six invariant stages that represent successively more complex ways of organizing the meaning of faith. Stage six is characterized by an awareness that one's ultimate environment includes all beings. The seven structural aspects of faith are: (1) the form of logic, (2) role taking and social relationships, (3) forms of moral judgment, (4) bounds of social awareness of primary reference groups, (5) locus of authority, (6) ways of forming and holding a comprehensive sense of unified meanings, and (7) symbolic functioning.

Worthington (1989) recommends that counselors understand not only the processes of the development of religious clients but also the substantive content of some of the issues that they confront in their lives across the life span. People will deal with issues that may directly involve religion or stimulate them to consider the role of religion in their lives. In particular, stressful life events and life transitions can bring issues of religion into counseling.

Related entries: PERLS, FREDERICK S.; VALUES.

References

Allport, G. W. (1950). *The individual and his religion.* London: Macmillan.

Fowler, J. W. (1981). *Stages of faith.* New York: Harper and Row.

Pargament, K. I. (1987, August). God help me: Towards a theoretical framework of coping for the psychology of religion. Paper presented at the meeting of the American Psychological Association, New York City.

Spilka, B., Shaver, P., and Kirkpatrick, L. A. (1985). A general attribution theory for psychology of religion. *Journal for the Scientific Study of Religion 24,* 1–20.

Worthington, E. L., Jr. (1989). Religious faith across the life span: Implications for counseling and research. *The Counseling Psychologist 17,* 555–612.

RESEARCH. Research in counseling is for the most part applied research that links basic science and theory to issues of counseling practice (see Tracey, 1991).

Forsyth and Strong (1986) described research in counseling as just another part of research on human behavior. In contrast, Gelso (1979) argued that counseling was a very different activity, unique unto itself, and that researchers needed to have specialized knowledge and to focus their efforts on issues that pertain directly to counseling.

It has been noted repeatedly by counselor practitioners and researchers that counseling research has had little impact on the practice of counseling (Elliott, 1983; Hayes & Nelson, 1981; Rice & Greenberg, 1984). Still, it needs to be generally acknowledged that no research study should be expected to provide directions to counselors for helping specific clients deal with specific problems at any particular point in time (see Tracey, 1991).

The scientist-practitioner model originally proposed by Pepinsky and Pepinsky (1954) argued that counselors should apply scientific principles to their clinical practices. The model has been used as an argument for employing the scientific method in practice as well as for encouraging counselors to engage in both clinical work and research.

Campbell (1965) presented an example of outcome research in counseling. He reported a study of counseled and noncounseled students twenty-five years later. His results suggested that the counseled students were mildly less satisfied with their station in life but had more accomplishments to show for their efforts than did the noncounseled students. The size of the differences is not dramatic, but that they should exist at all is.

Related entry: COUNSELING.

References

Campbell, D. P. (1965). *The results of counseling: Twenty-five years later.* Philadelphia: W. B. Saunders.

Elliott, R. (1983). Filtering process research to the practicing psychotherapist. *Psychotherapy: Theory, Research and Practice, 20,* 47–55.

Forsyth, O. R., & Strong, S. R. (1986). The scientific study of counseling and psychotherapy: A unificationist view. *American Psychologist, 41,* 113–119.

Gelso, C. J. (1979). Research in counseling: Methodological and professional issues. *The Counseling Psychologist, 8*(3), 7–35.

Hayes, S. C., & Nelson, R. O. (1981). Clinically relevant research: Requirements, problems and solutions. *Behavioral Assessment, 3,* 209–215.

Pepinsky, H. B., & Pepinsky, P. N. (1954). *Counseling theory and practice.* New York: Ronald Press.

Rice, L. N., & Greenberg, L. (1984). *Patterns of change.* New York: Guilford.

Tracey, T. J. (1991). Counseling research as an applied science. In C. E. Watkins & L. J. Schneider (Eds.), *Research in counseling* (pp. 3–31). Hillsdale, NJ: Lawrence Erlbaum.

ROGERS, CARL RANSOM (1902–1987). The major spokesperson for non-directive, client-centered, and person-centered counseling. In the 1960s he did much to foster the encounter group movement in education and industry.

Rogers graduated from the University of Wisconsin in 1924, and he then entered Union Theological Seminary. Two years later he transferred to Teachers College, Columbia University. After graduating he worked for twelve years at a child guidance center in Rochester, New York. In 1939 he joined the faculty at Ohio State University. His presentation at the University of Minnesota on December 11, 1940, entitled "Some Newer Concepts in Psychotherapy," was a critical event in the development of client-centered counseling. At that time he proposed that counselors could promote insight, independence, and positive attitudes in their clients by refraining from giving advice and making interpretations and by recognizing and accepting feelings.

After serving as Director of Counseling Services for the United Service Organization during World War II, he was appointed Professor of Psychology at the University of Chicago. In 1957 he described the necessary and sufficient conditions of counseling as congruence, unconditional positive regard, and empathy. At about this time, Rogers accepted a professorship in psychology and psychiatry at the University of Wisconsin. In 1964 he went to the Western Behavioral Sciences Institute. In 1968 he established the Center for the Studies of the Person in La Jolla, California. During the last fifteen years of his life he applied the person-centered approach to issues such as the reduction of racial tensions and the promotion of world peace.

Related entry: CLIENT-CENTERED COUNSELING.

References

Rogers, C. (1942). *Counseling and psychotherapy.* Boston: Houghton Mifflin.

Rogers, C. (1957). The necessary and sufficient conditions of therapeutic personality change. *Journal of Consulting Psychology, 21,* 95–103.

Rogers, C. (1970). *On encounter groups.* New York: Harper and Row.

S

SCHOOL COUNSELING. The provision of a program of counseling services covering such topics as career decision making, parent and family issues, interpersonal relationships, child abuse, AIDS, and abortion.

School counseling is considered a comprehensive program of services that is purposeful and sequential. It is both an integral part of and an independent component of the educational program, its major purpose being to facilitate the instructional process and students' academic success (Myrick, 1987).

A wide range of activities occurs in counseling offices from elementary through university levels of education. The basic services include counseling; consultation and coordination of services; evaluation and testing; and group guidance and information. Elementary, middle level, high school, and higher education counselors have somewhat distinct roles because of the differences in the chronological ages and developmental stages of their clients.

Elementary counselors are often involved in consultation with teachers and parents. They combine classroom guidance with individual and small group counseling. Counselors in middle schools frequently work with interdisciplinary teams of teachers. They are apt to employ group counseling techniques to deal with career and educational issues and adolescent development concerns. These counselors may also work with the teacher-advisory programs as consultants and trainers. High school counselors spend a considerable amount of time in educational and career counseling. Often they may specialize in one or another grade level in high school. These school counselors are apt to find themselves confronted with clients having significant personal problems that demand high levels of counseling skills and specialized knowledge about sexuality and substance abuse. College and university counseling is more specialized than elementary or secondary school counseling. Under the umbrella of student personal services, special counselors deal with admissions, career counseling and placement, residence hall counseling, and personal counseling.

Counselors in all of these various educational settings have somewhat similar missions. They are to help students benefit from their instructional experiences. Most of them are working with students who have no serious psychological impairments. Finally, school counselors are usually accountable to administrators that have broad educational responsibilities.

Borders and Drury (1992) concluded from their literature review of thirty years that school counseling interventions have a substantial impact on students' educational and personal development. Individual and small group counseling, classroom guidance, and consultation activities all seem to contribute to success in the classroom.

Related entry: STUDENT PERSONNEL.

References

Borders, L. D., & Drury, S. M. (1992). Comprehensive school counseling programs: A review for policy makers and practitioners. *Journal of Counseling and Development, 70,* 487–498.

Cole, C. G. (1991). School counseling. In D. Capuzzi & D. R. Gross (Eds.), *Introduction to counseling: Perspectives for the 1990s* (pp. 233–249). Boston: Allyn and Bacon.

Myrick, R. D. (1987). *Developmental guidance and counseling: A practical approach.* Minneapolis: Educational Media Corporation.

SCHOOL PSYCHOLOGIST. A professional mental health worker who provides psychological services to clients involved in educational settings from preschool through higher education for the protection and promotion of their mental health and the facilitation of their learning (APA, 1981).

The school psychologist provides (a) psychological and psychoeducational evaluation and assessment of school functioning; (b) interventions to facilitate the functioning of individuals or groups; (c) educational services and child care functions of school personnel, parents, and community agencies; (d) consultation regarding school related problems of students and professional problems of staff; and (e) program development services to schools and community agencies.

School psychological services have been a part of education since about 1900. In Philadelphia in 1896, Lightner Witmer established the first psychological clinic and initiated the journal *The Psychological Clinic.* He is considered the founder of clinical psychology, and to him is also attributed parentage of school psychology. In 1946 the American Psychological Association created the Division of School Psychology.

School psychologists possess either a sixty-credit master's degree from a university program approved by the National Association of School Psychologists or a doctoral degree (Ph.D., Ed.D., or Psy.D.) in school psychology from a program approved by the American Psychological Association. They may offer counseling or psychotherapeutic services to clients who are having school related problems.

References

American Psychological Association (1981). Specialty guidelines for the delivery of services by school psychologists. *American Psychologist, 36,* 670–681.
Baker, D. B. (1988). The psychology of Lightner Witmer. *Professional School Psychology, 3*(2), 109–121.

SELF-ACTUALIZATION. A basic human need toward growth, health, self-
realization, and autonomy (Maslow, 1970/1954). Self-actualized persons are
characterized by seventeen attributes. They are:

1. perceive reality accurately

2. accept themselves and others

3. act spontaneously and naturally

4. focus on problems

5. prefer privacy and have an air of detachment

6. are independent and autonomous

7. appreciate and enjoy new experiences and life

8. are mystical and transcendent; have peak experiences

9. possess strong social identity and social interest

10. have strong relationships with a few friends

11. are oriented toward democratic values

12. have a strong sense of moral values

13. have a philosophical sense of humor

14. are creative and inventive; have fresh perspectives on ideas

15. resist conformity and acculturation

16. are well-integrated, total, whole, coherent

17. transcend dichotomies, bring opposites in harmony

Self-actualized people are motivated by metamotives or enduring values of
human history. These include truth, beauty, wisdom, peace, unity, and freedom
(Maslow, 1971).

Goldstein (1942) also discusses the concept of self-actualization. He argues
that all behavior is undertaken to enhance or preserve self-actualization. However, not all behavior is equally effective. Denial of illness may be seen as an
attempt to restore personal integrity that is not effective behavior.

Related entries: ACTUALIZING TENDENCY; CLIENT-CENTERED
COUNSELING.

References

Goldstein, K. (1942). *Human nature in the light of psychopathology.* Cambridge, MA:
Harvard University Press.

Maslow, A. (1970). *Motivation and personality.* New York: Harper and Row. (Originally published 1954)

Maslow, A. (1971). *The farther reaches of human nature.* New York: Viking.

SELF-CONCEPT. As infants grow older, they slowly build up an increasingly differentiated field of experiences, called self-experiences; later, through interactions with others, these experiences become the self-concept or their definitions of their personal attributes, including their "good points" and "bad points."

When the individual experiences the physical self as separate from the environment, the configuration of the self-concept begins. At about the same time that the physical self differentiates from the environment, the social self emerges as part of the physical self. Once the self-concept is formed, a need for positive regard from others develops. This need is considered universal and is of utmost importance for the optimum development of a person. The need for love influences perceptions that have a significant effect on the self-concept.

The self-concept may become inaccurate, unrealistic, and rigid over time. Individuals who are seeking positive regard from others may even falsify some of the values that they experience and perceive them only in terms of their value to others. When experiences that are discrepant with the self-concept are symbolized in awareness, the integrated balance of the self-concept is broken and the person may experience anxiety and sometimes act in a disorganized manner.

Related entries: ACTUALIZING TENDENCY; CLIENT-CENTERED COUNSELING.

Reference

Holdstock, T. L., & Rogers, C. R. (1983). Person centered theory. In R. J. Corsini & A. J. Marsella (Eds.), *Personality theories, research and assessment* (pp. 189–227). Itasca, IL: F. E. Peacock.

SELF-DIRECTED SEARCH. An instrument designed to provide vocational planning assistance. It is self-administered, self-scored, and self-interpreted.

Items concern competencies, preferred activities, and self-ratings of abilities. Scores are reported in terms of six types of personality orientations and environments: realistic (R), investigative (I), artistic (A), social (S), enterprising (E), and conventional (C).

The Self-Directed Search (SDS) includes an assessment booklet, an occupational classification booklet or Occupations Finder, as well as an interpretative booklet entitled *Understanding Yourself and Your Career.* The first edition was published in 1970. In the 1977 edition, the scoring procedure was simplified, a total of fifty job titles were added to the Occupations Finder, and the Occupations Scale was revised to improve the list of occupational titles. The 1985 edition of this test has very few modifications, but it is supposed to be more reliable than the 1977 edition. Form E of the SDS, first published in 1970, then revised in 1973 and 1979, is for adolescents and adults with limited reading skills.

The self-assessment booklet of the SDS has five sections, covering occupational daydreams, preferred activities, competencies, preferred occupations, and self-estimates of abilities and skills. Items are keyed as realistic, investigative, artistic, social, enterprising, or conventional and then summed to get a three-letter code or profile.

Related entries: CAREER COUNSELING; KUDER GENERAL INTEREST SURVEY (FORM E); KUDER OCCUPATIONAL INTEREST SURVEY (FORM D-1956 AND FORM DD-1966); STRONG-CAMPBELL INTEREST INVENTORY (STRONG VOCATIONAL INTEREST BLANK).

References

Holland, J. L. (1959). A theory of vocational choice. *Journal of Counseling Psychology, 6,* 35–45.
Holland, J. L. (1985). *The Self-Directed Search, professional manual.* Odessa, FL: Psychological Assessment Resources Inc.

SELF-HELP GROUP. A group of laypersons with perceived common needs and problems who provide support and encouragement to each other.

Examples of self-help groups include Alcoholics Anonymous, the Society for Compassionate Friends, Overeaters Anonymous, Al-Anon, Mended Hearts, Inc., and Alateen, to name only a few (Vinogradov & Yalom, 1988). Such support groups are an essential link in prevention services at the community level. They can provide participants with personal attention, a source of information, and guidance. Alcoholics Anonymous (AA) provides individualized rehabilitation support and crisis intervention. Through the use of a buddy system, it helps members reestablish equilibrium after being confronted with a critical situation that they are ill-prepared to handle. Persons in crisis can turn to a support group for intensive help that is not readily accessible through professional mental health services. Cassem (1978) found that the bereaved have been effectively helped by support groups. Organizations like the Society for Compassionate Friends or the Candlelighters provide a compassionate setting where the bereaved can get in touch with their feelings and rebuild their self-esteem.

Related entries: GROUP COUNSELING; PARAPROFESSIONALS; PRIMARY PREVENTIVE COUNSELING.

References

Cassem, N. (1978). Treating the person confronting death. In A. Nicholi (Ed.), *Harvard guide to modern psychiatry* (pp. 579–608). Cambridge, MA: Belknap Press.
Lieberman, M., & Borman, L. (1979). *Self-help groups for coping with crisis.* San Francisco: Basic Books.
Macht, L. (1978). Community psychiatry. In A. Nicholi (Ed.), *Harvard guide to modern psychiatry* (pp. 627–650). Cambridge, MA: Belknap Press.
Vinogradov, S., & Yalom, I. (1988). Group therapy. In J. Talbott, R. Hales, & S. Yu-

dofsky (Eds.), *Textbook of psychiatry* (pp. 951–984). Washington, DC: American Psychiatric Association.

SELF-INSTRUCTIONAL TRAINING. A cognitive-behavioral intervention in which clients learn to use self-talk to better manage their behaviors.

Self-instructional training has been used to treat many problems of children (Kendall & Braswell, 1982). Meichenbaum and Goodman (1971) describe how impulsive children were trained to use self-talk to help them successfully complete academic tasks.

Initially, a client is provided with a verbal set, an explanation of the task and the process. The counselor then models the task while explaining each step out loud. Next, the counselor verbally guides the client through the task, providing overt external guidance as needed. The process moves to overt self-guidance, where the clients direct themselves through the task with verbal directions spoken out loud. In the next transition phase, overt self-guidance is faded to the client's whispered self-instruction while completing the task. Finally, the client is able to complete the desired task independently, relying solely on covert mental self-instructions to guide the task process.

Related entries: COGNITIVE-BEHAVIORAL COUNSELING; META-COGNITION.

References

Cormier, W., & Cormier, L. (1979). *Interviewing strategies for helpers: A guide to assessment, treatment, and evaluation.* Monterey, CA: Brooks/Cole.

Hughes, J. (1988). *Cognitive behavior therapy with children in the schools.* New York: Pergamon.

Kendall, P., & Braswell, L. (1982). Cognitive-behavioral self-control therapy for children: A components analysis. *Journal of Consulting and Clinical Psychology, 50,* 672–689.

Meichenbaum, D. H., & Goodman, J. (1971). Training impulsive children to talk to themselves: A means of developing self-control. *Journal of Abnormal Psychology, 77,* 115–126.

SEX-ROLE STEREOTYPES. Preconceptions about persons on the basis of their gender with little or no consideration of their personal characteristics.

Stereotyping is a rigid schema or representation of the traits of a particular gender. While the traits may reflect in a very general way certain characteristics that have come to be associated with a particular gender, stereotypical thinking is misleading because it is never sufficiently flexible to allow for individual differences. While stereotypes can be valued either positively or negatively by society, stereotypes of groups such as women that have traditionally been assigned second-class status typically legitimize their mistreatment and are perceived as negative and demeaning.

The effect of stereotypical thinking is circular and self-reinforcing because expectations rooted in stereotypes can shape our perceptions of persons and

events, which in turn reinforce the original stereotypes. Stereotypes and prejudices function similarly in that both contain elements that are false or inaccurate,
evoke emotional feelings, and result from routinized habits of judgment and
expectations.

Related entry: FEMINIST COUNSELING.

References

Axelson, J. (1985). *Counseling and development in a multicultural society.* Monterey,
   CA: Brooks/Cole.
Deaux, K., & Wrightson, L. (1984). *Social psychology in the Eighties* (4th ed.). Mon-
   terey, CA: Brooks/Cole.

SEXUAL EXPLOITATION ISSUES. A category of clients' problems dealing
with issues surrounding violations of a person's sexual rights.

In 1986 a survey of 930 women found that 38 percent had been sexually
abused before they were 18 years of age (Russell, 1986). The incidence of
sexual abuse had quadrupled from 1909 to 1973. Prevalence rates of sexual
abuse for men in various studies range from 3 to 31 percent (Finkelhor et al.,
1986).

An example of a serious sexual exploitation issue of youth and adults is
that of sexual harassment. The most commonly held conception of sexual harassment involves an implicit or explicit bargain whereby the harasser promises rewards or threatens punishment depending on the victim's response
(Crocker & Simon, 1981). The second type of harassment includes the creation of a hostile environment that may include suggestive remarks but no implied or stated threat.

Summaries of research studies on sexual harassment suggest that 20 to 30
percent of women are victims of sexual harassment. A conservative estimate
is that over one million women students are sexually harassed (Sandler,
1990).

Clients may be very hesitant to discuss either sexual abuse or sexual harassment. Many of them have blamed themselves or have tried to repress their
memories of these experiences. Denial may be used by these clients to argue
that these experiences have had little or no impact on them. Counselors need to
deal sensitively with these issues without prematurely forcing clients to disclose
instances of sexual abuse or sexual harassment. Feelings should be let out slowly
so as not to overwhelm the clients (Ratican, 1992).

Related entries: COUNSELING; FEMINIST COUNSELING.

References

Crocker, P. L., & Simon, A. S. (1981). Sexual harassment in education. *Capital Univer-
   sity Law Review, 10*(3), 541–584.
Finkelhor, O., Araje, S., Baron, L., Broune, A., Peters, S. D., & Wyatt, G. E. (1986).
   Sourcebook on child sexual abuse. Newberry Park, CA: Sage.
Hotelling, K. (1991). Sexual harassment: A problem shielded by silence. *Journal of
   Counseling and Development, 69*(6), 497–501.

Ratican, K. L. (1992). Sexual abuse survivors: Identifying symptoms and special treat-
    ment considerations. *Journal of Counseling and Development, 71*(1), 33–47.
Russell, D. E. H. (1986). *The secret trauma: Incest in the lives of girls and women.* New
    York: Basic Books.
Sandler, B. R. (1990). Sexual harassment: A new issue for institutions. *Intiatives.* 52(4),
    5–10.

SIXTEEN PERSONALITY FACTOR QUESTIONNAIRE. This test, also
known as the 16 PF, was developed to tap a wide range of ongoing personality functioning, including traits and conflicts. It yields scores on sixteen different dimensions that were derived from a factor analysis of personality
descriptors.

There are six forms of the 16 PF. Form A is most commonly used and is
composed of 187 items, or about 10 to 13 items for each scale. The 16 PF
allows three response choices. Raw scores are converted to stens (standard ten
scores) that range from 1 to 10. A sten score of 5 or 6 is average. The 16 PF
can also be scored for faking good and faking bad. The scales on the 16 PF are
as follows:

A. Sizothymia (reserved) versus Affectothymia (outgoing)

B. Lower Scholastic Capacity (less intelligent) versus Higher Scholastic Capac-
    ity (more intelligent)

C. Lower Ego Strength (affected by feelings) versus Higher Ego Strength (emo-
    tionally stable)

E. Submissiveness (humble) versus Dominance (assertive)

F. Desurgency (sober) versus Surgency (happy-go-lucky)

G. Weaker Superego Strength (expedient) versus Stronger Superego Strength
    (conscientious)

H. Threctia (shy) versus Parmia (venturesome)

I. Harria (tough minded) versus Premsia (tender minded)

L. Alaxia (trusting) versus Protension (suspicious)

M. Praxemia (practical) versus Autia (imaginative)

N. Artlessness (forthright) versus Shrewdness (astute)

O. Untroubled Adequacy (self-assured) versus Guilt Proneness (apprehensive)

Q_1. Conservatism of Temperament (conservative) versus Radicalism (experi-
    menting)

Q_2. Group Adherence (group-dependent) versus Self-Sufficiency (self-sufficient)

Q_3. Low Integration (undisciplined self-conflict) versus High Strength of Self-
    Sentiment (controlled)

Q_4. Low Ergic Tension (relaxed) versus High Ergic Tension (tense)

Related entries: PERSONALITY THEORY; TRAIT AND FACTOR
COUNSELING.

Reference

Cattell, R., Eber, H., & Tatsuoka, M. (1970). *Handbook for the Sixteen Personality Factors Questionnaire.* Champaign, IL: IPAT.

SKINNER, BURRHUS F. (1904–1990). Skinner is considered the major psychologist who defined the concepts and methods of behaviorism.

He was born on March 20, 1904, in Susquehanna, Pennsylvania. In 1931 he received his Ph.D. in experimental psychology from Harvard University. He accepted his first faculty position at the University of Minnesota, then he became chair of the psychology department at Indiana University. He returned to Harvard University in 1948 and became professor emeritus in 1974.

Skinner received various American Psychological Association awards for his contributions to psychology. He is said to have considered his most important work to be *Verbal Behavior* (1957).

Delprato and Midgley (1992) present what they consider to be twelve fundamental points of Skinner's behaviorism. They address such points as the purpose of science, methodology, determinism, locus of behavioral control, consequential causality, materialism, behavior as subject matter, reductionism, nonreductionism, organism as the locus of biological change, classification of behavior into respondent and operant, stimulus control of operant behavior, and the generality of behavioral principles.

Related entries: APPLIED BEHAVIOR ANALYSIS; BEHAVIOR MODIFICATION; BEHAVIORAL ASSESSMENT; BEHAVIORAL COUNSELING; FUNCTIONAL ANALYSIS.

References

Delprato, D. J., & Midgley, B. O. (1992). Some fundamentals of B. F. Skinner's behaviorism. *The American Psychologist, 47,* 1507–1520.
Skinner, B. F. (1957). *Verbal behavior.* New York: Appleton-Century-Crofts.
Skinner, B. F. (1976). *Particulars of my life.* New York: Knopf.
Skinner, B. F. (1990). Can psychology be a science of mind? *The American Psychologist, 45,* 1206–1210.

SOCIAL DARWINISM. A theory that the most powerful groups in a society have become that way because they adapted best to that society. Anna Y. Reed in Seattle and Eli Weaver in New York established early twentieth century counseling services based on Social Darwinian concepts (see Rockwell, 1958).

Anna Reed urged that schools use the example of business and keep before children the dollar sign, which she believed every pupil understood (Reed, 1916). For her, the goal of counseling was to get youth to emulate successful business people. A person's worth was judged by his or her acceptability to employers.

In 1906 Eli Weaver and some of his colleagues organized the Students Aid Committee of the Boys High School in Brooklyn, New York. Weaver also saw counseling as a way of promoting the industrial and economic goals of the society. Counseling was to prepare young people to enter the world of work. He claimed that by 1910 every high school in New York City had a committee of teachers actively helping boys and girls to secure jobs in which their abilities could be used to full advantage.

References

Reed, A. Y. (1916). *Vocational guidance report 1913–1916.* Seattle: Board of School Directors.

Reed, A. Y. (1944). *Guidance and personnel services in education.* Ithaca, NY: Cornell University Press.

Rockwell, P. J., Jr. (1958). *Social concepts in the published writings of some pioneers in guidance.* Doctoral dissertation, University of Wisconsin, Madison.

SOCIAL LEARNING THEORY. A theory of human behavior that emphasizes the importance of cognition in the person-environment interactions that are the basis of social learning.

Bandura (1969) challenged the view of traditional behavioral theorists that the cause of behavior is unidirectional—that environmental stimuli are the sole causes of human behavior. Instead, he argued that behavioral causality is bidirectional—that it is a reciprocal process of mutual influence between the individual and the environment. Humans are somewhat independent of external environmental factors because of cognitive processes which enable them to regulate their behavior. Observational learning is an important element of social learning theory and is comprised of underlying cognitive mechanisms such as attentional processes, memory functions, the capacity for covert rehearsal, motor reproduction processes, incentive processes, and motivational processes. Individuals are able to reinforce themselves through the exercise or manipulation of attention, incentives, and expectancies.

Social learning theory is the basis for the cognitive behavior approach to counseling. Self-monitoring, self-reinforcement, and modeling are essential elements of cognitive-behavioral strategies such as self-instructional training, social skills training, self-control therapies, or cognitive therapy.

Related entry: COGNITIVE-BEHAVIORAL COUNSELING.

References

Bandura, A. (1969). *Principles of behavior modification.* New York: Holt, Rinehart and Winston.

Bandura, A. (1977). *Social learning theory.* Englewood Cliffs, NJ: Prentice-Hall.

Hughes, J. (1988). *Cognitive behavior therapy with children in the schools.* New York: Pergamon.

SOCIAL SKILLS TRAINING. Cognitive-behavioral instruction in the skills and strategies necessary for successful social interactions.

Social skills training is used to treat a variety of social competence problems ranging from depression due to rejection or nonacceptance by peers to aggressive, hostile behavior attributable to ignorance of more effective ways of interacting. Social skills training can involve instructional methods such as the discussion of hypothetical situations, role playing, modeling, and problem-solving social dilemmas.

Related entries: ASSERTIVENESS TRAINING; COGNITIVE-BEHAVIORAL COUNSELING.

References

Cartledge, G., & Milburn, J. (Eds.) (1986). *Teaching social skills to children* (2nd ed.). New York: Pergamon.

Hughes, J. (1988). *Cognitive behavior therapy with children in schools.* New York: Pergamon.

Wielkiewicz, R. (1986). *Behavior management in the schools: Principles and procedures.* New York: Pergamon.

SOCIAL WORKERS. Mental health professionals who are trained in case work, group work, and community organization approaches.

A fully trained social worker usually possesses a master's degree in social work and the professional certification ACSW (Academy of Certified Social Workers). Many states also require licensing of social workers.

Social workers provide social services and counseling to individuals and families with medical, legal, economic, or social problems. They work with youth groups, senior citizen groups, and minority groups in community or institutional settings, and they work with civic, religious, political, or industrial groups to develop community wide programs to address particular social problems in a community. Psychiatric social workers using casework approaches assist psychiatric patients and their families in coping with social and economic problems associated with illness, hospitalization, and return to home and the community. They very often provide counseling services for their clients who are experiencing problems of living.

References

Babcock, C. (1955). Social work as work. *Social Casework, 34,* 415–422.

Brian, S. (1971). Social case work and social group work: Historical foundations. In R. Morris (Ed.), *Encyclopedia of social work* (16th ed.). New York: National Association of Social Workers.

Hamilton, G. (1939). Social case work. In R. H. Kurtz (Ed.), *Social work yearbook.* New York: Russell Sage Foundation.

National Association of Social Workers (1990). *Code of ethics.* Silver Spring, MD: National Association of Social Workers.

Toren, N. (1972). *Social work: The case of a semi profession.* Beverly Hills, CA: Sage.

SPIRITUAL EMERGENCE/EMERGENCY. Natural transpersonal experiences that fall on a continuum in terms of their disruptiveness to ordinary life.

According to Bragdon (1990), spiritual emergence is a natural process of human development in which an individual goes beyond normal personal feelings and desires—ego—into the transpersonal, increasing relatedness to Higher Power, or God. Typically this process is initiated by some form of spiritual practice such as meditation or prayer, although sometimes experiences are spontaneous, with seemingly no causative factors. The experiences associated with emergence are considered positive and transformational as evidenced by observable increases in compassion, creativity, and a desire to be of service to all life.

Spiritual emergence may cause minor disruptions in daily life; it occurs when the normal developmental, transpersonal process becomes a crisis. According to Bragdon (1990), a person undergoing a spiritual emergency may experience profound emotions, visions, psychosomatic illness, and compelling desires to behave in unusual ways, including suicidal thoughts. Grof and Grof (1989) warn that counselors and other mental health professionals must not confuse the extreme mental and physical phenomena associated with spiritual emergency with psychosis or any other form of mental illness. Instead, they should seek to understand the client's experience and support the client so as to bring the crisis (which is merely an extreme manifestation of an otherwise normal, if unfamiliar, developmental process) to a positive resolution. Such an intervention requires a knowledge of what Grof and Grof call the "inner maps" of spiritual development which the great spiritual traditions have attempted to plot. They lament that traditional Western science has routinely dismissed the findings and practices of these spiritual traditions despite their long, systematic study of human consciousness (Grof & Grof, 1989).

The concepts of spiritual emergence/emergency were first formulated by Christina and Stanislov Grof. The groundwork for the concept of spiritual emergency was an outgrowth of Stanislov Grof's pioneering research in consciousness studies. Christina Grof established the Spiritual Emergence Network (SEN) in Menlo Park, California, which serves as a resource center for laypersons and professionals interested in psychotherapeutic strategies for supporting the processes of spiritual opening and integration (Bragdon, 1990).

The classic forms of spiritual emergency identified by Bragdon (1990) are (a) shamanic crisis, (b) awakening the Kundalini, (c) episodes of unitive consciousness or peak experiences, (d) psychological renewal through return to the center, (e) crisis of psychic opening, (f) past-life experiences, (g) mediumistic or "channeling" experiences, (h) near-death experiences, (i) unusual UFO-related experiences such as abductions or close encounters, and (j) possession experiences.

Related entries: PASTORAL COUNSELING; RELIGION.

References

Bragdon, E. (1990). *Call of spiritual emergency.* New York: Harper and Row.

Grof, S., & Grof, C. (1989). Spiritual emergency: Understanding evolutionary crisis. In S. Grof & C. Grof (Eds.), *Spiritual emergency: When personal transformation becomes crisis* (pp. 1–26). Los Angeles: Jeremy Tarcher.

STANDARDS FOR CLINICAL PRACTICE (AMERICAN MENTAL HEALTH COUNSELORS ASSOCIATION). The American Mental Health Counselors Association publishes *Standards of the Clinical Practice of Mental Health Counseling,* which can be used to identify the "good" practice of mental health counseling.

These standards are designed to protect the welfare of clients and to improve the quality of mental health counseling. State counselor regulatory bodies may find these standards helpful in making decisions on complaints against counselors.

There are eighteen standards for the delivery of clinical services. The American Mental Health Counselors Association plans to develop a companion set of standards for the practice of preventive and developmental counseling.

Related entries: AMERICAN ASSOCIATION FOR COUNSELING (AAC); ETHICS; MENTAL HEALTH COUNSELING; NATIONAL BOARD FOR CERTIFIED COUNSELORS.

References

American Mental Health Counselors Association (1993). *Standards of the clinical practice of mental health counseling.* Alexandria, VA: American Mental Health Counselors Association.

Anderson, D. (1992). A case for standards of counseling practice. *Journal of Counseling and Development, 71*(11), 22–26.

Covin Theron, M., & Robinson, G. (1993). AMHCA adopts national standards for clinical practice. *Guidepost/American Counseling Association, 136,* 44–45.

STRATEGIC PROBLEM-SOLVING COUNSELING. Problem-solving counseling focuses on counseling families of triads or larger system structures and emphasizes interventions involving the relational context of a problem.

A problem is defined as a type of behavior that is part of a sequence of acts among several persons. This repeating sequence of behaviors is the focus of counseling. The counselor develops and utilizes therapeutic directives to solve these problems.

Analogic communication, or communication that has multiple referents, is nonverbal, informal, and contextual. These kinds of messages, in contrast to digital or more specific messages, are very important in human interpersonal communication and critical in defining the dynamics of relationships and in understanding the context in which interpersonal problems arise and maintain themselves. For Jay Haley, the founder of strategic problem-solving counseling, the counselor's task was to affect the analogic communication dynamics that support unwanted or symptomatic behaviors. He believed that problems were specific to relationships, so to change symptoms it was necessary for relationships to change.

The initial interview in strategic problem-solving counseling is a structured family interview that has five stages: (1) a social stage that includes greetings and making the family comfortable; (2) a problem stage in which each member is asked to define the presenting problem; (3) an interaction stage that places family members in various types of social interactions; (4) a goal setting stage in which family members define their goals for change and expected outcomes from counseling; and (5) a task setting stage that involves establishing the tasks to be completed in the second session and settling issues regarding logistics.

Directives used throughout counseling are recommended tasks presented to the family as a means of studying or influencing a problem. The first directive usually does not occur until the end of the second session, but sometimes is given at the end of the first session. Therapeutic directives are frequently aimed at solving a problem, and they provide a means for the counselor to maintain a degree of control over the counseling process. When the counselor meets resistance, a back-door directive or "prescription of the symptom" may be utilized: the family may be asked to produce the symptom. As a consequence, resistant families may refuse to follow this directive and thereby change in such ways as to remove the presenting symptoms.

The counselor is to be a strategist, and this may involve placing clients in therapeutic binds, such as prescribing symptoms or making it very difficult for a person to have a symptom. In Haley's 1984 book, he discussed the uses of ordeals to produce changes in clients. Ordeals are prescribed activities that are burdensome and unpleasant but nevertheless appropriate and good or valuable for the client.

Related entry: FAMILY COUNSELING.

References

Haley, J. (1976). *Problem solving therapy.* New York: Harper and Row.
Haley, J. (1984). *Ordeal therapy.* San Francisco: Jossey-Bass.

STRESS. Models of stress describe it as a stimulus condition, a response to environmental conditions, and/or a type of person-environment interaction (Matheny, Aycock, Pugh, Curlette, & Silva Panella, 1986).

Stress has been defined as clusters of events that involve significant life changes and events that involve hassles or everyday irritations (Holmes & Rahe, 1967; Lazarus & Folkman, 1984). However, Redfield and Stone (1979) concluded from their research that it may be important to understand more about the characteristics of individuals that determine their responses to stressful life events than it is to describe the characteristics of the events themselves.

Stress has been defined as inappropriate physiological, behavioral, and/or psychological responses to environmental/stimulus conditions. Still, it may be that the conditions influencing particular stress responses will change over time, and responses at one point in time may have an independent influence on responses at a later time. Individuals who experience stress responses may try to influence their situations so as to lessen their stress (primary control), or they may try to modify their responses to the environmental conditions (secondary control) (see Weiss, Rothbaum, & Blackburn, 1984).

Stress has been described as a dynamic social interaction process in a particular context. This process may be mediated by one's cognitive appraisals of the demands on one and one's appraisals of the adequacy of one's resources for coping with these demands (Lazarus & Cohen, 1977). The perception and interpretation of the environmental conditions as well as personal goals will influence the perceived level of stress, perceived coping resources, and choice of coping strategies. These person-environment relationships are dynamic because of the changing nature of the interactions among actions, responses, and appraisals.

Related entry: ANXIETY.

References

Holmes, T. H., & Rahe, R. H. (1967). The social readjustment rating scale. *Journal of Psychosomatic Research, 11,* 213–218.

Lazarus, R. S., & Cohen, J. B. (1977). Environmental stress. In I. Altman & J. Y. Wohlwill (Eds.), *Human behavior and environment* (Vol. 2, pp. 89–128). New York: Plenum Press.

Lazarus, R. S., & Folkman, S. (1984). *Stress: Appraisal and coping.* New York: Springer.

Matheny, K. B., Aycock, D. W., Pugh, J. L., Curlette, W. L., & Silva Panella, K. A. (1986). Stress: Coping—A qualitative and quantitative synthesis with implications for treatment. *The Counseling Psychologist, 14,* 499–549.

Redfield, J., & Stone, A. (1979). Individual viewpoints of stressful life events. *Journal of Consulting and Clinical Psychology, 47,* 147–154.

Weiss, J. R., Rothbaum, F. M., & Blackburn, R. C. (1984). Standing out or standing in: The psychology of control in America and Japan. *American Psychologist, 39,* 955–969.

STRESS MANAGEMENT. A family of techniques used to reduce physical tension, emotional arousal, and symptoms such as insomnia, headache, indigestion, poor concentration, or reduced work performance.

Counselors often use meditation or muscle relaxation techniques such as progressive relaxation to alleviate the debilitating effects of chronic stress. One useful cognitive-behavioral technique for managing stress in an anxious client is stress inoculation. Three components in stress inoculation are (1) the client learns about stress and its effects on mind and body, as well as specific coping techniques; (2) the client rehearses the cognitive and behavioral coping strategies; and (3) the client applies these techniques to real-life situations.

A more general application of stress management occurs in a form of psychotherapy called supportive therapy. In contrast to conventional psychoanalytic counseling, supportive therapy attempts to encourage and reassure clients by building up their defenses and reinforcing existing coping mechanisms. The goal is to strengthen and build up a client to undertake psychoanalytic counseling.

Related entries: BEHAVIORAL COUNSELING; COGNITIVE-BEHAVIORAL COUNSELING.

References

Agras, W., & Berkowitz, R. (1988). Behavior therapy. In J. Talbott, R. Hales, & S. Yudofsky (Eds.), *Textbook of psychiatry* (pp. 891–906). Washington, DC: American Psychiatric Association.

Cormier, W., & Cormier, L. (1979). *Interviewing strategies for helpers: A guide to assessment, treatment, and evaluation.* Monterey, CA: Brooks/Cole.

Meissner, W., & Nicholi, A. (1978). The psychotherapies: Individual, family, and group. In A. Nicholi (Ed.), *Harvard guide to modern psychiatry* (pp. 357–386). Cambridge, MA: Belknap Press.

STRONG-CAMPBELL INTEREST INVENTORY (STRONG VOCATIONAL INTEREST BLANK). This measure has 325 items and asks about individuals' interest in occupations, school subjects, activities, amusements, and types of people as well as their preferences between specified activities. They are also asked to describe their characteristics by indicating whether fourteen different statements apply to them or not.

Five types of scales included are as follows: (1) Occupational Themes, (2) Basic Interests, (3) Occupations, (4) special scales such as Academic Comfort and Introversion-Extroversion, and (5) administrative indices such as Total Response, Infrequent Response, and the Relative Frequency Distribution on Response Alternatives.

The original Strong Vocational Interest Blank as well as the present Strong-Campbell Interest Inventory occupational scales contain items that discriminate between successful persons in an occupation and a reference group of people in general. The assumption has been that it is possible to differentiate the interests of successful persons in an occupation from others in general and thereby identify the distinctive interest pattern of an occupation. When a person's interests and traits match the interest patterns of a number of similar occupations, the person might wish to give them serious consideration and explore them as part of career counseling.

The Strong Vocational Interest Blank was originally published in 1927 with 420 items and was used to differentiate male certified accountants from other occupational groups. Since the publication of a manual in 1928, this test has undergone a series of changes: (a) the publication of the women's form in 1933 and a manual in 1935; (b) the revision of the men's form in 1938; (c) the revision of the women's form in parallel with the men's form in 1946; (d) the revision of the men's form in 1966 with 399 items; (e) the revision of the women's form in 1969 with 398 items; (f) the publication of a handbook in 1971; (g) the publication of the 1974 edition, which merged the men's and women's forms and provided a theoretical framework for the interpretation of test scores (this revision was identified as the Strong-Campbell Interest Inventory); and (h) the publication of the User's Guide in 1984.

The items on this test are at about a sixth grade reading level. It takes an average of twenty-five to thirty minutes to complete the test. It is not recommended for students below the ages of 13 or 14. The test is often used in counseling high school and university students as well as working adults who need to make educational and career decisions.

Related entries: KUDER GENERAL INTEREST SURVEY (FORM E); KUDER OCCUPATIONAL INTEREST SURVEY (FORM D-1956 AND FORM DD-1966); SELF-DIRECTED SEARCH.

References

Campbell, D. P., & Hansen, J. C. (1981). Manual for the Strong-Campbell Interest Inventory (3rd ed.). Stanford, CA: Stanford University Press.
Strong, E. K., Jr. (1927). *Strong Vocational Interest Blank.* Stanford, CA: Stanford University Press.

STUDENT PERSONNEL. An early statement of the student personnel point of view in higher education held that even though the major responsibility for students' growth rests with themselves, their development will be influenced by the different backgrounds, traits, and expectancies that they bring to college as well as by their classroom experiences and their reactions to them (American Council on Education, 1949). Student personnel services have traditionally provided assistance in helping students resolve their adjustment problems in higher education settings.

The purpose of student personnel work was described in the 1930s as delivering students to their classrooms in optimum condition for profiting by instruction. In order to accommodate this task there were to be four types of personnel workers: group, advisory, instructional, and clinical (Williamson, 1950). These workers differed in respect to the complexity and technicalities of the problems that they were able to diagnose and help students resolve.

Williamson and Biggs (1975), in their book *Student Personnel Work: A Program of Developmental Relationships,* said that student personnel work was designed to aid students to strive for self-fulfillment as humane persons. They restricted the concept of student personnel work to those developmental relationships that take place outside of the classroom. Its goal was to prepare students to be constructive individuals within an organized society. The mission of student personnel work was to develop informed and actively involved citizens who were able to promote responsible social change.

Related entries: SCHOOL COUNSELING; WILLIAMSON, EDMUND G.

References

American Council on Education (1949, September). *The student personnel point of view* (Studies Series 6, Vol. 13, No. 13). Washington, DC: American Council on Education.
Williamson, E. G. (1950). *Counseling adolescents.* New York: McGraw-Hill.
Williamson, E. G., & Biggs, D. A. (1975). *Student personnel work: A program of developmental relationships.* New York: John Wiley and Sons.

SUBLIMATION. Sublimation is a special variation of the defense mechanism of displacement.

The subjects unconsciously channel their sexual and aggressive energies into activities that are socially acceptable. Normally, displacement involves the redirection of libidinal energies from one object to another. When the original object loses its ability to reduce tension or satisfy desire, an alternative that is more accessible and/or acceptable takes its place. The substituted object is never as satisfying as the original for tension reduction, which accounts for the continual seeking and dissatisfaction that characterize human societies.

Related entry: PSYCHOANALYTIC COUNSELING.

Reference

Hansen, J., Stevic, R., & Warner, R. (1977). *Counseling: Theory and practice* (2nd ed.). Boston: Allyn and Bacon.

SUGGESTION. The process of influencing a client to accept an idea, belief, or attitude suggested by the counselor.

Suggestion is a basic counseling technique used to encourage clients to function in a more healthy or productive way. The term is most commonly used within the context of hypnosis, when clients suspend the usual conscious editing functions and are less concerned with the origin of directives, whether from themselves or from others, than they might be in their normal state. In hypnosis, clients are inclined to act as if the content and source of a suggestion were in themselves. Because of the subject's increased responsiveness, hypnosis has the potential for damaging results in some circumstances.

Related entries: DIRECTIVES; HYPNOSIS OR HYPNOSUGGESTIVE PROCEDURES.

References

Spiegel, D. (1988). Hypnosis. In J. Talbott, R. Hales, & S. Yudofsky (Eds.), *Textbook of psychiatry* (pp. 907–928). Washington, DC: American Psychiatric Association Press.
Stoudemire, G. (1988). Somatoform disorders, factitious disorders, and malingering. In J. Talbott, R. Hales, & S. Yudofsky (Eds.), *Textbook of psychiatry* (pp. 533–556). Washington, DC: American Psychiatric Association Press.

SUPER, DONALD E. (b. 1910). The major advocate for developmental career counseling and the author of a theory of vocational development as stages in the process of implementing a self-concept.

Donald Super graduated with a baccalaureate degree from Oxford University in 1932. In 1936 he received his M.A. from Oxford, and in 1940 he received his Ph.D. from Columbia University. From 1945 until 1975 he was Professor of Psychology and Education at Columbia University. He has written more than 120 articles, books, and monographs.

Related entry: LIFE CAREER DEVELOPMENT.

References

Super, D. E. (1957). *The psychology of careers.* New York: Harper and Bros.
Super, D. E. (1970). *The work values inventory.* Boston: Houghton Mifflin.
Super, D. E. (1981). The relative importance of work. *Bulletin: International Association of Educational and Vocational Guidance, 37,* 26–36.

SUPEREGO. The aspect of the psyche which represents the conscience of the individual and embodies the ethical and moral attitudes of the culture in which the individual lives his or her life.

The superego is supposed to represent the internalization of social standards as presented by an individual's parents. A sense of personal goals and ideals is also attributed to superego processes.

Neurotic symptoms are related to conflicts between a powerful id seeking immediate gratification of instinctual drives and an overpunitive and inhibitory superego.

Related entries: EGO; ID; PSYCHOANALYTIC COUNSELING.

References

Arlow, J. A. (1989). Psychoanalysis. In R. J. Corsini & D. Wedding (Eds.), *Current psychotherapies* (4th ed., pp. 19–62). Itasca, IL: F. E. Peacock.
Freud, S. (1961). The ego and the id. In J. Strachey (Ed. and Trans.), *The standard edition of the complete psychological works of Sigmund Freud* (Vol. 19, pp. 3–66). London: Hogarth Press. (Original work published 1923)

SUPERVISION. An intensive, interpersonally focused, one-to-one relationship in which one person is designated to facilitate the development of therapeutic competence in the other person.

One of the four primary functions of supervision focuses on the client, while the other three focus on the supervisee. The first function attends to the supervisor's ethical imperative to ensure the welfare of the client; the second deals with the enhancement of the supervisee's growth within each stage of development; the third deals with promoting the transition of the supervisee from stage to stage within the course of his or her development; and the fourth presents the evaluative function of supervision (Loganbill, Hardy, & Delworth, 1982).

One major component of the supervisory relationship is the authoritative nature of supervision. The supervisor is held accountable for the actions of the supervisee.

Matarazzo (1978) identifies five methods of teaching and supervising: didactic instruction; supervisor modeling; direct observations of actual or role play interviews; in-process supervisor interventions; and feedback on audio or video tapes after counseling sessions are completed. Combinations of all or some of these methods have been identified in various models of supervision.

References

Loganbill, D., Hardy, E., & Delworth, U. (1982). Supervision: A conceptual model. *The Counseling Psychologist, 10,* 3–42.

Matarazzo, R. G. (1978). Research on teaching and learning of psychotherapeutic skills. In S. L. Garfield & A. E. Bergin (Eds.), *Handbook of psychotherapy and behavior change: An empirical analysis* (2nd ed.). New York: Wiley.

SYSTEMATIC COUNSELING. A counseling model in which the various aspects of the process are clearly identified and organized into a sequence designed to resolve the client's concerns as efficiently as possible.

Systematic counseling represents a synthesis of three scientific approaches: learning theory, systems analysis, and educational technology. Learning theory and the principles of behavior modification provide the theoretical and experimental rationale; systems analysis provides the organizational framework; and educational technology is the source of methods and materials.

This approach first establishes mutually agreed upon objectives stated in terms of specific observable behaviors. Then the counselor's role is to direct specific learning experiences that are designed to help clients attain these objectives. Counseling is viewed as a learning process in which clients learn new ways of obtaining information, new ways of making decisions, and new ways of responding to the environment. In addition, the clients learn how to generalize new knowledge and skills to other problem situations.

Reference

Stewart, N. R., Winborn, B. B., Burks, H. M., Jr., Johnson, R. R., & Engelkes, J. R. (1978). *Systematic counseling.* Englewood Cliffs, NJ: Prentice-Hall.

T

TARASOFF VS. BOARD OF REGENTS AT THE UNIVERSITY OF CALIFORNIA. In August 1969, Prosenjet Poddar was a voluntary client at the Student Health Service on the Berkeley campus of the University of California. He informed a counselor that he planned to kill his girlfriend.

The counselor called the police and told them of the threat. He asked them to observe the client, who was questioned and released. The counselor also sent a letter requesting the assistance of the campus police chief. Later the counselor's supervisor asked that the letter be returned and ordered that the letter and the counselor's notes be destroyed and that no further actions be taken by the counselor. In this whole process, no warning was given to the intended victim or her parents. Two months later, the client killed Tatiana Tarasoff. In 1976 the California Supreme Court ruled that the failure of the counselor to warn the intended victim had been irresponsible.

The most significant implication of this court decision for counseling was that protection of the confidential nature of the counseling relationship must yield when disclosure is essential to avert danger to others. Counselors must accurately diagnose a client's propensity for behaving in dangerous ways toward others and then use reasonable care and take the necessary steps to protect a potential victim against any dangers. Knapp and Vandercreek (1982) suggest that counselors are bound only to follow reasonable standards in predicting violence. However, they are also responsible for keeping abreast of ways of dealing with violent clients, of evaluating dangerousness, and of any recent legislation that bears on the nature of their duty to warn and to protect.

Related entries: CONFIDENTIALITY; ETHICAL GUIDELINES FOR GROUP COUNSELORS; ETHICS.

References

Corey, G. (1991). *Theory and practice of counseling and psychotherapy* (4th ed., pp. 72–73). Pacific Grove, CA: Brooks/Cole.

Fulero, S. M. (1988). Tarasoff: 10 years later. *Professional psychology: Research and Practice, 19,* 184–190.

Knapp, S., & Vandercreek, L. (1982). Tarasoff: Five years later. *Professional Psychology, 13,* 511–516.

TEACHER-COUNSELOR. The teacher who has counseling responsibilities may hold initial and mid-term group sessions and even short interviews with students to discuss their academic schedules and/or to discuss any conditions or obstacles to the successful achievement of their academic goals (Strang, 1946).

In 1939 Williamson argued that all teachers should be trained to work with individual students because the effects on them may be beneficial. Although their counseling might be ineffective, such teachers may become more pupil-minded than subject-matter–minded. In particular, these teachers may be able to contribute valuable anecdotal data to the diagnoses of students by trained workers. In addition, teachers can play an important role in preventing the development of maladjustments in students, and when necessary refer students to trained counselors.

Strang (1946) described two levels of teacher-counseling. The first is the one at which the classroom teacher generally works. Group experiences may be used to help students discover what they can do and become, find ways of meeting daily situations, and gain the affection, recognition, and security that is needed in their lives. Short face-to-face counseling relationships may allow these teachers to supplement, reinforce, and further individualize these group experiences.

The teacher's success on this level of counseling depends largely on (a) personal relationships with students, (b) knowledge of individual students, (c) level of insight into the meaning of student behavior, and (d) level of ingenuity in helping students to get needed experiences.

The second level of counseling at which teachers work goes a little more deeply into the needs that give rise to observed student behavior. This type of counseling may occur in private interviews when the counselor tries to help students know themselves better, accept their best selves, and work out satisfying relationships in their environment.

Related entry: SCHOOL COUNSELING.

References

Strang, R. (1946). *The role of the teacher in personnel work.* New York: Teachers College, Columbia University, Bureau of Publications.

Williamson, E. G. (1939). *How to counsel students.* New York: McGraw-Hill.

THOUGHT STOPPING. This counseling technique is used to help a client control unproductive or self-defeating thoughts and images by suppressing or eliminating these negative cognitions.

The thought control procedure of thought stopping was developed by Taylor (1963) and later described by both Wolpe (1982) and Lazarus (1971). Cautela

(1977) describes a thought stopping survey that can help clients to identify maladaptive thoughts.

Thought stopping is particularly appropriate with clients who ruminate about past events that cannot be changed, those who ruminate about events that are unlikely to occur, and those who engage in repetitive, unproductive, anxiety producing, or self-defeating images. Thought stopping may be most effective with clients who are troubled by intermittent rather than continuous self-defeating thoughts.

The thought stopping strategy has six major components: treatment rationale, counselor directed thought stopping, client directed thought stopping, a shift to positive, assertive or neutral thoughts, homework, and follow-up (see Cormier & Cormier, 1985).

Related entries: AUTOMATIC THOUGHTS; COGNITIVE-BEHAVIORAL COUNSELING; COGNITIVE COUNSELING.

References

Cautela, J. R. (1977). *Behavior analysis forms for clinical intervention.* Champaign, IL: Research Press.

Cormier, W. H., & Cormier, L. S. (1985). *Interviewing strategies for helpers.* Monterey, CA: Brooks/Cole.

Lazarus, A. A. (1971). *Behavior therapy and beyond.* New York: McGraw-Hill.

Taylor, J. G. (1963). A behavioral interpretation of obsessive-compulsive neurosis. *Behavior Research and Therapy, 1,* 237–244.

Wolpe, J. (1982). *The practice of behavior therapy* (3rd ed.). New York: Pergamon.

TRAIT AND FACTOR COUNSELING. The purpose of counseling is to help clients improve their skills in self-appraisal and use the resulting data in their decision making. Counseling is a means of teaching clients how to apply the scientific method to personal problem solving.

Hall and Lindzey (1957) described trait and factor theory as follows: ''The essence of such theories is customarily a set of carefully specified variables or factors that are seen as underlying and accounting for the broad complexity of behavior'' (p. 378). Berdie (1972) identified the following assumptions in the trait and factor approach to counseling: (a) to some extent, individuals differ from one another in every behavioral respect; (b) within broad limits that are genetic in origin, behavior is modifiable through personal and environmental changes; (c) consistency of individual behaviors allows for generalizations and predictions over time; (d) behavior is a product of current status, previous experiences, and the present physical and social setting; (e) differences in human behaviors can be conceptualized along dimensions of ability, personality, temperament, and motivation; (f) social and interpersonal conflicts are inevitable and necessary, and may yield constructive or destructive outcomes.

Pepinsky and Pepinsky (1954) identified three stages in the development of the trait and factor approach to counseling. The first period began about the turn of the century and ended about the time of World War II. During this time, a number of tests were developed to measure attributes of clients, such as aptitudes, abilities, achievements, interests, values, and personality characteristics. The goal was to develop scientific tools that would improve selection and guidance programs and help match clients and appropriate educational and vocational alternatives. In World War I, a corps of army psychologists had used the Army Alpha and Beta tests for assignment of recruits. Later W. D. Scott at Northwestern University and D. G. Patterson at the University of Minnesota applied these new testing methods to problems in industry and education (Williamson & Biggs, 1979).

In the second period in the development of trait and factor counseling, starting about the time of World War II, attempts were made to describe models of the counseling process that went beyond educational and vocational advisement. Williamson and Darley (1937) outlined a model of trait and factor counseling that involved six steps: analysis, synthesis, diagnosis, prognosis, counseling (treatment), and follow-up. The emphasis was on differential diagnosis. The counselor's task was to perceive "the dynamic and multidimensional character of personality and thus seek an understanding of its unique pattern or individuality" (Williamson, 1939, p. 103). Later Bordin (1946) and Pepinsky (1948) provided a model of diagnostic categories for trait and factor counselors.

Pepinsky and Pepinsky (1954) described the third period in the history of trait and factor counseling as the age of factorization studies. At that time, both predictor and criterion data were subjected to factor analyses in attempts to more clearly define significant differences among traits.

Williamson and Biggs (1979) identified a fourth stage in the development of the trait and factor approach to counseling, which they portrayed as philosophical and theoretical. Williamson (1950) and Hahn and Maclean (1955) described more sophisticated and complex models of the trait and factor approach to counseling, while Williamson (1958) provided a philosophical critique of the concept of value neutrality in counseling.

Related entries: CLINICAL COUNSELING; WILLIAMSON, EDMUND G.

References

Berdie, R. F. (1972). Differential psychology as a basis for counseling. *The Counseling Psychologist, 3,* 76–81.

Bordin, E. S. (1946). Diagnoses in counseling and psychotherapy. *Educational and Psychological Measurement, 6,* 169–184.

Hahn, M. E., & Maclean, M. S. (1955). *Counseling psychology.* New York: McGraw-Hill.

Hall, C. S., & Lindzey, G. (1957). *Theories of personality.* New York: Wiley.

Pepinsky, H. B. (1948). The selection and use of diagnostic categories. *Applied Psychology Monographs, 15.*

Pepinsky, H. B., & Pepinsky, P. N. (1954). *Counseling theory and practice.* New York: Ronald Press.

Williamson, E. G. (1939). *How to counsel students: A manual of techniques for clinical counselors.* New York: McGraw-Hill.

Williamson, E. G. (1950). *Counseling adolescents.* New York: McGraw-Hill.
Williamson, E. G. (1958). Value orientation in counseling. *Personnel and Guidance Journal, 37,* 521–528.
Williamson, E. G., & Biggs, D. A. (1979). Trait and factor theory and individual differences. In H. M. Birks, Jr., & B. Steffire (Eds.), *Theories of counseling* (3rd ed., pp. 91–131). New York: McGraw-Hill.
Williamson, E. G., & Darley, J. S. (1937). *Student personnel work.* New York: McGraw-Hill.

TRANSACTIONAL ANALYSIS (TA). Transactional analysis deals with three primary counseling mechanisms: egogram state energy shifts, game interruptions, and script redecisions. Efforts are made to ensure that no ego state in the personality has minimal energy; that a client is aware of the games he/she plays; and that a client is free from influences of parental injunctions.

In the first phase (1955–1962) of transactional analysis, the emphasis was on observing and paying attention to here and now behaviors of clients in order to identify ego states. The second phase (1962–1966) focused on identifying transactions and games, while the third phase (1966–1970) involved script analysis and encouraged strong emotional experiences of decisive moments in childhood. The fourth and present phase (1970 onward) includes the employment of egograms as well as Gestalt, psychodrama, and encounter techniques (Dusay & Dusay, 1989).

To facilitate client responsibility, the TA counselor uses a simple common vocabulary, establishes a contractual treatment goal, and uses specific techniques designed to enhance a client's power and responsibility. The vocabulary of ego states (parent-adult-child), games, scripts, and strokes is easily learned and understood by most clients. A key question in establishing a TA contract is "How will you and I know when you get what you came for?" The client and counselor are to be allies trying to achieve a mutual goal, and the contract is between their adult ego states. It should frequently be reviewed, updated, and changed.

Clients may be seen individually, in families, as couples, in marathons, in prisons, and in business and industry settings. Specific kinds of TA interventions may include (a) game analysis by confrontation, (b) game interruption by psychodrama, (c) script treatment or reversing basic life scripts, (d) script reversal by receiving a potent counter-injunction, (e) reparenting, (f) redecision, (g) egostate oppositions or changing weaknesses into strengths, and (h) egogram transfer of energy (Dusay & Dusay, 1989).

Game interruptions will bring to awareness a client's involvement with different ego states and will establish the adult ego state in control. TA counselors try to help clients exercise their adult options to get better. When games are interrupted, clients will have more social control. Script redecision will help clients to overcome early childhood decisions by applying an opposing injunction to reverse early negative script injunctions of a mother or father. Ego state energy shifts can help to build up weak areas on an egogram. For example, TA counselors may encourage their clients to express humor, to air hunches and intuitions, and/or to provide nurturing behaviors to strengthen specific ego states.

Counseling may begin with a structural analysis that allows clients to become more aware of their ego states. Then clients are helped to understand more fully the nature of any self-destructive games and unhealthy life scripts that may be influencing their present problem situations. They can learn to analyze these troublesome interpersonal situations in their lives and assess whether the conflicts are due to their games or scripts or whether they are possibly being drawn into other people's games and scripts.

Related entries: ADULT EGO STATE; BERNE, ERIC; CHILD EGO STATE; EGO; EGO STATES; EGOGRAM; PARENT EGO STATE.

References

Berne, E. (1964). *Games people play.* New York: Grove Press.
Dusay, J. M., & Dusay, K. M. (1989). Transactional analysis. In R. J. Corsini & D. Wedding (Eds.), *Current psychotherapies* (4th ed., pp. 405–454). Itasca, IL: F. E. Peacock.
Steiner, C. (1974). *Scripts people live.* New York: Grove Press.

TRANSFERENCE. Transference occurs when a person unconsciously reenacts a latter-day version of forgotten childhood memories and repressed unconscious fantasies in the counseling session.

It is a form of memory in which repetition in action replaces recollection of events. It is evident in the counseling situation in which the client responds to the counselor as though he or she were a significant figure in the client's past, usually a parent.

Analysis of transference is one of the major elements in the psychoanalytic approach. Clients are helped to understand how one misperceives, misinterprets, and relates to the present in terms of the past. They are then able to evaluate the unrealistic nature of impulses and anxieties and to make appropriate decisions on a more mature and realistic level.

At a certain stage in counseling, counselors may assume major significance in the life of clients. As a result, client perceptions and demands on their counselors may be inappropriate. The professional relationship may become distorted by the introduction of personal considerations that have their roots in childhood experiences. An important part of counseling is the recognition and subsequent working through of an analysis of transference. The resolution of transference is the termination phase of psychoanalytic counseling.

Related entries: COUNTER-TRANSFERENCE; PSYCHOANALYTIC COUNSELING.

References

Arlow, J. A. (1989). Psychoanalysis. In R. J. Corsini & D. Wedding (Eds.), *Current psychotherapies* (4th ed., pp. 19–64). Itasca, IL: F. E. Peacock.

Giovacchini, P. L. (1983). Psychoanalysis. In R. J. Corsini & A. J. Marsella (Eds.), *Personality theories, research and assessment.* Itasca, IL: F. E. Peacock.

TYLER, LEONA (1906–1993). Tyler was a major contributor to the development of professional counseling in the United States and the author of eight books, including *The Work of the Counselor,* published in 1953.

In the 1980s she was President of the American Psychological Association and also received the National Vocational Guidance Association's Eminent Career Award. Leona Tyler is a recognized authority and scholar in the area of interest development and measurement.

In 1959 Tyler wrote that what makes one person different from everybody else is what one chooses from life's offerings and the kinds of constructs one uses to organize one's experiences. There are differences in the possibility structures controlling the choices individuals make. She defines possibility structures as including interests, values, problem-solving strategies, and cognitive styles. She proposed that we need to answer questions about how people process their experiences rather than questions about how much of some hypothetical ability people possess. Further, counseling is the process of examining possibility structures and choosing with awareness what one will do with one's life.

Related entry: INTERESTS.

References

Gilmore, S. K., Nichols, M. E., & Chernoff, S. P. (1990). Mountain iron woman: A case of androgyny—Leona Elizabeth Tyler. In P. Paul Heppner (Ed.), *Pioneers in counseling and development: Personal and professional perspectives.* Alexandria, VA: American Association for Counseling and Development.

Tyler, L. (1953). *The work of the counselor.* New York: Appleton-Century-Crofts.

Tyler, L. (1959). Toward a workable psychology of individuality. *American Psychologist, 14,* 75–81.

U

UMWELT. This term in existential counseling refers to the "world around," the biological world or the environment.

Umwelt is the world of objects or the natural world. It includes biological needs, drives, and instincts. Umwelt is the world of natural law and natural cycles of sleep and awakeness, of being born and dying, of desire and relief.

Related entries: EIGENWELT; EXISTENTIAL COUNSELING; EXISTENTIALISM; MITWELT.

Reference

May, R., & Yalom, I. (1989). Existential psychotherapy. In R. J. Corsini & D. Wedding (Eds.), *Current psychotherapies* (4th ed., pp. 363–402). Itasca, IL: F. E. Peacock.

UNCONDITIONAL POSITIVE REGARD. The essence of this facilitative condition in person-centered counseling is that the counselor experiences a deep and genuine but nonpossessive caring for the client as a person.

The counselor genuinely accepts and cares for the client and experiences none of the client's self-experiences as being more or less worthy of positive regard. This term does not imply that the counselor approves of the client's behaviors.

Butler (1952) used the term *prizing* to help define this concept. To prize other persons means to value or esteem them. Thus, the concept of unconditional positive regard implies that the counselor is not appraising the client but prizing him or her whether he or she expresses good or bad feelings.

Rogers (1957) identified unconditional positive regard, genuineness, and empathy as the three conditions necessary for personality change to occur in counseling.

Related entries: ACCEPTANCE; ANALYTICAL COUNSELING; AUTHENTICITY; CLIENT-CENTERED COUNSELING; EMPATHY; HUMAN-

ISTIC APPROACHES TO COUNSELING; RATIONAL-EMOTIVE COUNSELING.

References

Butler, J. M. (1952). *The evaluative attitude of the client centered counselor: A linguistic-behavioral formulation.* Chicago: University of Chicago, Counseling Center.

Rogers, C. R. (1957). The necessary and sufficient conditions for therapeutic personality change. *Journal of Consulting Psychology, 21,* 95–103.

V

VALIDITY. Evidence presented that a test measures certain traits, characteristics, behaviors, or constructs. The concept of validity refers to the kind of evidence used to identify the behaviors being elicited by a pool of test items.

The term *validity* indicates the extent to which a test measures what it purports to measure. An intelligence test is valid if it relates to independent observations of behaviors that have been defined as intelligent behaviors. Tests do not have general validity, but they are valid for specific purposes within a given context.

Anastasi (1982) described three types of validity: content, construct, and criterion-based. Construct validity is a particularly important source of validity because it describes the extent to which certain psychological concepts explain or account for performance on a test. Construct validity requires logical as well as empirical evidence.

Related entry: RELIABILITY.

References

Anastasi, A. (1982). *Psychological testing* (5th ed.) New York: Macmillan.
Cronbach, L. J., & Meehl, P. E. (1955). Construct validity in psychological tests. *Psychological Bulletin, 52,* 281–302.

VALUES. Personal, social, and cultural standards or codes that define obligations or required actions.

Smith (1954) said, "By values I shall mean a person's implicit or explicit standards of choice, insofar as these are invested with obligation or requiredness" (p. 513). Kluckhohn et al. (1952) defined values as a concept of "the desirable which influences the selection from available modes, means and ends of action. . . . Value implies a code or standard which has some persistence through time, or put more broadly, which organizes a system of action. Values, conveniently and in accord with received usage, place things, acts, ways of behaving, goals of action on the approval-disapproval continuum'' (p. 395). Moral values are those values that relate to interpersonal relationships and attitudes toward actions that affect other persons. The counselor's attitudes toward clients may be considered moral values.

Rogers (1942) differentiated the directive and nondirective philosophies and values of counseling. The former were assumed to place a higher value on social conformity and the rights of the more able to direct the less able, while the latter placed a higher value on the rights of every individual to be psychologically independent and to maintain his/her psychological integrity. Rogers and the early nondirective counselors pleaded for "value neutrality" in counseling. Patterson (1992), a contemporary advocate of the nondirective approach, described two similar philosophies in counseling as "manipulative" and "understanding." He, too, argued that counselors should not impose their values on clients. However, he thought that they should be willing to discuss values, ethics, or philosophy and that, at the request of clients, they might express their own values.

A somewhat different perspective on values in counseling was expressed by Murphy (1955), who wrote, "Shall personnel and guidance work . . . attempt to impart a philosophy of life?" His reply was that "no one knows enough to construct an adequate philosophy of life," but "nevertheless if he who offers guidance is a whole person, with real roots in human culture, he cannot help conveying directly or indirectly to every client what he himself sees and feels and the perspective in which his own life is lived." He went on to say that "it is not true that the wise man's sharing of a philosophy of life is an arrogant imposition upon a defenseless client." But he warned counselors not to "attempt the arrogant and self-defeating task of guiding men and women without a rich, flexible, and ever growing system of values of your own" (p. 8).

Related entries: MULTICULTURAL COUNSELING; RELIGION.

References

Kluckhohn, C., et al. (1952). Values and value orientation in the theory of action. In T. Parsons & E. A. Shils (Eds.), *Toward a general theory of action* (pp. 288–443). Cambridge, MA: Harvard University Press.

Murphy, G. (1955). The cultural context of guidance. *Personnel and Guidance Journal, 34,* 4–9.

Patterson, C. H. (1992). Values in counseling and psychotherapy. In M. T. Burke & J. G. Miranti (Eds.), *Ethical and spiritual values in counseling* (pp. 106–119). Alexandria, VA: American Association for Counseling and Development.

Rogers, C. R. (1942). *Counseling and psychotherapy.* Cambridge, MA: Riverside.

Smith, M. B. (1954). Toward scientific and professional responsibility. *American Psychologist, 1,* 513–516.

VOCATIONAL GUIDANCE. The giving of information, experience, and advice in regard to choosing an occupation, preparing for it, entering upon it, and progressing in it (Allen, 1923).

In 1937 a committee of the National Vocational Guidance Association stated that the process of vocational guidance entailed assisting individuals in their efforts to choose occupations, to prepare themselves for entrance into them, to enter them, and to make progress in them. The major change in these two early definitions of vocational guidance involved the shift from "giving" clients information to "assisting" clients to gather and interpret information and choose a vocation.

Among the earliest books on vocational guidance were Nathaniel C. Fowler's *Starting in Life,* published in 1906, and Frank W. Rollins' *What Can a Young Man Do?,* published in 1907. In 1910 and 1911 national conferences on vocational guidance were held in Boston and New York City. The development of vocational guidance during the early 1900s was strongly influenced by the rise of scientific management and cooperative education, as well as the development of the standardized testing or measurement movement.

In 1954 Humphreys and Traxler described the process of making wise vocational choices as being complex. The counselor and client should have knowledge of the essential steps in choosing an occupation; knowledge of the basic facts about occupations; and knowledge of the fundamental characteristics of the counselee. These authors gave four reasons why vocational guidance was so complex. First, it was time consuming and could not be consummated quickly. Second, the client was an individual whose personality was complex and had many facets that could influence a vocational choice. Third, the world of work was fluid; conditions differed from one area of the country to another, and they also were apt to change over time. Fourth, vocational guidance needed to consider personal, social, and educational decisions that were steps in the process of choosing a vocation.

Related entries: CAREER COUNSELING; CAREER DEVELOPMENT; GUIDANCE.

References

Allen, F. (1923, November). Editorial. *National Vocational Guidance Association: Bulletin,* p. 26.

Committee of the National Vocational Guidance Association (1937). The principles and practices of educational and vocational guidance. *Occupations, 15,* 772–778.

Humphreys, J. A., & Traxler, A. E. (1954). *Guidance services.* Chicago: Science Research Associates.

W

WILLIAMSON, EDMUND G. (1900–1979). The architect of the Minnesota point of view or trait and factor approach to counseling.

Williamson earned his B.A. in psychology from the University of Illinois in 1925 and his Ph.D. in psychology at the University of Minnesota in 1931. In 1932 he organized and directed the University Testing Bureau at the University of Minnesota. From 1941 until 1969 he was the Dean of Students at the University of Minnesota. In 1962 he received the American Personnel and Guidance Association's Nancy C. Wimmer Award for organization of the first integrated program of student personnel services in the United States.

In 1939 he published the book *How to Counsel Students: A Manual of Techniques for Clinical Counselors,* which articulated the trait and factor approach or Minnesota point of view in counseling. In his lifetime he authored over 400 publications, at least a dozen of which were books.

Related entry: TRAIT AND FACTOR COUNSELING.

Reference

Ewing, D. B. (1990). Direct from Minnesota: E. G. Williamson. In P. Paul Heppner (Ed.), *Pioneers in counseling and development* (pp. 104–111). Alexandria, VA: American Association for Counseling and Development.

WORK ADJUSTMENT THEORY. This theory focuses on the interaction between work personality and work environment as a way of conceptualizing the process by which a person adjusts to work.

The theoretical model identifies vocational abilities and vocational needs as the two significant elements of work personality. The ability requirements and reinforcer systems are the key factors in the work environment. Satisfactoriness, satisfaction, and tenure are the outcomes of work personality–work environment interactions. The continuous and dynamic process by which an individual seeks to achieve and maintain correspondence with the work environment is called work adjustment.

Related entry: CAREER DEVELOPMENT.

Reference

Lofquist, L. H., & Dawis, R. V. (1972). *Application of the theory of work adjustment to rehabilitation and counseling* (Minnesota Studies in Vocational Rehabilitation, 30). Minneapolis: University of Minnesota, Industrial Relations Center.

Y

YAVIS SYNDROME. The tendency of professional counselors and other mental health workers to primarily serve and to prefer young, attractive, verbal, intelligent, and successful clients (Schofield, 1964, 1986).

References

Schofield, W. (1964). *Psychotherapy: The purchase of friendship*. Englewood Cliffs, NJ: Prentice-Hall.

Schofield, W. (1986). 2nd Ed. *Psychotherapy: The purchase of friendship*. New Brunswick, NJ: Transaction Books.

Index

Page numbers in bold refer to the location of main entry.

About the Author

DONALD A. BIGGS, Professor of Counseling Psychology, Educational Psychology, and Religious Studies at the State University of New York at Albany, has served as assistant to the Vice President for Student Affairs at the University of Minnesota and as a consultant to various national and international organizations. His recent books with D. Blocher include *Counseling Psychology in Community Settings* (1983) and *Foundations of Ethical Counseling* (1987).